A HISTORY OF
LSU SCHOOL OF MEDICINE
NEW ORLEANS

To Dr. Walter Preau Jr.
With all good wishes

Russell Klein

ളൽ

for DGK

ളൽ

A HISTORY OF
LSU SCHOOL OF MEDICINE
NEW ORLEANS

by

Russell C. Klein, MD
and
Victoria Barreto Harkin, MA

AuthorHouse™
1663 Liberty Drive
Bloomington, IN 47403
www.authorhouse.com
Phone: 1-800-839-8640

PUBLISHED BY

LSU MEDICAL ALUMNI ASSOCIATION

NEW ORLEANS

COPYRIGHT 2010

First published by AuthorHouse 8/24/2010

ISBN: 978-1-4520-3094-4 (sc)

Library of Congress Control Number: 2010907598

Printed in the United States of America
Bloomington, Indiana

This book is printed on acid-free paper.

Layout and Design by
Virginia Howard

PRINTED BY AUTHORHOUSE

Contents

THE President and Board of Administrators of Louisiana State University announce the opening, October, 1931, of the State University's Medical Center, to be domiciled in its own quarters in New Orleans. For the session 1931-1932, the Medical Center will offer instruction in the first and third years of medicine. Four years' instruction will be offered beginning with the 1932-1933 session. A fifth year of hospital residency will be required before awarding the degree of doctor of medicine. The Medical Center offers superior clinical facilities due to its location within the grounds of, and its operating connection with the great 1756 bed Charity Hospital of New Orleans, a State owned and operated institution.

Practical instruction in all the branches of medicine and surgery will be stressed, and particular attention will be given tropical medicine, industrial surgery and the diseases indigenous to the Southland. Preventive medicine will occupy a prominent place in the curriculum. An abundance of anatomical and pathological material will, at all times, be available for proper instruction in the important branches of anatomy and pathology. The Medical Center, throughout its organization, is meeting all of the requirements of a class A medical school as outlined by the Council on Medical Education of the American Medical Association.

Applications for admission are now being received. Preference will be given to applicants possessing a collegiate degree. For admission, 15 high school units with a minimum of 2 years collegiate work consisting of no less than 60 semester hours are required. The pre-medical training must include no less than one year instruction in biology, physics, general chemistry, French or German, general and organic chemistry, with courses including at least 3 hours lecture and 4 hours laboratory periods weekly for a minimum of 32 weeks yearly per course. Application blanks may be had by communicating with the Dean, Dr. Arthur Vidrine, Louisiana State University Medical Center, Charity Hospital, New Orleans, Louisiana. No tuition will be charged to residents of Louisiana. For students who are residents of other states tuition fee of $300.00 per year will be charged.

Preface

This book is an attempt to record a history of the LSU School of Medicine in New Orleans from its founding in 1931 through its first 75 years of history, its 2006 Diamond Jubilee. Because of the devastating effect in 2005 of Hurricane Katrina on the School and the City of New Orleans it includes a post-Katrina epilogue through 2009.

It also includes biographical vignettes of famous and, in rare cases, notorious faculty members, and some history of the Medical Alumni Association and Medical Alumni. Since it would be impossible to discuss the accomplishments of all the alumni in all spheres, we have concentrated principally on the accomplishments of alumni in areas such as government service, the military, art, literature, and other public service and only to some extent in medical practice and academic achievement.

In this work I have been greatly aided by my coauthor and by a devoted support staff, most notably Virginia Howard, JoAnn Roloff and Carmen Barreto. The staff of the Medical Library has provided outstanding access to its collections of books, journals and photographs. Jenny Melillo interviewed several former faculty for this project and Leslie Capo of the Chancellor's Office and the staff of the Historic New Orleans Collection have been most helpful. The staff of the Hill Memorial Library, Louisiana State University, Baton Rouge, also gave unlimited access to their "Special Collections." The support of Dr. **Paul Azar** of the Class of 1970 and the support of Dr. **A. J. Friedman** and the Class of 1976 for this project are acknowledged with gratitude.

Every effort has been made to insure the accuracy of this work; the sources used are listed elsewhere. Dozens upon dozens of people have provided unprecedented amounts of help, information and cooperation in this effort and I thank them all. As with all history, there are many details that might have been included and many alumni and faculty who surely deserved mention but it is simply impossible to include everything and everybody. Forgive me if I have slighted some person or fact. If there are any errors in the text, I humbly apologize for them as they are unintentional.

Finally, I offer thanks to Bill Kelly and the staff of AuthorHouse our publishers for the encouragement, advice and help.

—*Russell C. Klein, MD*
12 March 2010

BE IT RESOLVED by the Board of Supervisors of Louisiana State University and Agricultural and Mechanical College, that, in order to comply with the mandates of the laws granting its charters, as well as to meeting its growing needs, it does hereby establish in the Louisiana State University and Agricultural and Mechanical College a School of Medicine.

January 3, 1931, New Orleans, La.

Chapter I

Founding the School

Huey Pierce Long, the then Governor of Louisiana, devised a plan in late 1930 to build a medical school in New Orleans as a branch of the Baton Rouge campus. His aim was to provide a medical education for the "poor boys" of Louisiana. The presence of "Big Charity" Hospital dictated its location in New Orleans.

In his planning Long was strongly influenced by Dr. Arthur Vidrine, Sr., his appointee as Superintendent of Charity Hospital. Vidrine, a former Rhodes Scholar and National Regent of the International College of Surgeons, was a talented and politically connected surgeon from Ville Platte. He had operated a hospital in Eunice, Louisiana, and had twice been President of the Louisiana Hospital Association before accepting the Charity position. He had served a two-year internship at Charity Hospital before training in surgery in London and Paris for two years. He proved to be a valuable guide in an area unfamiliar to Long.

The idea for a School of Medicine was not new. LSU's predecessor, the Louisiana State Seminary and Military Academy in Alexandria, Louisiana, "established" a School of Medicine in 1866 and decided (for reasons lost to history) to combine it with the School of Civil Engineering and award a dual degree of engineer and physician. They advertised for faculty who could teach medicine, surgery, geology, chemistry, and mineralogy; found two, Dr. J W Wilson of Missouri and Dr. J R Page of Virginia, and hired them. Not a single student was enrolled and the offering disappeared from the catalog in 1867, never to be seen again. By 1877, the charter of the LSU System, now in Baton Rouge, allowed creation of a School of Medicine, but further action awaited the coming of Huey Long.

On January 3, 1931, members of the LSU Board of Supervisors and the Charity Hospital Governing Board were summoned to Huey's suite in the Roosevelt (later Fairmont) Hotel in New Orleans. It is said that Huey conducted the

Governor Huey Long

The Historic New Orleans Collection, DETAIL from Acc. No. 1990.7.1

meeting in his pajamas, which was not long in any case. He proposed the establishment of a School of Medicine in New Orleans and that Vidrine continue both as Superintendent of Charity Hospital, and to serve also as its Dean.

"With little discussion," Huey's proposals were adopted. The School was born. Huey needed a site and the Charity Board obligingly donated vacant land in the 1500 block of Tulane Avenue. The matter of financing the construction was easily handled. The Baton Rouge campus would sell some land to the State Highway Department and the proceeds would fund construction. That the Baton Rouge campus did not

Woodcut caricature of Arthur Vidrine by W. B. Stewart, Head of the Medical Art Department

wish to sell the land or that the Highway Department did not need to acquire it were irrelevant details. Huey had his school, a Dean, a site, and most importantly funding. With his usual flare for the dramatic Huey announced what he had accomplished in a letter to the "Citizens of Louisiana," proclaiming that he was "justly proud" of the "outstanding accomplishments of my administration."

What Huey had done to fund the construction was probably quite illegal and a newspaper promptly accused Huey of stealing a million dollars from the Highway Trust Fund. Huey is said to have retorted that he had stolen two million and to "publish what you want but we will have a medical school for the poor boys of Louisiana." A suit was filed eventually to halt the land sale but by the time it was heard the contracts had been signed, the building was under construction and the court shrugged its shoulders and dismissed the suit.

There was another predictable backlash when news of the school's approval was publicized. Some felt Tulane was being threatened and the "Spite School" theory was born. The theory postulated that revenge was Long's motive for building the school. Actually there were several versions of the theory. The first involved Huey's desire to avenge himself against Esmond Phelps, a prominent New Orleans attorney and the president of Tulane's Board of Administrators, who in 1928 had attempted, quite unsuccessfully, to have Huey impeached. The second theory involved Charles C. Bass, DDS, MD, Dean of the Tulane Medical School, inventor of dental floss and a New Orleans "blue blood," who was particularly upset by this perceived threat and said so openly to the Tulane Board, which was mostly anti-Long. Huey, it was said, had been denied an honorary doctorate from the Tulane Law School, and some guessed that building a School of Medicine was his revenge. That Huey had never sought such an honor from Tulane was irrelevant. Historian James Duffy noted that others, most notably Tinsley Harrison, the Superintendent of Education, had argued that Huey, a recognized expert on Louisiana constitutional law, deserved such an honor but no evidence exists that Huey was even aware of their efforts. How building a medical school damaged Tulane's law school was not obvious to some bystanders.

Huey was ruthless, dictatorial, and power-hungry, but there is no real evidence to support any "Spite School" theory. Rather, a love of LSU and a concern for the health of the poor, Huey's source of political power, drove his actions. In an interesting sidelight Loyola University in New Orleans did award Huey an honorary law degree.

Construction of the Medical School building began in March 1931. Organization of the School was by then already well under way. Huey, who designed plays for the LSU football team and led the Tiger Band when the mood struck him, proved equally adept at meddling in the day-to-day affairs of the School of Medicine. This tendency proved short-lived, but ultimately nearly disastrous, years later.

The method of filling most faculty positions was simply to target Tulane. Some significant outsiders, however, were brought aboard. Aristides Agramonte, for example, a Cuban physician who helped conquer yellow fever, was named the head of the Tropical Medicine Department and Rigney D'Aunoy, Head of Pathology at Charity, was named Head of the combined Department of Pathology and Bacteriology and Associate Dean. Ray McLean Van Wort, Director of the State Colony for the Feebleminded, was recruited to head Neuropsychiatry. Joseph Clark Stephenson came from Oklahoma to Chair Anatomy, and Clyde Brooks, who boasted not only an MD and a PhD but also an LLD, came from Wisconsin, to lead the combined departments of Pharmacology and Physiology.

Raiding the Greenies, however, was the order of the day. P. Jorda Kahle in Urology, Homer Dupuy in Otolaryngology, Philip Carter in Obstetrics, John Signorelli in Pediatrics, J. Bernie Guthrie in Medicine, Amadee Granger in Radiology, Henry Blum in Ophthalmology and Peter Graffagnino in Gynecology all came over to LSU from Tulane to head their departments. All were outstanding catches, and in most cases nationally known. Granger, who had served as Chief of Radiology at Charity since 1921, for example, had been awarded the Gold Medal of Radiological Society of North America for his work on sinus x-ray interpretation and had been decorated by the French Government for his use of x-rays to locate bullets in wounded World War I soldiers. Graffagnino had introduced spinal anesthesia to the practice of gynecology. Guthrie would contract pericarditis in 1932 and pass away. He would be succeeded by the equally well-known Dr. George Sam Bel, who had at one time served as Professor of Medicine at Tulane and was on the Charity staff.

Huey had particularly wanted to land Urban Maes, MD, a hero of World War I, a surgeon of national repute, and second in command to Alton Ochsner, Sr., the Chair of Surgery at Tulane, as LSU Surgery Chairman. Maes turned Huey down flat, distrusting that Huey would produce a "Class A," i.e., fully accredited, medical school and angry that the year earlier Ochsner had been summarily booted from the staff of Charity Hospital. In 1930,

Ochsner had written a letter to Dr. Allen O. Whipple, an out-of-state surgical colleague in which he strongly criticized the politicized operation of Charity Hospital (read: "Huey meddling"), a copy of which somehow came into the possession of Arthur Vidrine, who apparently was not a fan of Ochsner. Three explanations have been offered for how this happened. The first is that a copy was stolen from Ochsner's coat pocket and given to Vidrine; the second is that a copy was found on the street and given to Vidrine; and the third is that someone on the Tulane faculty or staff mailed a copy to Vidrine. Take your pick.

However it happened, Ochsner, an immensely popular figure in New Orleans society, but someone who had clashed repeatedly with Vidrine over Charity policies, was soon dismissed from Charity's staff. It is unlikely that Vidrine did this without an approval from Huey. Ochsner's dismissal caused the expected firestorm and gave rise ultimately to a third alternative and equally improbable "Spite School" theory, namely that Huey formed the LSU Medical School to avenge himself on Ochsner. In an interesting footnote Huey at about the time of Ochsner's dismissal was recommending the appointment of Dr. Isidore Cohn, Sr., a Tulane clinical faculty member, to be a senior visiting surgeon at Charity. So much for Huey's blanket animosity toward Tulane.

Failing to get Maes, Huey settled on Emmitt Lee Irwin, an Assistant Professor of Surgery at Tulane, to head Surgery. This choice did not sit well with the organizations, such as the AMA, that would rate the fledgling school. The School was going to need, Huey was told, someone of real academic stature in Surgery, considered the most important clinical department, for the coveted "Class A" designation to be awarded. And that wasn't Irwin.

Hat in hand, Huey eventually went back to Maes. By now, money had been committed and a large building was under construction. They struck a deal. Maes would take the position on three conditions: Ochsner would be reinstated to the Charity Staff, Tulane would control an equitable number of beds at Charity Hospital, and Huey would

MEDICAL CENTER SCIENCE BUILDING   WEISS, DREYFOUS & SEIFERT, ARCHITECTS

Medical Center Science Building, architect's rendering

quit meddling in the Medical School. Huey made good on the agreement, and Irwin's brief tenure was over. He left after sending an angry letter of resignation to the Dean.

Maes became Chairman of Surgery and brought with him a talented protégé, Dr. James D. Rives. Maes would serve as Chairman until 1954, when Rives succeeded him.

Many years later, Irwin, still bearing a big grudge, reappeared on the LSU stage. But the LSU School of Medicine officially opened on October 1, 1931.

Dedication of the School was postponed until May 1932 to coincide with the AMA convention that was being held in New Orleans. The School was showcased to many visiting dignitaries who toured it and several were invited to give speeches at the dedication. Huey

LSU School of Medicine
original façade, before expansion

brought the Tiger Band from Baton Rouge. They played before each speech. Huey spoke last, promising "friendly relations" all around. Before he spoke, the band played "Hail to the Chief," the anthem of the President of the United States. Modesty was not a virtue that Huey cultivated. Clearly, the pomp and circumstance—and there was a lot of pomp and circumstance—was designed to impress the visitors and help the campaign for "Class A" status. The School would receive full accreditation in 1933 before the first class would graduate. That class and all subsequent classes through 1939 would receive a Bachelor of Medicine (MB) and after successfully completing a year of internship, an MD would be awarded. This was typical for newly established schools.

And that's how Huey got his medical school. In the space of 10 months it went from dream to reality. Seventy-five plus years later, the School of Medicine continues to fulfill the dream of giving a quality medical education to the men and women of Louisiana and through them providing excellent care for patients around the world.

෯෬

Chapter II

The Early Years

It was warm on October 1, 1931, but the students, a freshman class and a transfer class of junior students, crowded into the unairconditioned and still-unfinished building at 1542 Tulane Avenue. LSU School of Medicine had officially opened its doors for classes. The junior transfer class came mostly from the University of Alabama, which had a two-year medical program. Between the two classes, sixteen states and two foreign countries were represented. Louisiana residents paid no tuition. All others paid $300 a year. Students had to trek up five floors to reach their classes, since only the building's fifth floor was open for business and the elevators did not work. There was only a little office and research space for new faculty members. Four departments shared a single office and a single secretary.

Still, Huey Long's shadow hovered above the medical school. Despite all of the challenges, the school that opened its doors that day changed the face of medical education in Louisiana forever. Many of its students were from impoverished rural areas, and their new medical school was a symbol of the increasing opportunities for higher education open to the poor. It was the Depression era, and most Americans were busy working for survival. The promise of an affordable medical education for everyone was exciting and important. The School of Medicine in New Orleans was an important part of Huey Long's agenda for improving his poor rural state.

It was also central to improving the medical care of Louisiana's indigent patient population. The School was situated next to Charity Hospital, which allowed students and faculty members to treat one of the largest and most diverse patient groups in the country. From its inception, LSU was intricately linked to patient care and clinical excellence.

The original School of Medicine building was a testament to its time and position. The imposing eight-story structure was designed in the Art Deco style. One of the most striking Art Deco features of the building was a metal bas-relief over the original entrance designed by noted Louisiana artist Enrique Alferez. The relief depicted the conquest of yellow fever, the result of work by the Walter Reed commission in Cuba in the early twentieth century.

Later, when the additions to the School of Medicine covered the sculpture, the art piece was hung in the school library. Over time it became obvious that it was deteriorating and was taken down and sent for restoration.

In the aftermath of Hurricane Katrina, the sculpture disappeared temporarily. After the school returned to New Orleans, the sculpture was located by the Office of Alumni Affairs and now hangs prominently in the library today.

The sculpture was, in part, meant to honor Dr. Aristides Agramonte, a member of Reed's group who had been named head of the school's Tropical Medicine Department. Agramonte unfortunately died before he could take his position at LSU, but his influence continued to be felt, as the School of Medicine purchased his personal medical library and used it to form the nucleus of the Medical School's library, which was named for Dr. Agramonte. Within the first decade of the School's history, additions to the library forced its move out of its original space In 1931 it consisted of 412 books, 100 bound volumes of journals, and 128 journal subscriptions. By 1937 it had grown to 2,861 books, 3,158 bound journals, and 174 journal subscriptions. It was opened to healthcare professionals from around the city. During World War II, officers from the armed services borrowed heavily from the medical school library. It was only one of the ways in which the School of Medicine performed an important role in the medical education needs of the New Orleans community.

Upon Agramonte's death, his position as Chair of Tropical Medicine would be filled temporarily by Dr. Joseph O'Hara, who was head of the State Board of Health and Orleans Parish Coroner. In 1932, he would give way to Dr. Thomas B. Anderson, Chief of Staff at the U.S. Public Health Service Hospital in New Orleans. O'Hara, who was nationally known for his work in tuberculosis control and traffic safety, would remain on the faculty until 1940.

Medical students followed a traditional course of study. Basic science classes were taught in the first two years, including anatomy, pharmacology, physiology, biochemistry, bacteriology and pathology. The final two years of medical school were occupied with clinical instruction. Students did not receive their MD degree, however, until they finished one year of internship. This arrangement, whereby a Bachelor of Medicine degree was awarded after four years and an MD

Library as it looked at the opening of the school

degree after the intern year, was typical for new medical schools and persisted until 1940, when the School began to award the MD degree upon graduation.

The medical school was immediately distinguished for the quality of its educators. There were many giants at the School of Medicine. George Sam Bel, a renowned internist and former president of the Louisiana State Medical Society, was a professor of Internal Medicine and served as Departmental Chair, succeeding Dr. J. Bernie Guthrie. He was also on the Charity Hospital Board and a close friend of Arthur Vidrine. Richard Ashman was recruited from Vanderbilt by Clyde Brooks, first chairman of the combined Department of Pharmacology and Physiology, as a faculty member in Physiology. Ashman's work in electrocardiography would forever change the way doctors looked at diagnosing heart disease. In 1932 the combined department would be separated, Brooks retaining the chairmanship of Pharmacology and Ashman becoming Head of Physiology and Director of the Charity Hospital Heart Station.

In a testament to his longevity, Ashman would serve as head of the department until 1951. He was succeeded by Dr. A. Sidney Harris, a pupil of Dr. Charles Wiggers, the greatest American physiologist of the time. Harris would remain until 1973. Incredibly, their records would be surpassed by Dr. John Spitzer, Harris' successor, who would serve until 2002, when Dr. William Chilian from the University of Wisconsin succeeded him.

The School of Medicine had other up-and-coming physicians. In 1931, Edgar Hull joined the faculty as an instructor in the Medicine Department, and later became a key figure both in the Department and in the school as a whole. Other faculty members included Walter Moss, an instructor in the Department of Surgery and junior house surgeon at Charity Hospital since 1929, who eventually had the Lake Charles Charity Hospital named in his honor in recognition of a distinguished career. Howard Beard, recruited from Case Western Reserve School of Medicine, became Chairman of Biochemistry. Henry Nathan Blum joined the faculty from Tulane to chair Ophthalmology after advanced study in Paris and Vienna. Dr. Abraham Louis Levin, inventor of the Levin tube came from Touro Infirmary to head the Section of Gastroenterology. His son Irving and two grandsons, Alan and Louis, would graduate from the School, and Irving and Alan would both eventually be faculty members. Visiting faculty included Allen O. Whipple from Columbia University, Isidor Ravdin from the University of Pennsylvania, Priscilla White from the Joslyn Clinic and Tufts University, and M. Edward Davis from the University of Chicago, all giants in their fields. Another visitor was Walter Alvarez, MD, Chief of Medicine at the Mayo Clinic and author of a nationally syndicated newspaper column that provided answers to medical questions posed to him by nonphysicians.

Faculty members were quickly cited for important work. In 1936, Dr. Rigney D'Aunoy, who served as Chairman and Professor in the combined Department of Pathology and Bacteriology and Associate Dean of the School of Medicine, along with Emmerich von

Hamm, who in 1938 would become Chairman of Pathology at Ohio State University School of Medicine, were recognized by the American Society of Clinical Pathologists with a "Gold Medal" for their research on the cause of granuloma inguinale and Dr. Frederick Fitzhugh Boyce, Assistant Professor of Surgery, would be awarded the Samuel D. Gross Prize for surgical research by the Philadelphia Academy of Surgery, a prize awarded only every five years. The following year, Drs. Richard Ashman and Edgar Hull published *Essentials of Electrocardiography*, a trailblazing text in the recognition of electrocardiography as one of the most important diagnostic tools available to physicians.

In this they were greatly aided by the newly formed Department of Medical Illustrations under the direction of the noted medical illustrator, William B. Stewart. Incredibly the Department had only four heads in its almost 75-year history, Stewart, Gerald Hodge, Donald Alvarado and Eugene New.

In the aftermath of Katrina and with the advent of sophisticated computer illustration software, the Department was dissolved.

As the school grew in size and influence, the activities of the school began to have an increasing impact in the health of New Orleanians and the practice of medicine. By the fall of 1932, the School of Medicine had four functioning classes, with 66 freshmen, 50 sophomores, a new transfer class of 27 juniors, and 28 seniors. All 28 seniors graduated in the spring of 1933, the first graduating class in School of Medicine history. Graduation of the first four-year class would take place in 1935, an epochal year in the school's history.

Students, residents, and faculty members benefited from varied and extensive experience at Charity Hospital. Senior medical students routinely saw a large number of autopsies performed by LSU faculty. In addition, the patient population seen on Charity Hospital's wards and clinic service gave medical students a first-class medical education. Clearly, their time at LSU exposed them to the realities of medicine, as well as testing their fortitude and honing their skills.

Not all medical practice involved patient care at a hospital. Beginning in the 1930s, LSU medical students and residents delivered many babies at the expectant mothers' homes. In what could be a terrifying experience, medical students were sometimes left to their own devices in managing a delivery and providing immediate post-partum care to new mothers.

Home delivery gave students experience in obstetrics. As school officials realized, students performing home deliveries provided a valuable service and also caught a glimpse of a future in rural medical practice.

This glimpse may have had an unintended effect. After internship most early graduates opted for residency training rather than rural general practice. **Julius Mullins, Sr. ('36)**, offered an explanation. He was better off with a small resident's salary, a hospital room, and three meals a day than he would be trying to start a general practice in an impoverished depression-era Louisiana town. Mullins would become a leading Baton Rouge obstetrician, would found Women's Hospital there, would become an early and unofficial school historian, and in 1986 the first president of the modern Medical Alumni Association.

LSU also provided a valuable service in helping to combat venereal diseases in the New Orleans area. Supplying staff members for clinics around the city, the school joined national efforts to raise awareness about venereal diseases. Additionally, the School of Medicine afforded healthcare professionals an important education in this area by holding classes geared toward practicing doctors, nurses, and technicians and helping them combat these diseases. These classes were especially important to doctors from rural areas. It was an early foray into the area of Continuing Medical Education.

A number of faculty participated in preventive medicine courses in conjunction with state agencies. Dr. John Signorelli, Sr., the first chairman of Pediatrics and a popular medical figure, organized the first program in child welfare in the city. Efforts such as these were symbols of LSU's commitment to public health initiatives and the well-being of the community.

Students also received education through various guest speakers who came through the New Orleans area. Organizations such as the Southern Medical Association, second only to the AMA in importance to organized medicine at that time, the Orleans Parish Medical Society, and the Southern Medical Women's Association routinely sponsored guest lecturers from around the country, while other physicians made individual trips to New Orleans for research or speaking engagements. It was this flourishing intellectual environment that made LSU an emerging leader in medical education.

The early to mid-1930s were also an exciting, though fluid, time for the medical field. Women were entering the ranks of physicians at a slow but increasing pace, and this pattern was also seen at LSU. The school's first graduating class included a single female physician, Virginia Webb. Despite the advances of women in medicine, there were still a number of hurdles for female physicians to traverse.

Navigating largely uncharted waters, women doctors faced many challenges. For example, female medical students at LSU were given a lecture to help them learn how to adapt to working in a traditionally male environment. The lecturer, herself a woman, reminded her audience to not lose their femininity. Other speakers were less kind. During a talk in New Orleans in the mid 1930s, Morris Fishbein, President of the American Medical Association, a man described as having a lightning rod for a personality, rebuked the presence of women in the American medical workforce. He contended that women had no place in medicine and ridiculed them for spending too much money on cosmetics, saying that a look at his audience would prove his point. Fishbein, who was editor of the *Journal of the American Medical Association*, would mellow over time or at least learn to hold his tongue better.

This stigma against women in medicine would pervade the medical profession for decades. Certainly, the women at LSU during this early period felt the effects of discrimination and criticism most acutely. Their trailblazing path, however, provided a benchmark of achievement for those who followed. Things have changed a lot. At present, nearly 50% of the entering classes are women and often they are the student leaders.

LSU School of Medicine came of age in a time of great change in medicine. Advancements in surgical and medical technology would develop rapidly through World War II and the 1950s. Medical students could be cheered by these new advancements because better medicine directly impacted the health and studies of medical students themselves. A number of maladies regularly claimed the health of medical students. They were susceptible to tuberculosis and gastrointestinal problems, among other conditions. Many students lived in close quarters near the campus of the medical school. Dean Beryl Burns reported in 1939 to LSU President Campbell B. Hodges that the condition of student housing near the LSUSOM campus was deplorable. Students were also exposed to a variety of infections during their service at Charity Hospital, where crowded conditions contributed to a great risk for communicable diseases, particularly tuberculosis.

In 1938 and 1939, Drs. Joe and Alice Baker Holoubek conducted a study of tuberculosis prevalence among medical students. Their results were striking: 98% of senior medical students at the School of Medicine showed evidence on their chest x-rays of primary tuberculosis, compared with 94% of juniors, 90% of sophomores, and 68% of freshmen. Thankfully, only nine students showed evidence of active disease. In 1938, according to Dr. J. Clyde Schwartzwelder, of the Department of Tropical Medicine, 10% of students harbored intestinal parasites. Studies such as these demonstrated the dangers facing medical students in the pre-antibiotic era, making medical school and internship life particularly risky.

The School ultimately established a special committee to study the effects of tuberculosis on the medical school and to recommend measures that could be taken to minimize the devastating impact among the medical school population. Faculty members on the special committee recommended tuberculosis testing for all incoming freshmen. In this way, active disease could be detected and treated.

To further combat this and other health problems, the School of Medicine adopted a student health program in the early 1940s. Paid for by a student health fee, this program allowed students to receive tuberculosis testing, as well as access to clinic staff drawn from the LSU faculty, consults from other LSU faculty members, and hospitalization near the School of Medicine, if needed.

Faculty members had many pressures in the early days. First and foremost, they were greatly pressed for time, with a combination of hospital, clinic, private practice, and consults. The School of Medicine, moreover, suffered from a constant shortage of funds in cash-poor

Louisiana. For these reasons, part-time faculty members were the mainstay of the educational program of the School of Medicine.

Part-time faculty members held a wide variety of teaching positions. Indeed, many clinical departments were almost entirely made up of part-time faculty members, including the Departments of Surgery and the surgical subspecialties, Obstetrics and Gynecology, and Pediatrics. There was not one full-time faculty member in Pediatrics until 1938 when Dr. G.S. Kenney was hired by Department Chair John Signorelli, Sr. Full-time faculty members often held numerous administrative posts, while part-time faculty members bore much of the burden of teaching.

Despite the numerous challenges facing the medical school it was able to attract an impressive array of talent. Faculty members often had impressive experience that they brought to LSU. For example, George McCoy, MD, was the Head of the United States Public Health Service and former Director of the National Institutes of Health before joining the LSU faculty as Chairman of the Department of Public Health in 1938. He was the first person to discover the etiologic agent of tularemia. Chevalier Jackson, the nation's leading expert in bronchoscopy and esophagoscopy served as visiting professor annually from 1932 to 1937. In 1939, John Adriani, MD, came to New Orleans from New York to be Chief of Anesthesiology at Charity Hospital. He would become one of the world's foremost anesthesiologists. Because LSU had no separate Department of Anesthesia (and would not have one for many years), Adriani became Clinical Professor of Surgery and Pharmacology, posts he would hold until retirement in 1977. LSU would not have a separate Department of Anesthesiology until 1977, when one would be organized by Dr. Mohammed Naraghi.

Early on, LSU also drew faculty from around the world. Julius Bauer was a noted internist at the University of Vienna, who joined the LSU faculty ranks in 1938 as a clinical professor of Internal Medicine. Erwin Wexberg, an internationally known psychoanayst also from Vienna served as visiting professor from 1935 through 1937. Sir Aldo Castellani, "the leading physician in Italy," came to LSU for three to six months several times during the 1930s to teach Tropical Medicine and Dermatology. During his career he treated members of the British Royal Family and the Italian dictator Benito Mussolini. In 1939 he was named to lead the Institute of Tropical Medicine in London. As of that same year, 13 out of 200 LSU faculty members hailed from foreign medical schools.

Long was the school's benefactor throughout its early years. It was not in Huey's character to watch from the sidelines, either in his gubernatorial duties or even during LSU football games. As a result, he was there with the School of Medicine when money or influence was needed. When political battles threatened the prerogative of New Orleans' newest medical school, Long sided with the medical school and secured its development. Even though Long had been elected to the United States Senate and would have logically stepped out of the minutiae of the state's governance, he did not abandon his beloved medical school.

Indeed, before he was murdered in 1935, Long had made even grander plans for the medical complex surrounding Charity Hospital, including a dental school, a nursing school, a pharmacy school and a graduate school of medicine. Huey, it is said, wanted a dental school in downtown New Orleans because Loyola University, which had a dental school, had denied Long the unrestricted use of its powerful, clear channel radio station, WWL.

Huey had personally selected the Dental School site, immediately behind the building at 1542 Tulane Avenue. The new 12-story building would front on Gravier Street and be connected to the original building by a series of sky bridges.

There was one small problem, the "contagion building" an ancient but useful structure, occupied Long's chosen site. He had a simple, elegant solution. Move the building. It was an immense four-story structure but where there is a will there's a way. The building was jacked up and railroad tracks were laid under the building and down Gravier Street. The building was set down on a series of metal rollers and a small train engine called a "donkey engine" was brought in.

The building was being slowly moved at the time that Long was shot. The moving halted. When Huey died, the plan died with him. No one knew what to do and none of Huey's henchmen cared for the project. Months after Huey's burial, the building was returned in the middle of the night to its original site, lowered to the ground and the engine removed. The whole episode cost half a million dollars. When the building was razed decades later to make room for a parking garage the train tracks and rollers were still there under it.

Long's death cast a pall over the school. His black-bordered portrait filled the front page of "The Tiger," the student newspaper that had begun publishing in 1932. His dreams would be scaled back dramatically. A Department of Nursing would be created in 1937 to act as liaison between Baton Rouge campus and the Charity School of Nursing. In this way selected students could obtain both an RN and a BS degree.

A Graduate School of Medicine was established in 1936 under Drs. C. J. Tripoli and J. T. Nix, but war preparations brought it to an end and a true

moving the old C Building

The Charles L. Franck Collection of the Historic New Orleans Collection, Acc. No. 1979.325.998

Officially preparing to move the old contagion building

Graduate School would not be established until 1965. A Dental School would be approved in 1966 and a separate School of Nursing in 1967. The School of Allied Health would be established in 1970, completing the Schools that would be established in New Orleans until the Department of Public Health became a separate school in 2003. A School of Pharmacy never materialized.

The death of Huey Long was a severe blow to the fortunes of the School of Medicine. The circumstances of his death have been recounted in various books, most notably the biography by T. Harry Williams. Most of the facts have been gotten right, but some of them, especially the story that Huey bled to death, are perhaps quite wrong.

After Huey was shot in the Capitol, he was taken to Our Lady of the Lake Hospital and Arthur Vidrine was called. Although Vidrine was a competent surgeon, he called Urban Maes to come to Baton Rouge. Maes and his young associate Dr. Jimmy Rives started to Baton Rouge with Rives driving. To avoid a head-on collision on the two-lane road, Rives was forced to drive on the muddy shoulder of the road and the car got stuck. It took hours before the car was freed and they could continue to Baton Rouge. Vidrine decided he couldn't wait for the two to arrive, so he operated, finding two perforations in Huey's colon.

Edgar Hull and P. Jorda Kahle, the Head of LSU Urology, were also called in. A suspicion of perirenal bleeding was raised because small amounts of blood were present in the urine. Hull arrived first, followed by Rives and Maes, and separately by Kahle. Kahle inserted needles into both perirenal spaces and said there was no bleeding. Blood counts apparently confirmed this. Rives and Maes felt there was nothing more that could be done. Hull examined Huey and diagnosed fulminant peritonitis. Huey died 36 hours after being shot. Although Hull argued for an autopsy, permission was denied. Hull confirmed all of the above in an *LSU Medicinews* interview in 1983. Williams never interviewed Hull for his book but suggested to Hull years after its publication that he might have written it differently if they had talked.

Arthur Vidrine survived for only a short time after Long's death. With his patron gone, Vidrine lost influence and resigned first as Superintendent of Charity Hospital in 1936 and as Dean in 1937. He would then open a surgical practice in the Lafayette area. Many years later, his son, Arthur Vidrine Jr., would attend the School of Medicine and graduate in 1959.

Dr. George Sam Bel, a member of the Charity Board, succeeded Vidrine as Superintendent at Charity in 1936. Dr. Bel, who had been Professor of Medicine at Tulane, was at the time also serving as Chairman of Medicine at LSU. Bel would die in 1939 of coronary occlusion and would be succeeded as Chair of Medicine by Dr. Edgar Hull. Joseph Rigney D'Aunoy, Associate Dean and Chair of Pathology, took up the deanship following Vidrine's departure. Just two years later, in 1939, D'Aunoy resigned as Dean and was replaced by Beryl I. Burns, Chairman of Anatomy.

That was a welcome transition for the medical school. The differences between the leadership styles of D'Aunoy and Burns could not have been greater. D'Aunoy was a competent physician but a harsh taskmaster and feared by faculty and students. It has been said that he had more enemies than Huey Long, a remarkable feat for a pathologist. Burns, on the other hand was highly respected and well liked.

A dedicated, nationally known, and talented doctor, D'Aunoy had chagrined many with his treatment of students and faculty. **Alice Baker Holoubek ('38)** remembered everyone being petrified with fear of Dr. D'Aunoy.

D'Aunoy's fate as Dean was sealed by a survey visit to the School of Medicine from members of the American Association of Medical Colleges. Whether the visit was a routine inspection or inspired by faculty discontent is unclear. At any rate, the visitors reported that unfavorable relations between dean and faculty seriously hampered the effectiveness of both D'Aunoy's leadership and the school's performance.

Actually, two reports were issued – a long one to D'Aunoy and a second, very short one to LSU President Paul Hebert. The one to D'Aunoy suggested, among other things, that the School should drop the requirement of an intern year to grant the MD degree and award it after the fourth year. This would occur in 1940. Another suggestion was that D'Aunoy should "delegate" many of his responsibilities as Dean.

The blunter report made to Hebert said that the written report to D'Aunoy was "tempered with considerable mercy … but our conversations … were very much more to the point." They had made "an urgent plea to resign the deanship because of his dictatorial methods," which had lost him the support of the faculty. Within weeks, D'Aunoy was gone as Dean.

Assuming the deanship at LSU in 1939, Burns was a solid choice. He was well liked and eminently qualified as an anatomist and administrator. Burns received his Doctor of Medicine degree from the University of Iowa in 1922 and his PhD in anatomy from the University of Chicago in 1931. He came to LSU in 1932 as a professor in the Anatomy

Department. From 1939 to 1945, Burns led the School of Medicine through one of the most critical times ever faced by the country at large, not just the medical school.

Burns later admitted that he strove "to maintain, not to improve" the medical school during his years as Dean. As the School's students and faculty were thrown into the furor of World War II, simply maintaining the school on an even keel proved to be a formidable task.

Despite the critical times faced by the School of Medicine, it was clear that scholastic excellence was expected and recognized by both faculty and students. In April 1940, the School founded The Circle, a society established to honor those students who achieved the highest levels of academic excellence. Membership in The Circle was limited to the upper ten percent of the senior class, while only the top three junior classmen were selected for the group. Later, The Circle would metamorphose into the local chapter of Alpha Omega Alpha, the national honor medical society.

Initial members of The Circle included **Norman C. Woody ('40)**, who would become Professor of Pediatrics at Tulane, and the legendary **Abe Mickal ('40)**, Commandant of Cadets at LSU in Baton Rouge and a football All-American. Abe so fascinated Huey Long that Huey had offered Abe an appointment as a State Senator, which Abe, an LSU undergraduate at the time, wisely declined. Still, Abe as a medical student had a twice weekly sports radio program while maintaining a nearly perfect academic record. He would become one of America's premier obstetricians/gynecologists and ultimately Departmental Chair in 1959. Other noteworthy early members of the Circle who would go on to academic greatness included **Walter Hollis ('45)** and **Albert Hyman ('45)**. Both would become outstanding cardiologists, Hyman as Professor of Medicine at Tulane and Hollis as Professor of Medicine at LSU.

Several faculty changes occurred during the 1930s. Dr. Rudolph Kampmeier, who had been a faculty member since 1932, took a position at Vanderbilt in 1939. He would go on to write a famous text in Physical Diagnosis and return as a Visiting Professor of Medicine on many occasions. Dr. J. B. L. Howles, a noted author and teacher, would become Chair of Dermatology in 1937, replacing Joseph Numa Roussel, who had been Chief of Dermatology at Touro Infirmary before coming to LSU. Howles, a product of the University of Cincinnati, would head the Department for 16 years. He would be succeeded by C. Barrett Kennedy, a close associate who would serve from 1953 to 1968. In 1939, Dr. John Signorelli, the first Chairman of Pediatrics, would die and be succeeded by Dr. Edwin Socola as Acting Chairman.

෧෬

Chapter III

The War Years

By 1940 it was obvious to many that the United States would eventually be drawn into the Second World War and that medical care would be essential. Thus, Dean Beryl I. Burns and senior faculty members began preparing the school for a wartime footing long before the war began. Faculty members also began considering their own service in the armed forces. On November 5, 1940, the faculty of the School of Medicine met at the insistence of the Dean and the Department of Surgery chairman Urban Maes, himself a decorated World War I battlefield surgeon, to discuss the formation of a general hospital that would be affiliated with the School of Medicine.

In many ways, the School's mission during the Second World War would be the same both overseas and at home. LSU doctors everywhere strove to deliver care to all of their patients to the best of their ability. Charity Hospital was a good training ground for either civilian or military service. The patient population was widely diverse, physical facilities could often be makeshift, and trauma and infectious diseases were common. In this way, LSU's doctors had trained for trench medicine well before the start of the Second World War.

By 1941, LSU was on a mission to produce doctors for both the military and civilian populations at a faster rate than before. The School of Medicine had a twofold challenge. Not only would the school adopt an accelerated curriculum, but it also would sacrifice many of its faculty members who would either staff a medical unit sponsored by the school or be assigned elsewhere. For the next four years, the School of Medicine would be fully engaged in the war effort, participating in the care of civilians and soldiers alike.

Also of major concern was the possible shortage in medical personnel for the civilian population. The scope and intensity of the fighting ensured that any mobilization would include the activation of tens of thousands of doctors, as well, as millions of men and women into the Army, Navy, and Marines. In rural Louisiana, this was particularly important, as surveys showed that many parishes depended upon small numbers of doctors. How would the United States replenish its supply of doctors if the war lasted longer than a few years?

Howard Buechner ('43M), who kept meticulous contemporary records, noted that he and many of his classmates initially thought that Japan would be quickly defeated, but hopes for a short war were soon dashed. The American Navy and Marines mobilized in the Pacific while Hitler's armies threatened Allies in Europe, North Africa, and Russia. Fifty years after graduation, Buechner recalled, "Optimism soon turned to gloom, however, as one ominous sign after another made its appearance." LSU President Campbell B. Hodges announced that he expected every male student at LSU to serve in the armed forces during the war.

Many LSU medical students during World War II were actually student soldiers—enrolled in the Army Specialized Training Program and the Navy's V-12 program. Eligible students were told that they could either apply for commissions in the army and finish medical school or be drafted into the infantry immediately. It was not a hard choice. By February 9, 1942, Dean Burns announced, 65 students of an 81-member senior class at the School of Medicine had applied for their commissions in the Army, Navy, or Public Health Services. Ninety percent of their classmates in the junior class followed their example. These students embarked on a medical school career designed to make them military doctors. Since flunking out of medical school meant immediate induction into the army as a private, scholarship was the order of the day. Those few not in the Army or Navy programs were ineligible for health reasons, such as heart murmurs from prior rheumatic fever or severe myopia.

The School of Medicine's curriculum during the war was hectic and difficult, as it went to an accelerated status. Summer vacations were cut out of the school calendar, and a new freshman class was admitted every nine months. After completing a shortened nine-month internship period, new doctors were ready to enter either the civilian or military medical professions in just over four years. The Class of 1942 graduated three months early and two classes graduated in 1943, one in March and one in December. From 1943 until 1945, the students accepted into the Army Specialized Training Program (ASTP) and the Navy's V-12 program received military pay and expenses, and Army officials took over part of the school. By September 1943, two hundred sixty-two students were enrolled in the Army and Navy Specialized Training Programs, approximately 70 percent of the school's enrollment.

Military programs were tightly controlled. Student soldiers dressed in military uniforms, and were disciplined under a version of the military's cadet system. The students drilled as a part of their regular training regime, usually along South Claiborne Avenue and other city streets. The accelerated program initiated by the LSU faculty proved highly successful, and the Army, using the LSU model, expanded the expedited curriculum nationwide continuously until 1944.

The School of Medicine was supposed to teach students to be effective military doctors, do it in less time than would normally be afforded for medical education, and without some of its most talented faculty. There were also no guarantees that these doctors would return for civilian practice in Louisiana after the war. The original mandate for the LSU School of Medicine, therefore, changed from one of providing the state of Louisiana with qualified doctors to one of participating in a nationwide effort against foreign enemies. Dean Beryl Burns made it clear that the Medical School was another willing cog in the wartime machine. "It is your assignment in the national emergency," Burns wrote to students. "To fail to carry out that assignment to the best of your ability would be a very grave matter indeed." The student soldiers would be expected to sacrifice themselves to the war effort through their medical education if not in immediately joining the armies in battle.

Students were keenly aware of the sacrifices that everyone was forced to make in wartime. Government

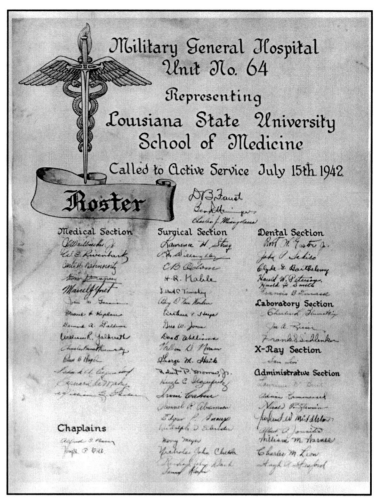

roster of the 64th General Hospital

officials strictly limited nonessential professional activities, and faculty members and students alike suffered the consequences. "We have just received word from Mr. R. H. Clare, Secretary, War Committee on Conventions," reads one announcement, "that permit is denied to hold the ninth annual meeting of The New Orleans Graduate Medical Assembly." Students were also forced to give up some of their recreational activities. Students enrolled in the Navy's specialized training program, for example, could not travel beyond a forty-mile radius. This meant LSU Navy medical students could not go to LSU's football games in Baton Rouge. Students made sacrifices willingly. Phi Lambda Kappa Medical Fraternity cancelled its formal dance and contributed the money reserved for that event to the United Community War Chest. These were just tiny examples of the effect of the sacrifices students made to preserve American society.

Other changes in wartime were far more potentially damaging. Howard Buechner remembered that one classmate, Kay Kohara, an American-born woman of Japanese ancestry was considered a suspect by many after Pearl Harbor. As the U.S. began to set up internment centers for Japanese-Americans in the western United States, some at the Medical School feared that Kohara would be placed in one of these camps. Buechner comments, "We were told that Kay would be pulled out of medical school and interned in a relocation camp ... but luckily this never came to pass." The effects of the war were coming nearer, and no one could know how they would be touched by the conflict's effects.

Meanwhile, accelerating a medical school's educational program produced many difficulties. First, the strain on the faculty as a result of shortened and continuously running school years was intense. This pressure was increased as more faculty members went off to war. As of July 1, 1943, thirty-eight members of the School of Medicine's faculty were already on military leave, and twenty more full- and part-time faculty had resigned. Those who stayed behind faced additional teaching duties and patient care responsibilities.

Throughout this critical time, alumni and faculty members were departing for active military service. Identical twins **Lee** and **Sam Hartman** of the class of (**'41**) entered the Army Air Force together. They were perhaps the only twins to serve as Flight Surgeons in WWII. Lee was posted to India while Sam served in Europe. In that capacity Sam participated in 1945 in "Operation Manna-Chowhound," a relief effort to drop food to the starving people of the Netherlands.

Though diminutive in size (they did not top five feet, four inches), they were extremely brave and received numerous campaign medals. Both had been members of the LSU Tiger Marching Band. When Huey Long saw Lee struggling under the weight of a tuba he insisted that he be given a baritone horn to play.

Clifford Keller (**'37**) served in the South Pacific as a member of a medical battalion attached to a Marine amphibious corps near the Solomon Islands. **Philip Cenac** (**'43**) also served four years in the Navy in the Pacific theater of operations. Three of his sons would ultimately graduate from his Alma Mater – Chris in 1971, Paul in 1983 and William Andre in 1984. Cenac would be honored many years later when his family created a Professorship of Medical Ethics in his honor. Buechner served gallantly in Europe, received several medals and became the first American physician to enter the Nazi death camp, Dachau. During the Dachau liberation several German guards were killed by Jewish inmates while American soldiers apparently looked the other way. The American officers including Buechner were threatened with court martial but it never came to pass. He would later write an account of the whole incident, a book entitled *Dachau: Hour of the Avenger* (Thunderbird Press, 1986). He would serve for many years on the faculty of the School of Medicine, and a Professorship of Medicine would eventually be created by admiring former students.

Major **Vincent Culotta, Sr., MD** (**'43**) was about to board a ship in California for service in the Pacific when he was informed of an abrupt change in orders and was told to report to New York for "specialized service" in the European theater. The specialized service had little to do with medicine but hinged on the fact that he spoke Italian fluently.

During the war he did practice medicine but because of his linguistic ability he was also made commandant of an Italian Prisoner of War camp that had been established in England and his patients were the prisoners.

A total of 450 alumni and 37 faculty answered the call to duty and many suffered greatly as a result of their war service. Lieutenant **John Vernon Ward**, class of 1939, served in the Army's Air Corps. He was shot down during the Allies' famous raid on Eastern Europe's Ploesti oil fields and taken prisoner by German forces. According to his wife, he was awarded the Distinguished Flying Cross and the Air Medal with Oak Leaf Cluster. Major **James Schonlau ('38)** was made a B29 bomber pilot by the Air Force and never did practice medicine during the war. In 1941, Capt. **C. A. Dwyer ('38),** a member of the Marine Corps, was sent to Manila. He was captured by the Japanese in 1942 and remained a prisoner of war until freed by American forces in 1945. **Ralph Nix Jr. ('41),** 25 years old, was killed in June 1943 while serving with the Coast Guard and the Public Health Service. He left behind a wife and a weeks-old son. He had received a Commendation Medal for his part in the rescue of 133 survivors of a troop ship torpedoed by a German submarine. His Coast Guard Cutter was subsequently sunk while on another mission. **Samuel Barkoff ('37)** was an Army Medical Corps wing surgeon stationed at MacDill Field in Florida when he died in a plane crash. In all, eight graduates of the School of Medicine died in service during World War II.

In 1946 Dr. Urban Maes would design a special flag and present it to the School of Medicine. One hundred blue stars were sewn on a red-and-white background, each star representing an alumnus still in military service. In the center of the banner were eight gold stars representing those who gave the ultimate sacrifice. A bronze plaque was also hung in the School of Medicine listing their names.

The Maes "battle flag" would be on display in the school library for many years. When the library moved to another building, the flag was relegated to basement storage. Before Katrina hit, a maintenance worker brought it to the Office of Alumni Affairs along with a number of records and artifacts. He had no particular reason to do this except that he had cared for these relics for many years and was retiring. By accident he had saved some of the School's irreplaceable history. The flag is now back on display in the Center for Advanced Practice.

An important facet of the School's survival was the retention of faculty for teaching and clinical care. Burns requested an increase in salaries for those who were forced to handle added teaching responsibilities as faculty departed to serve either in the 64th General Hospital or as part of other units. Clinical duties at Charity would consume more time, for example, because critical clinical departments would be especially hard-hit by departures and leaves of absence. Burns reported to his superiors, "I am sure that every one of them [the

The LSU School of Medicine Flag

This "battle flag" (right in the photograph) was presented to the LSU School of Medicine in 1945 by Dr. Urban Maes, Chairman and Professor of Surgery and a decorated battlefield surgeon in World War I. Dr. Maes was a consultant to the War Department and was the driving force behind LSU's preparation in World War II and the formation of the 64th General Hospital, LSU's Hospital that served with distinction in Sicily, Italy and North Africa.

Dr. Maes devised the accelerated curriculum that LSU adopted in 1942. That allowed the school to graduate the Class of 1942 three months early and to graduate two different classes in 1943. The LSU program was widely copied by medical schools across the nation.

Thirty-seven faculty members and 450 alumni served during the war. The 100 blue stars represent alumni and faculty still in service at the time of presentation. The eight gold stars represent the actual alumni killed in the war.

This flag was displayed in the library for many years and then stored in the basement. It was rescued from the basement and given to the Alumni Association for safekeeping before Hurricane Katrina.

A generous grant from Dr. and Mrs. **James Leonard** ('63) funded the conservation and framing of the flag.

faculty] will give this additional service if they remain with us, without thought of extra compensation." However, he added worriedly, "This is not to say that some will not leave in order to accept more advantageous positions just as in normal times." Burns therefore highlighted the importance of staying both competitive and competent during the war.

In late February 1942, the School of Medicine graduated the first medical students in the country under an accelerated program. As reported, commencement speaker C.S. Boucher, Chancellor of the University of Nebraska, "contrasted the American ideals with those of the Nazis, which 'condemn universal education and advocate illiteracy for the masses.' " Students clearly shared these feelings of professional obligation to the war effort.

"We will not follow the orthodox route of our predecessors," wrote Mac Woodward, president of the early class of 1942, to his classmates just before graduation. "No, the foolish rattle of guns and swords and the quick whisp of pens have provided for our immediate tomorrows." Leaving the School of Medicine meant getting one step closer to the shores of the South Pacific or the battle fields of Europe. A group of faculty members from the LSU School of Medicine, meanwhile, had already begun preparations for overseas service.

As early as October of 1940, doctors from LSU were called for military service as reserve officers. School administrators tried to defer their faculty members' service. They hoped that the military would allow LSU to fully staff the 64th General Hospital. Some faculty members, however, were not fortunate enough to have their service deferred. **Claude Craighead ('39),** who would ultimately serve for many years as Professor of Surgery, was simply instructed to comply with orders to join the Medical Reserve until the 64th General was ordered to active duty. He was assigned to the 344th Medical Regiment and never joined the 64th General; he served largely in Ireland and Northern Europe.

Most faculty members who were eligible for military service, nonetheless, formed the nucleus for the 64th General Hospital. A testimonial dinner was held at the Roosevelt Hotel on July 9, 1942, in honor of the 64th and on July 15, 1942, it was finally called for active duty. The 64th General Hospital was originally organized as a 1,000-bed hospital. The unit was first assigned for training at Fort Jackson in South Carolina, where the doctors were joined by the rest of the hospital's staff, including nurses, technicians, and enlisted men assigned to them by the Army. The staff of the hospital unit was immediately acquainted at Fort Jackson with the tangled web that was the Army's mobilization process.

The men and women who made up many of the medical units during World War II quickly found that their medical expertise alone would not carry them through the war. That is, war service would require a great amount of flexibility and patience. Many had trouble adjusting to Army life and culture. For one thing, the 64th was almost always commanded by a non-LSU military doctor. An enlisted man once wandered past the unit's commanding officer, Colonel Daniel Faust, without saluting him. The Colonel plaintively asked the soldier, "Say, son, don't you realize you are a soldier?" The soldier replied just as seriously, "No Sir, I'm just a civilian in uniform." Similar to what Army and Navy students at home experienced throughout the war, the personnel assigned to the 64th were asked to be two different types of the soldier—the kind that could manage the medical challenges, and the kind who could conform to Army life.

Many of the most odious tasks were administrative in nature, tedious but necessary. At Fort Jackson, the 64th was weighed down with unfamiliar organizational functions. "There was much confusion and loss of time in processing … as there was no one present familiar with the procedure and the work had to be done by inexperienced medical officers," complained Colonel Thomas Reagan, the 64th's commanding officer at the time. Forms were

64th General Hospital, Italy

incorrect and personal equipment was sometimes inadequately inspected before being given to the men and women for use.

Other problems, resulting from the Army's lackluster administrative apparatus were more serious. "Immunizations and inoculations not being given or recorded or both," unit commanders complained. "Typhoid shots given at intervals of two to four weeks, necessitating whole new series being started. Smallpox vaccinations not given or recorded." For a medical unit to be effective, all of these problems, both medical and administrative in nature, had to be ironed out quickly and effectively.

Other challenges were caused by limited training space. The Army activated a large number of technical and professional units during a short amount of time. The 64th was at Fort Jackson, for instance, for more than a year before its deployment to North Africa. In that time, the unit was rotated in and out of medical service at the Post Station Hospital at Fort Jackson for quite a while. Valuable training time was lost when the 64th did not have regular access to an army hospital, as the base hospital was sometimes too full to accommodate the unit. This forced the 64th to improvise training procedures. The unit's commander at Fort Jackson, Daniel Faust, observed in the unit diary, "We do have journal clubs, twice a week, to keep from getting too rusty."

The unit did not embark for its overseas assignment until July 14, 1943. The staff members of the 64th General Hospital also experienced the vital differences between military and civilian medicine. A civilian doctor, especially in a largely rural state like Louisiana, was expected to bond with his patient, listen to them attentively and to get to know them as individuals. A military doctor, however, did not have the luxury of time to devote to each patient. Instead, he was part of a larger military structure that emphasized healthcare in furtherance of the Army's goals.

Lou Peveto Scott, a nurse assigned to the unit in South Carolina, remembers one young patient whose stay with the 64th was extended because he was suffering from a fever. Though his condition was not serious, Scott tried to find other reasons to keep the young man hospitalized. When her superior was forced to send him back to his unit, he said, "Miss Peveto, how can we ever win this war if we don't discharge the boys because they look too young to be on the front lines." Military medicine was quite different from civilian practice; doctors and nurses sent men back to war every day, even though they knew they could be hurt or killed in action.

As troop movements were most often kept secret, the 64th General Hospital finally departed for destinations still unknown to them on August 21, 1943. The unit realized they were heading into the Mediterranean only after recognizing the telltale land formation of Gibraltar and the North African mainland to the south. One night, the unit was treated to an impressive display of airpower. "Our ship didn't give the alarm until after the fireworks started," Lou Scott wrote. "An aircraft carrier began shooting and put on a beautiful show with a shower of tracer bullets prettier than any Fourth of July celebration I have ever seen." Another air raid followed a few days later, but the *Barry*, their troop ship, reached its destination in Tunisia, safely, on September 4, 1943.

On October 23, 1943, the unit formally opened as a General Hospital six miles south of Ferryville, Tunisia, and served troops in the North African and Sicilian campaigns until the middle of February 1944. There was a large concentration of hospital facilities in the Bizerte area, which included the 24th General Hospital formed by the Tulane University School of Medicine. The LSU and Tulane Units and a nearby British Army Hospital formed the "Bizerte County Medical Society" and held regular educational meetings for several months. On Thanksgiving Day,

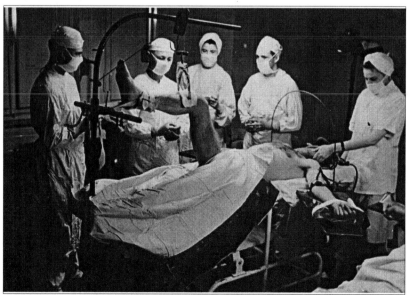

Surgery in Italy – 64th General Hospital

Tulane and LSU played a touch football game. Tulane was reported to have narrowly won the game but was soundly defeated in the post-game drinking contest. All of these units were kept busy. In its first nine days of operation, the 64th General admitted 363 patients to the Medical Service. This admission rate remained constant throughout the early period of the hospital's operation and grew as the 64th gained more responsibilities.

Communicable and infectious diseases were an especially important part of medical care required by ground forces during World War II. The close quarters and primitive conditions in which soldiers had to live for months on end made the risk of diseases such as typhus, tuberculosis, and hepatitis very high. They were also vulnerable to the threat of infection because of the bad condition of the sewerage and water supply around the 64th postings. On October 22, 1944, the unit diary mentions, "There are quite a large number of personnel being hospitalized for hepatitis." The entry also noted, "[The] absence [of hospital personnel] is being keenly felt as the minimum hospitalization period is 30 days." The spread of water-borne illnesses was consequently a serious problem as sidelined staff reduced the efficiency of the hospital, and put lives at risk.

For this reason, immunization and other preventive measures were very important. Herald R. Cox, a medical researcher with the U.S. Department of Agriculture, found ways to produce substantial quantities of a typhus vaccine, which greatly helped American armed service personnel. Other preventive medicine procedures included delousing procedures, insecticide use, and regulations that placed brothels off-limits to servicemen. Measures like these prevented epidemics of communicable disease, which would have severely stressed the Army's medical capabilities.

Malaria was a big concern, and 31 cases of the disease were admitted to the Medicine Service in December 1943. Twenty-two members of the 64th General itself were diagnosed the following month. The primary preventive treatment for malaria was Atabrine, but the anti-malarial drug was unpopular. Lou Scott remembered, "It nauseated me so that I vomited and vomited." Despite its side effects, Atabrine, or quinacrine as it was also known, was extremely effective against the deadliest type of malaria, *falciparum*, but only when soldiers were persuaded to take it.

In the meantime, public health measures were also taken. In February 1944, Colonel Reagan reported that the 64th was searching for the breeding grounds of malarial vectors in the form of adult mosquitoes and their larvae. The 64th General addressed drainage systems and used the pesticide DDT to maintain their area free of pest-borne diseases. These efforts were part of an effort in which the Army provided nonmedical malaria control officers and anti-malaria training materials at every level of its organization.

Military doctors welcomed the ready availability of sulfa drugs and penicillin. The technology was so new that researchers did not yet understand how the medications worked, but their effectiveness undercut any reluctance that physicians might have had in using them extensively. Penicillin was discovered in Britain in 1929 but not developed commercially until the Second World War. It proved to be a lifesaver, along with the sulfonamides, for many sick or injured servicemen. Unfortunately, it was not until 1945 that penicillin was available widely for civilian use.

Despite the difficulties inherent in their mission, the 64th General Hospital treated more than 3,100 patients in their roughly four months in the North African theater. "The largest number of patients received during a [twenty-four-hour] period," reported commanding officer Colonel Reagan, "was three hundred and forty-two." In North Africa, the unit lost only six patients, one of whom was a member of the unit and the first casualty for the 64th General. All of these deaths occurred with the patients admitted under the surgical service, while the medical service did not lose any patients. This suggests that traumatic injury was primarily responsible for the deaths. The unit's mortality while stationed in North Africa was less than one percent, a rate that it would duplicate in other locations.

The 64th General Hospital moved closer to the front lines and opened in Maddaloni, Italy, on March 17, 1944, only to move again a few months later near the town of Leghorn, Italy, officially opening on August 8, 1944, at the site of a former Italian paratrooper school. By now, the unit was attached to U.S. Fifth Army under the command of Lt. Gen. George S. Patton, and was a part of the Italian campaign in the Allied assault ascending through Italy in pursuit of Axis forces. While in Maddaloni, Dr. Kahle, the Chief of Urology and an avid peacetime sailor, found an abandoned sailboat and decided to take it out into the harbor. Promptly a navy patrol boat approached him and the crew suggested he dock because he was sailing into a German mine field.

When the hospital moved closer to the fighting lines, the risk of enemy attack increased. Military historian Charles Wiltse notes, "Leghorn was still within range of German guns when the 64th General began taking patients in that city." Lou Scott remembers, "There was fierce fighting at Anzio Beach, and Germans were holed up in an ancient monastery on Monte Cassino." Despite the dangers, more hospitals crept closer to the fighting, in support of the very busy fighting units north of Rome. On

General George Patton (left) and
64th General Hospital physician Charles Odom

one occasion enemy patrols were reported near the hospital and the physicians were issued side arms. Almost immediately the physicians were disarmed. Line officers apparently concluded that armed physicians represented a greater danger to each other than the Germans.

During 1944, the 64th General Hospital cared for an increasing number of foreign patients. Scott vividly remembered members of the French Foreign Legion—the "Free French," as they were known in contrast to troops of the Fascist Vichy government then still in power. Scott remembers that many Arab and Senegalese patients were admitted to the 64th, forcing the doctors to use their French skills. The hospital supplied these patients with information as well as medical care. The presence of non-American personnel nevertheless proved tricky. Free French patients, for example, had to be taught American sanitation procedures, not an easy task when there were so many to treat. More than 600 French casualties were admitted to the hospital on May 13, 1944, alone. In time, most of the soldiers complied with these regulations, and the task of treating these patients became much easier.

The 64th also began to take on other technical and medical services that augmented their capabilities. "Plans were also made to create a convalescent hospital for two hundred … patients which began to function shortly thereafter under one (1) officer and six (6) [non-commissioned officers] attached to the unit for that purpose." While they were stationed near Leghorn, the 64th General's laboratory provided "general laboratory service for all medical and service installations requiring laboratory units in this surrounding area." This laboratory provided sanitation and medical testing. "Our laboratory services," the unit's annual report proudly states, "have been utilized by all units north of Livorno to the [Italian] border and by all units south of Livorno as far as Rome." In the last year of the war, the 64th General Hospital's facilities also ran the area's blood bank, morgue, and animal care services.

In July 1945, the 64th was made the headquarters' dispensary for the Peninsular Base Section, servicing 37 units in and around Leghorn, Caserta, and Livorno. In addition to furnishing medical supplies, the dispensary inspected bars, officers' clubs, a transient hotel in the area, and Red Cross facilities. It also provided immunizations and routine exams to troops in the area. It dispensed a lot of penicillin.

The 64th General also treated civilians. In August 1945, the 64th established a pre- and post-natal division in order to deliver and treat the babies of American servicemen and their Italian wives. By December 1945, eight babies fathered by G.I.s were born at the 64th General Hospital. Clearly, Italian women had found their own way to surrender.

In March 1944, as the unit sat in the Bay of Naples awaiting disembarkation, the members of the 64th witnessed the 1944 eruption of Mount Vesuvius. "Such drama, such force shooting fire high into the darkness," recounts Louise Holland Bick, a physical therapist with the unit. "For hours we watched fascinated. No one will ever forget that." Like many of her colleagues, Lou Scott visited numerous sites in both North Africa and Italy, including the Casbah, the ruins of Carthage, Pompei, Capri, Pisa, and Florence.

Within the confines of hospital grounds, there were several forms of recreation that helped personnel relax, enjoy each other's company, and get to know more of the local population. Students and staff from the School of Medicine collected money to send a record player called a Victrola, phonograph records, and reading materials to the unit after hearing the following from one of the LSU officers: "I think you can definitely feel that the University could make no better contribution to the happiness of the officers and nurses than to help us in getting a nice radio and Victrola and a good set of records and books unless it were to get the war over and get us back to good old New Orleans."

Regularly shown movies and live performances also entertained the unit. In January 1944, for example, the 64th hosted a performance by a German Prisoner of War band. Bingo parties, ping pong, chess, and checkers tournaments, and a crafts shop for soldiers were also part of an abundant recreation program.

The men and women of the 64th also enjoyed a number of social events that attracted Army personnel and civilians. On June 11, 1944, the unit's diary reported, "This week, the first dance for enlisted men overseas was held at the Santa Maria Red Cross. Civilian girls were invited." Other events either hosted or attended by members of the 64th General included quiz shows and sporting events against other units. The 64th organized a baseball team, known as the 64th Barons, and sponsored a basketball team while in North Africa, in addition to its previously mentioned football team.

Like thousands of other American servicemen and women of the time, the members of the 64th General Hospital had a unique perspective as members of a liberation army. Many soldiers, therefore, including the medical officers working at the 64th General Hospital, paid close attention to military updates. Indeed, administrators created a "War Information Room" for both staffers and patients. This room maintained maps, press releases, and other war news-related material to keep soldiers informed.

In the spring of 1945, the 64th General Hospital celebrated with everyone else as the war in Italy ended with a Nazi defeat. Eventually, as the war in the Pacific Theater also ended, rumors about the hospital's possible redeployment to the Pacific died down. Many doctors, nurses, and enlisted personnel were now reassigned to different posts on their way home. Most of the original members of the 64th, including the core group of doctors from LSU, went home in the late summer and early fall of 1945, but not before they were honored with a number of awards and distinctions for their service and valor.

A homecoming banquet would finally be held in July 1946.

Members of the 64th were authorized to wear the Bronze Star in recognition of their part in the Rome-Arno Campaign in the summer of 1944. A year later, the unit was collectively recognized for its service throughout the North Africa and Italian campaigns as a hospital that efficiently provided vital medical services for ill and wounded soldiers. "The superior care of medical patients and battle casualties was consistent with the unselfish ideals of the medical service of the United States Army," the citation read in part. "With rigid discipline, full knowledge of and devotion to its mission, the 64th General Hospital upheld the highest traditions of the United States and of the allied nations."

A few months after proudly announcing news of the unit's citation, the School of Medicine also reported a letter received from General Joseph T. McNarney from the Army headquarters of the Mediterranean Theater of Operations. "The standards of excellence established by the Sixty-Fourth General Hospital in its overseas service," McNarney wrote, "reflect great credit on the medical officers and nurses as individuals, and on the School of Medicine of Louisiana State University, their sponsor."

Irvin Cahen, a member of LSU's Department of Orthopaedics, received the Legion of Merit on September 2, 1945, in recognition of his work with the hospital's orthopedic service and "his high professional skill, intense personal interest and devotion to duty." Interestingly, much of his research focused on methods used by German doctors on injured Germans soldiers and American POWs. These doctors had pioneered the use of plates, screws, rods and other reconstructive devices in bone fractures and traumatic injuries. Learning to use this state-of-the-art—but German—technology, Dr. Cahen would treat American patients with great success.

Charles Miangolarra, a faculty member and the hospital's chief surgeon, was also awarded the Legion of Merit on September 14, 1945. Margaret Bussey was one of the nurses with the 64th that was also honored for her service. She was given the Bronze Star in December 1945 "for her services in the Surgical Service at the time the hospital was overtaxed with casualties during the drives on the north Italian front." For their care of thousands of soldiers during their service in the Mediterranean, these medical professionals

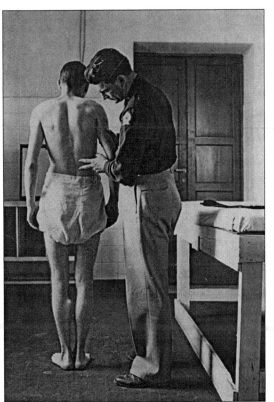

Cahen Clinic in Italy – Irvin Cahen examining a patient

received honors that rewarded their hard work in support of Allied troops.

Most of the original members of the 64th General Hospital left for home and their pre-war lives before the official closing of the unit in October 1945. The School of Medicine began to resume normal operations, discontinuing the accelerated program and began making plans to accommodate the many physicians who would be looking for residency training programs.

The School of Medicine would also offer a series of refresher courses in 1946 to returning physicians who had completed training before beginning military service. This allowed them to brush up on the "latest" in civilian medicine.

ಬಂ

Chapter IV

The Faculty Revolts

The end of World War II should have brought a period of peace and stability to the school. It brought exactly the opposite courtesy of an appointment to the LSU Board of Supervisors by former Governor Sam Jones. The appointee was Dr. Emmitt Lee Irwin, the same surgeon who had served ever so briefly as Chairman of Surgery in 1931.

And Irwin apparently brought an old grudge against the school to an already tense situation. As part of the war effort the federal government had funneled huge sums of money to the LSU System. The School of Medicine, which had labored so mightily in the war effort, was anxious to rebuild its faculty and felt entitled to a fair share.

LSU President William Hatcher was not in a sharing mood, and relations between him and the School of Medicine Dean Beryl Burns were strained. For the story of what happened next we are indebted to Gerald Schenken, MD, and **John Schenken, MD ('70),** who shared with the authors 58 pages of original documents compiled by their father, Jerold R. Schenken, Sr., MD, who was at the time Chairman of the school's combined Department of Pathology and Bacteriology, and a close friend of Burns.

The money issues, which had caused very strained relations between Burns and Hatcher, were unresolved when Irwin pressured Hatcher to have Burns fire Urban Maes, the Chairman of Surgery. Irwin apparently had two reasons: revenge against Maes and a desire to see a close friend and fellow surgeon, Dr. Charles Odom, named Assistant Dean at the School of Medicine. It would probably be only a small step, in that case, for Odom to assume the Chair of the Surgery Department. Dr. John Seabury of the Department of Medicine felt Irwin also bore a grudge against Dr. Edgar Hull, Chair of Medicine, and that he would be next to go if Maes was fired.

Odom had just been discharged from the Army and had been General George S. Patton's personal physician, treating the General for, among other things, a case of sandfly fever, and perhaps also performing a herniaplasty; he had become the General's physician when the 64th General Hospital was in Africa. He had been on the LSU faculty before the war as an assistant professor but had not yet been reappointed. Burns came under increasingly intense pressure from Hatcher to fire Maes and to hire Odom. The faculty, for their part, rallied to Burns' support and in July 1945 they sent Hatcher a sharply worded letter praising Burns.

Hatcher fired Burns in August and promptly appointed Wilbur "Bull" Smith, PhD, as Dean without any faculty input. Smith, a long-time Professor of Anatomy at Tulane, was fairly well known to many on the faculty, especially those who had been at Tulane, but he enjoyed no natural support. Smith was also Chairman of Intercollegiate Athletics at Tulane, a position that did not endear him much. A foul mouth helped him even less.

Hatcher, apparently capable of communicating with the great beyond, stated that Huey Long would have approved his actions. The faculty clearly did not agree. They heard about the dismissal of

Beryl Iles Burns (Dean, 1939-1945)

Burns at a mass meeting and left the meeting dispirited and angry. Dr. Edgar Hull, the Chair of Medicine, recalled going home and telling his wife that he felt he would have to leave LSU. Moments later, he received a call from Urban Maes, whom Hull affectionately described as a "tyrant." Maes told Hull that he planned to resign. A plan immediately began to take shape in their minds. Donald Duncan, an influential Professor of Anatomy, and Shenken, a close friend of Burns, who was an effective leader and a really well-liked man, joined in the plot. A number of informal meetings were held and the upshot was a mass resignation of the faculty. Every letter was the same and specified that the resignation was effective December 31, 1945. By January 1, 1946, entire departments and most department heads would disappear. Running a school without Medicine, Surgery, Dermatology, Pathology, Bacteriology, Biochemistry or Anatomy was going to be difficult.

Hatcher, caught very much by surprise, pointed out to the press that not every faculty member had resigned. The students pointed out that the ones who had elected to stay did only 20% of the teaching.

Hatcher was in a box, along with Irwin, Odom and Smith, and the newspapers in New Orleans and Baton Rouge had a field day. Medical students began a letter-writing campaign to the legislature and the

Wilbur Cleveland "Bull" Smith (Dean, 1945)

Alumni Association held an emergency meeting in a brewery and issued a loud protest. The instigator for this was then Senior Class President, Dr. William Stewart, a future United States Surgeon General. The AMA, the American Association of University Professors, and the Association of American Medical Colleges were drawn in and threatened investigations. It was a three-ring circus.

Members of the Board of Supervisors went from defending Hatcher to promising an investigation. Irwin professed innocence, but his position was not helped by Odom who, still supposedly a bystander, could not refrain from incessant public commentary and self-praise. Smith contributed to the situation by slamming his office door on reporters when he could and insulting them when he could not.

There was a brief attempt at diversion by the Supervisors. A few months earlier, Burns had dismissed Howard Beard as Chairman of Biochemistry. Senility had clearly rendered Beard incompetent. But now Burns was accused of violating Beard's rights and was thus himself deserving of dismissal. Reminded that Hatcher had approved the dismissal and had reported it to the Supervisors, they searched hopelessly for another fig leaf to hide behind but found none. The public mood turned increasingly nasty. In both New Orleans and Baton Rouge, letters to the editor appeared regularly, the papers ran almost daily articles on the situation, and the editorial cartoonists helped keep the pot boiling. A typical cartoon featured a drawing of the Medical School building with the caption "Is There A Doctor In The House?" and another featured a lifeboat full of medical students with a banner "Rescue Us."

With no faculty replacements in sight, Smith's position deteriorated by the moment and he resigned in November, just months after being named dean. Others, tired of the fight, also departed. Dr. Schenken became Chairman of Pathology at the University of Nebraska. Dr. Emma Moss, Chief Pathologist at Charity, briefly assumed the Chairmanship until Russell Holman, MD, was appointed in 1946. Burns left to become administrator of John Seely Hospital in Galveston and was succeeded by George Walter McCoy, Chair of Public Health, as Acting Dean. Described by a contemporary as a grand and wise old man, he had previously served as Surgeon General and as Director of the National Institutes of Health before coming to LSU. He was highly respected and brought a sense of calm to the school.

George W. McCoy
(Acting Dean, 1945-46)

Smith would return to Tulane. Hatcher would eventually resign as LSU President, citing ill health. Odom opened a surgical practice and later served as coroner of Jefferson Parish and as President of the State Board of Medical Examiners. Irwin ultimately left the Board of Supervisors and finished out his career as a segregationist rabble rouser, heading the White Citizens Councils of Louisiana. McCoy was named permanent Dean but died in early 1946.

The LSU System, now thoroughly chastened, allowed the faculty to choose McCoy's successor. In 1946 they chose Dr. Vernon Lippard, a New York trained pediatrician who was serving at Columbia University as Assistant Dean. Lippard recruited Charles Goss to Chair Anatomy, Russell Holman to Chair Pathology, and G. John Buddingh to Chair the now separate Department of Microbiology. Lippard left abruptly in 1948, to become Dean at the University of Virginia. Soon thereafter he would be named Dean at Yale, his alma mater. Apparently this was the prize he coveted, and LSU was merely viewed as a stepping stone. Dr. Edgar Hull, who had risen to the occasion so many times since 1931, became acting dean.

During the months that followed, Hull met on many occasions with William Frye, a newly hired Assistant Dean at Tulane. An MD and PhD who specialized in Tropical Medicine, Frye had a national reputation for science and would co-author with LSU faculty member Dr. J. Clyde Schwartzwelder the textbook *Tropical Medicine,* the bible of the specialty at that time.

Hull was duly impressed with Frye the educator and scientist and even more with Frye the administrator. William Frye became Dean of LSU School of Medicine in June 1949. Administrative stability, a quantity in short supply, would return to the School of Medicine. Frye would serve as Dean for 16 years, nearly as long as his six predecessors combined.

If Frye had spent much time musing over what disaster could next befall the school, it is unlikely that he would have selected the threat of a communist takeover of a major department. But that is what did indeed happen.

ဆာ

Chapter V

The Red Menace Invades LSU School of Medicine

Older readers and students of history will remember the political turmoil created in the early 1950s by Senator Joseph R. McCarthy, an ambitious and ruthless politician who saw exposing the menace of homegrown communism as his ticket to the White House and began discovering (mostly nonexistent) communists everywhere, especially in the media, the entertainment industry, government, and education. Hysteria prevailed for a long time. McCarthy would ultimately crash and burn on national television when he held hearings to find out why some obscure, allegedly communist dentist was promoted from captain to major by the army. He was undone by the Army's Chief Counsel, a crafty Boston lawyer, Joseph Welch, who during questioning revealed to the world that McCarthy was simply an unprincipled scoundrel. But much harm would be done everywhere before that day began the end of the Senator's career.

William Obrinski, MD

In due course LSU School of Medicine became embroiled in this issue. The year was 1951. Although most faculty were strongly conservative, though not necessarily McCarthy supporters, some others were described by contemporaries as left of center, perhaps very much left of center.

The Department of Pediatrics, led then by Dr. Myron Wegman, commanded a national reputation for research, education, and patient care. His two principal associates were Drs. Nelson Ordway and William Obrinski. Obrinski was particularly popular with students and was regarded as an excellent teacher. His wife, a non-faculty physician who went by her maiden name, was apparently very vocal in supporting a decidedly "left wing" agenda. A rumor began circulating around the School that Obrinski was a communist or a "fellow traveler," one who supported the party line but was not technically a party member. Many years earlier, he had served on the board of the Southern Conference Educational Fund, which later was run by James Dombroski, a suspected communist. A "reliable" unidentified confidential informant had brought all of this to the Dean's attention. Some felt that this was reason enough to dismiss Obrinski. A "Guide to Subversive Organizations," a 166-page US Government report published in 1951 was circulated on campus warning of the danger of tolerating this type of individual.

This all caused considerable upset in the faculty; according to several sources Wegman was pressured repeatedly by other Department Chairs to dismiss Obrinski. Wegman refused, arguing apparently that Obrinski, a tenured professor, was an excellent physician who was breaking no laws. Unwise choice of a marital partner was not a criminal offense, and the other "evidence" was thin indeed.

To appreciate the nuttiness that prevailed at that time, readers should know of one LSU medical student who was repeatedly accused by other students of communist sympathies because he had gone to Europe on a summer vacation and had visited some Eastern European countries. Although he was a decorated military veteran, he was subjected to a federal investigation and considerable harassment by some students. He had to go to court to obtain restraining orders against them and to clear his name. On graduation, he left the state, moved to California, and years later became a national figure in his specialty.

Pressure on Wegman increased by the day. He left LSU in late 1951 to become head of the World Health Organization and later Dean of the University of Michigan School of Medicine. He was succeeded by Nelson Ordway, who had developed Ordway's Solution, a popular treatment for rehydrating children suffering from diarrhea. Ordway stayed in the position only briefly, leaving in 1954 to become Chairman of Pediatrics at Yale. Ordway would be succeeded by Dr. Richard Fowler; a 31-year-old Duke-trained pediatric cardiologist, one of only 13 board-certified pediatric cardiologists in the U. S. at that time. Dr. Curtis Lund, Chairman of Obstetrics and Gynecology since 1947, also moved on, as did Andy Kerr of the Department of Medicine and Walter Burdette of the Department of Surgery. Burdette would become Chair of Surgery at the University of Missouri. Kerr would become a highly respected academic cardiologist in New York. Lund would become Department Chair at the University of Rochester (N.Y.) School of Medicine. John H. Seabury, MD, a towering figure in the Department of Medicine from 1945 to 1975, also planned to leave.

Richard Fowler, MD

Apolitical but tired of the turmoil, Seabury was urged to ride out the storm by his friend and long-time associate in the department, Dr. Harry Dascomb. In 1953, Obrinski also left, much to the collective relief of the faculty, and especially Bill Frye, the Dean, who was quoted as saying he was "glad to be rid on him." Frye was asked by the Faculty Council to submit a full report on the Obrinski affair but apparently he never did.

The departure of Obrinski should have ended the matter, but LSU's "involvement with communism" had one last brief Chapter. Members of the Louisiana legislature decided that an official hearing was just what was needed. They reckoned without Gen. Troy H. Middleton, the President of the LSU System, who had clearly had enough. Middleton, a highly decorated Louisiana hero of World War II, had served under then President Dwight Eisenhower as Eisenhower's Chief of Staff in Europe when Eisenhower was Supreme Allied Commander. He had been the mostly unrecognized architect of the German defeat at the Battle of Bastogne. General Middleton let it be known that if a hearing was held, he would be the first witness. And he would testify that there were no communists at the School of Medicine. The hearings never took place, the legislators apparently having recognized that tangling with Middleton was not a wise career-building move. Middleton was not a man to trifle with. People who command armies on the battlefield seldom are.

The Department of Pediatrics would struggle to rebuild for several years. Fortunately Fowler, who would lead the Department until 1982, a 29-year-run, had a right-hand man, Dr. Percy Rosenbaum. A Canadian by birth and education, Dr. Rosenbaum joined the faculty in 1950 and worked until his death in 2004. An expert in pediatric nephrology, he was a favorite of students and recruited many to the residency program, helping to rebuild the program.

Fowler, the then longest-serving Pediatrics Department Chair in the United States, would die in 1982, and toward the end, his duties as Chair would be assumed by **Dr. Nicholas Gagliano ('52)**, who would succeed as Chair, serving until 1984. When Dr. Gagliano stepped down he was succeeded

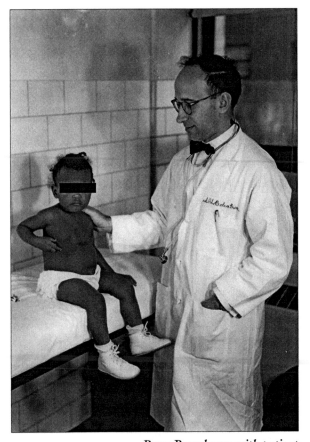

Percy Rosenbaum with patient

by Dr. Robert Suskind, who served until 1998, when he left to become Dean of the Chicago School of Medicine.

Suskind had previously served as Chair of Pediatrics at the University of South Alabama. He was internationally known for his work in childhood nutrition. Many faculty were added to the Department and it regained strength and stature under him.

Suskind would be succeeded by Dr. Ricardo Sorensen, who had been serving as Professor of Pediatrics. Sorensen would further strengthen the Department and would provide valuable leadership to the entire school in the aftermath of Hurricane Katrina. He would forge particularly strong bonds with Children's Hospital in New Orleans to the benefit of both organizations.

The Alumni Association would ultimately dedicate Professorships honoring both Fowler and Rosenbaum.

೮ාᲒ

Chapter VI

Bill Frye and Beyond
(1949 – 1977)

In June 1949, William W. Frye, MD, PhD, walked across the street from Tulane where he was Assistant Dean to take up residence at LSU School of Medicine as its new Dean. He would remain Dean until January 1966, then serve as the Medical Center's first Chancellor until 1969. Many changes would occur during his deanship.

Frye immediately faced several problems. In 1949, the school increased the size of the entering freshman class from 100 to 125, in response to health concerns in Louisiana and because many ex-servicemen who were filling colleges under government sponsored educational programs wanted to become physicians.

This began to put a strain on the physical facility and the budget because more students required more space and more faculty. The school could no longer rely on only volunteers to do the teaching. Frye was able to secure increased funding for faculty support and a $6,000,000 bond issue (an enormous amount at the time) for an addition to the original medical school building.

The T-shaped addition consisted of a four-story addition in front of and parallel to the original building on Tulane Avenue and was connected to the original by a nine-story addition. Construction was completed in 1954, adding greatly to the square footage. This addition provided office space for new junior faculty, research space and an auditorium, something the school had never had before. A second addition would be completed in 1964. This would consist of adding five floors to the four-story addition fronting Tulane Avenue, adding needed office and laboratory space.

Frye proved that he could be a creative sort. Faculty and staff at LSU School of Medicine, like all state employees in the 1950s, were paid via a paymaster, dispatched from Baton Rouge, who paid each employee in cash. Frye was in a quandary late one Friday when the paymaster hadn't arrived and the staff was getting anxious.

To solve the problem, Frye went down the street to Nick's Big Train Bar, where he often bent an elbow, and borrowed the cash from the proprietor, Nick Castrogiovanni, and paid the staff himself.

Frye, a widower, had a reputation as a bon vivant and lady's man. One day he held a party at his home for graduating seniors and offered several of them a guided tour of the house, which incidentally had many years previously been owned by Huey Long.

He led them to his upstairs master bedroom, where over the bed he had hung a large painting of an attractive young woman, totally nude. They stared open-mouthed from the painting to the Dean. "She's my housekeeper in Costa Rica," he said, eyes twinkling.

In the late 1950s Dr. Frye had extended his considerable interest in tropical medicine and had begun to establish close relations with Costa Rica, the only Central American country that did not have a medical school. In the early going he arranged for

William Frye (Dean, 1949-1977)

Costa Rican physicians and scientists to come and train at LSU to prepare for the opening of a medical school there. Over time Frye and LSU faculty, especially basic science faculty, began to spend long periods in Costa Rica. This was helpful to many LSU research programs but put strain on the day-to-day operation of the School of Medicine because Frye was often out of the country. Some cynics said that when problems developed at LSU, Frye headed for Costa Rica. Edgar Hull or Fred Brazda often found themselves as Acting Dean.

Dr. Frye was named Vice President of the LSU System in 1959 as well as Dean of the School of Medicine. This was designed to both give him more recognition and keep him home more. It worked to some extent. In 1961 the Medical School in Costa Rica would open its doors allowing LSU to scale back some of its day-to-day involvement. LSU would establish the Inter-American Center for Medical Research and Training a fellowship training program in New Orleans to continue its help to Costa Rica.

As Frye led the School's physical growth, such as overseeing the construction of the student dormitory in 1962, he also helped improve the School's educational offerings. Since the 1930s, for example, the School of Medicine had a Department of Nursing that trained nursing students in conjunction with the Baton Rouge campus. Frye enthusiastically supported its improvement. In 1962, the Department of Nursing won national accreditation for its baccalaureate nursing program. Six years later, it would be formally split off from the School of Medicine to form a separate LSU School of Nursing, eventually housed in a separate building on the downtown campus. The School of Nursing would ultimately offer Associate, Baccalaureate, Master's and Doctoral level degrees.

Another change occurred in 1962 that Frye didn't anticipate or even like. Since its founding, graduates of the School had journeyed to Baton Rouge to graduate with 3,000 or 4,000 others in the John Parker Agricultural Facility, sometimes known as "The Cow Palace."

The Class of 1962 decided that they would rather graduate in New Orleans. Frye said they had to go to Baton Rouge. The class, lead by Mack Thomas, said "no." Amazingly, Frye and the entire LSU System capitulated and graduation took place in the Roosevelt Hotel.

No more classes would graduate in Baton Rouge until the Class of 2006, because of the effects of Katrina on the City of New Orleans, graduated there. In 2007 graduations resumed in New Orleans.

In 1965 the School of Medicine produced another offshoot. At that time, the efforts of Dr. Roland Coulson paid off when he was appointed Associate Dean in charge of the School of Graduate Studies. Dr. Coulson had battled for years to eke out a comprehensive program of research opportunities for PhD candidates studying at the Medical School. Splitting away from the School of Medicine was just the first step in securing adequate funding and attention for graduate programs. The road was long and treacherous, but Dr. Coulson and the small group of dedicated faculty ensured that graduate programs prospered in the face of inadequate space, limited faculty support, and, occasionally, outright hostility from some members of the faculty, who felt that only the Baton Rouge campus should offer PhDs.

The Graduate Program was pivotal also in the integration of LSU as an educational institution. Thanks to the efforts of Dr. A. Sidney Harris of the Department of Physiology and with the blessing of Dean Frye, the first black technician, James Hawkins, had been hired to work in the student labs. He proved to be a valuable asset and with the ice broken, other departments followed suit.

Dr. Isidore Cohn, Jr., Chair of the Surgery Department, began extending invitations to black surgeons at Flint-Goodrich Hospital, the only private hospital for blacks in the area, to attend surgery conferences at LSU. The Department had also considered accepting an out-of-state applicant to its residency program, but the candidate was heavily involved in the civil rights movement and declined to cut back these activities as a condition of appointment.

But when the Department of Physiology, again with Frye's blessing, accepted Albert Bocage into its graduate program, integration really took a giant step forward. Dr. Bocage would join the faculty and serve until 1975, when a heart attack ended his life.

Integration of the student body of the School of Medicine did not take place until September 1966, when Claude Tellis, a Louisiana native who had taken his undergraduate training in Michigan, applied and was accepted.

Although he considered himself neither an activist nor a pioneer, he realized that this was a unique and groundbreaking opportunity, and with the encouragement of his family and Dr. Robert Simmons, Associate Dean of Students, he enrolled. Other faculty who helped greatly with advice and encouragement included Drs. Marilyn Zimny and Raymond Gasser of Anatomy, Jack Strong of Pathology, Fred Brazda of Biochemistry, John Bobear and Jorge Martinez of Medicine, Richard Paddison of Neurology and Dr. Cohn.

His four-year stint was, as he described it, mostly uneventful, and he graduated in 1970.

Since then hundreds have followed in his footsteps and many years ago the School set up the Office of Minority Affairs, under the direction of Dr. Edward Helm, to encourage minority enrollment in the School of Medicine.

In actuality a black New Iberia woman attempted to integrate the School of Medicine in 1946. Her name was Viola Coleman and she was a college graduate. Summarily rejected by the Board of Supervisors because of her race, she took them to court. Lower courts upheld the rulings of the Supervisors and she applied to and was accepted to Meharry Medical College.

When the appeals were heard, she was rejected, yet again, not on the merits of her suit but because, having moved to Tennessee, she wasn't a Louisiana citizen. She would settle in Midland, Texas, and practice there for half a century. In 1951, the case having now made its way to Federal Court, an order was issued by Judge J. Skelly Wright, barring the Board of Supervisors from denying access to the School of Medicine on the basis of race.

By the mid-1960s, the School of Medicine was growing at a rapid pace, but it was still training those who came from all over the state of Louisiana. Dr. Edgar Hull, whose dedication to the medical community of northern Louisiana communities was unparalleled, tried to establish a medical school in Shreveport. In 1965, his efforts bore fruit when the LSU School of Medicine in Shreveport opened its doors with Dr. Hull as its first Dean.

The School of Medicine had grown so much in 35 years, and produced so many offshoots, that the New Orleans campus of LSU was also reorganized in 1965. Dr. Frye was named the first chancellor of the LSU Medical Center. He would serve until 1969, when at age 65, he retired to Texas and was succeeded by **Dr. William Stewart, ('45).** Encompassed under this new organizational structure were the Schools of Medicine in New Orleans and Shreveport and the School of Graduate Studies. The School of Nursing, the School of Dentistry (founded in 1966), and the School of Allied Health (established in 1970) would soon join the Medical Center.

When Frye was promoted to Chancellor in 1965, new leadership was needed at the Medical School. After a national search, Dr. John C. Finerty, PhD, Professor of Anatomy and Associate Dean at the University of Miami School of Medicine, was named the School's new dean in 1966. For the first time in a long time, the School of Medicine was in a position to make long-term plans for the future, plans that included more than just what was necessary to survive in the immediate crisis. The most important changes in the School of Medicine would be new additions it received—both in space and in class size.

The most constant challenges in the history of the School were space and money. Dr. Finerty tried to remediate these problems by pushing a program of construction that would improve the amount of space available for basic science classes and researchers. This helped Finerty in his relationship with the preclinical departments, but his relationship with the clinical departments was at times strained. He was not a clinician and this put him at a distinct disadvantage in certain situations. Things eventually reached an impasse at Charity Hospital when Department Chairs told the hospital director not to take Finerty's advice in any matters that affected their services but to deal with them directly. Eventually, the strain would result in Finerty being named Vice Chancellor for Research, a more appropriate use of his considerable skill.

Finerty's successor in 1971 as Dean was Dr. Norman Crooks Nelson, Professor of Surgery at the School of Medicine and Associate Dean. A native of Minnesota, Nelson had journeyed south and taken his general surgery training under Dr. Isidore Cohn, Jr. Sensing that he had great potential, Dr. Cohn convinced him to do a fellowship in endocrine surgery and then join the faculty. After returning to New Orleans he immediately established a reputation as the go-to guy in New Orleans for surgical endocrinology.

Popular with residents, students and the private community, he seemed like an inspired choice for Dean because the faculty was anxious to push the clinical enterprise forward. In 1969 the Medical Center began to develop a long-range plan under the guidance of a planning organization, Lester Gorsline Associates. The result was a strong recommendation that the School needed an education and research building. Of greater importance to the clinical faculty was the recommendation that the Medical Center should have an Ambulatory Care Center and a University Hospital.

At the same time the state was developing an allegedly more comprehensive plan under the aegis of a new entity called the Health Education Authority of Louisiana (HEAL). It had the capacity to issue construction bonds and would bring together or so it was said, the plans of LSU, Tulane, and Charity Hospital. It was touted as something that would benefit LSU. The creation of HEAL was pushed heavily by Tulane. Darwin Fenner, a Tulane supporter, would be named its Chairman. It was never clear how LSU, a state agency, would benefit from the existence of HEAL unless the state exceeded its own capacity to issue revenue bonds.

Charismatic and full of ideas, Nelson had leaped into his job as Dean. Then slowly reality reared its ugly head. Inertia and push-back from upstream in the LSU System slowed his plans to upgrade the faculty practice. First, there were those who felt that LSU simply could not staff a private hospital and fulfill its "historic mission to care for the poor." And there was only a little more support at that time for an ambulatory care center.

HEAL would eventually issue bonds to help Tulane build its University Hospital. No one appeared to question Tulane's ability to serve both the poor and the affluent at the same time. Bonds were issued to help other private entities including the construction of a garage near the Superdome. How its construction helped health care was unclear to some observers. LSU was assured its turn would come to benefit from the creation of HEAL. Nelson pushed forward but nothing happened. HEAL would help finance other projects, none of which benefited LSU, and then become quiescent for several years. Its plans would eventually help with the construction of a power plant near the school, greatly reducing energy costs for the Health Sciences Center.

If HEAL wasn't enough to deal with, three other issues began to consume Nelson's time. The first issue involved Charity Hospital.

George Burch, MD, for decades the Henderson Professor and Chairman of Medicine at Tulane, reached the then mandatory retirement age of 65. Many at Tulane who viewed Burch as an autocrat were relieved to see that milestone come. Burch, still vigorous, did not want to just go away. So he approached the Director of Charity Hospital, **Dr. Charles Mary ('61)**, whom he knew well and had supported vigorously, with a plan. His plan was to establish a cardiovascular training center independent of either school, to be called the Louisiana Heart Institute. He also proposed the creation of a museum in the hospital dedicated to himself. Dr. Mary provided Burch with office space in the hospital and got started with the Museum and the Heart Institute, an idea that appealed to Dr. Mary.

The Heart Institute fitted with plans that Charity had toyed with for some time, namely to establish centers for specialized care. Initially the plan was to establish a Cancer Center. The idea was to tap into federal dollars outside of state appropriations.

The Cancer Center had never gotten very far because it required the ongoing cooperation of Tulane and LSU with Charity, especially in the area of research. The three entities could never agree on who would control the money, so the project never got beyond the talking stage.

From Charity's viewpoint heart disease would be almost as good a starting place as cancer. Burch was undeniably known well enough to open the dollar spigot and this would be a Charity program alone. It would involve only training and clinical care, not research, and would be independent of either school.

Burch's continued presence at Charity might simply aggravate some of his erstwhile buddies at Tulane, but what scared both schools was the loaded word: *independent*. For decades, from the 1930s till the 1960s, Charity had provided care through three services, LSU service, Tulane service, and Independent service. The Independent service, a relic of a simpler time, had been staffed by private physicians not allied with either school. Over time these physicians died or retired and were not replaced. The two schools gradually absorbed the hospital bed allotments and the trainees still attached to them.

Burch's proposal revived the possibility of the return of an Independent service, and that began to play out in the minds of both schools like a cheap horror movie. Tulane was especially nervous, apparently conjuring up George Burch as the Pied Piper, leading the cream of Tulane's faculty to Charity as full-time staff. LSU was only a few steps behind the Wave in its concern. Both vigorously lobbied against the proposal.

Things came to a head at a Charity Board meeting. After a vote was taken, Burch, et al, had narrowly lost. The Heart Institute was not approved. Brief attempts to revive the Independent service idea did continue until 1974, when LSU and Tulane would sign affiliation agreements with the Department of Health and Hospitals. Among other things, this would guarantee that the Schools, on a three-year rotating basis, would name the medical director of Charity Hospital. The idea of an Independent service was dead forever. The Burch Museum would close after a few years.

Another of Nelson's problems also involved Tulane. Some years earlier, Dr. Joseph Beasley, Tulane's Dean of Public Health, conceived an entity called the Family Health Foundation that would act as a conduit for funding family planning services and would provide obstetric care to indigent women in many parishes of Louisiana through a second nonprofit corporation called the Louisiana Family Planning Program, Inc. The federal government would ultimately provide millions in funding to these entities.

Ostensibly a private program, it was mostly a Tulane affair but LSU became involved when some faculty were paid, often handsomely, to provide clinical services, and at least one faculty member sat on the Foundation Board for a protracted period.

Nelson was also invited to join the Board. He did so, attending three meetings. What clearly impressed him most was the size of the enterprise and the sketchy financial details.

He was assured that all was well. This assurance came from an outfit that owned six airplanes, dined at expensive restaurants, regularly hired limousines, had according to one observer, a former Miss Arkansas on the payroll performing unspecified staff duties, and was joined at the hip to a number of state politicians and to the governor's brother. All the while it claimed that it was only helping the poor avoid unwanted pregnancies and deliver healthy babies. Nelson was unconvinced of its bona fides, and resigned. It was a wise move. Questions soon began to arise about financial irregularities that involved two different federal agencies being charged for the same services. Audits were ordered and the results were bad news. Double-dipping is a no-no, and the feds were not amused. Arrests soon followed.

In 1974, Beasley was convicted of fraud in federal court. His program was dead and Charity would have to pick up the clinical care. LSU would receive some mild criticism for its involvement, but otherwise emerged unscathed.

Nelson's third problem came when the School received a visit from the AMA and the American Association of Medical Colleges (AAMC). The school was bulging at the seams; built for 100 students, it now had 155 in each class. Classes had increased three times since 1931 with only minimal increases in teaching space. Actually the school had invited the two agencies to visit in hopes that they would support the school's quest for a new education building.

They obliged by immediately putting the school on probation because of overcrowding. Since the United States was facing a physician shortage, the threat of closing a medical school was unacceptable to everyone and the federal government soon offered $18,000,000 in construction money for an education building.

That was great news. There was only one catch. The state had to come up with a $14,000,000 match. The Governor, Edwin Edwards, was amenable but there was then a second catch. Edwards was under intensive political pressure to increase the size of the class yet again. Displaying remarkable chutzpah, Nelson and Medical Center Chancellor **William Stewart ('45)**, who had succeeded Frye in 1970, went to the AAMC asking for permission to increase the class size while being on probation for overcrowding. The AAMC, in the words of one observer, "had a coronary." They told LSU to be "creative." So LSU came up with an idea to add 30 students per year and educate them at the Dental School until the new Medical Education Building was constructed.

The basic science faculty would bear the brunt of the effort, having in essence to teach each subject twice, once at 1542 Tulane and then again at the Dental School. Only the promise of more space in the new building kept them from open revolt. The AAMC equally mollified by the plan agreed to the class expansion. The Medical Education Building would finally open in 1981.

But by then, Nelson, frustrated and looking for more progress, had long since left to become Chancellor of the University of Mississippi Medical Center in Jackson. It would flourish under his leadership.

In 1973 Nelson was followed as Dean by Silas E. O'Quinn, Professor and Chairman of Dermatology and Associate Dean. He lasted less than four years.

An excellent dermatologist and a popular faculty member, he inherited Nelson's fourth major problem. The faculty needed a place to practice and little progress had been made in the prior two years. The route that Silas chose involved getting the state to build a building. The state asked for a plan. So he planned and planned but the plans never moved much beyond the planning stage. Bids to build the building were judged "overpriced." It would have to be redesigned. The faculty practice moved from rented space to rented space but never resembled a multispecialty practice until much later, when the Lions Clinic Building opened in 1986. It would remain there until Katrina closed the building and the group practice dispersed to many locations.

There was much progress during O'Quinn's tenure on the academic front. Family Medicine, which had for some years been a section of the Department of Medicine, achieved full departmental status. **Dr. Gerald Gehringer ('52)** was named its first Chairman. Nationally known, he would later be named President of the American Academy of Family Physicians and preside over a popular residency program.

But attempting to help upgrade Family Medicine caused no end of problems for O'Quinn. He tried to develop a premier off-campus practice in Eastern New Orleans, which would have helped the Department and the area, but in insisting that patients seen at the site be hospitalized at Hotel Dieu Hospital rather than nearby at Methodist Hospital, he caused a firestorm of protest from the local medical community and the idea died.

He had other successes, however. Dr. Robert D'Ambrosia was brought in as the first full-time chair of the Department of Orthopaedics in 1976, replacing the newly retired Dr. Irving Cahen, who had served as Chair since 1959. Dr. D'Ambrosia reorganized the Department, adding new faculty and creating several subspecialty areas.

Dr. D'Ambrosia served until 2001, when he returned to his Western roots and became Chair at the University of Colorado. He was followed in 2002 by Dr. Barry Riemer, an expert in trauma, from Detroit's Henry Ford Hospital, who served until 2007, when an injury forced his retirement. Dr. Andrew King, a nationally known pediatric orthopedist, replaced him.

In 1977 the Division of Neurosurgery of the Surgery Department obtained independent departmental status. Its first Chairman, Dr. David Kline, served in that capacity for 30 years, and be succeeded in 2007 by Dr. Frank Culicchia.

In 1981, the Medical Education Building, begun under Dr. O'Quinn's leadership, opened for use by students, faculty, and staff. It was an impressive facility with sprawling lab space, a large number of classrooms, and several large lecture rooms, perfect for class lectures and faculty meetings.

Despite these successes, O'Quinn once said that he could never remember a problem-free day during his entire deanship. He would step up from dean to Vice-Chancellor for Clinical Affairs in 1978 and retire in 1980 to become a gentleman farmer in Mississippi.

When Dr. O'Quinn was promoted to Vice Chancellor in 1977, a successor as Dean was quickly anointed by then Chancellor, Dr. Allen Copping. He selected Dr. Paul Larson, Professor of Neurology and Associate Dean, as O'Quinn's replacement.

ℰↃℭℬ

Chapter VII

The Larson Regime

When Paul Larson, long-time Professor of Neurology and Associate Dean, was promoted to the Deanship in 1977, he took on a full administrative load but continued to provide clinical care, teaching and, important to him, research in movement disorders, especially those caused by spinal cord injury.

Dr. Larson threw himself into the job. A number of departments required upgrading as aging departmental chairmen prepared to retire. Encouraged by then Chancellor Dr. Alan Copping, Dr. Larson immediately began a search for a new Chairman of the Department of Ophthalmology to replace the retiring Dr. George M. Haik.

The search committee soon settled on Dr. Herbert Kaufmann, a brilliant research scientist and eye surgeon who had distinguished himself both in the areas of viral diseases of the eye and in corneal transplants. Dr. Kaufmann arrived in 1978 from the University of Florida with a view to change the culture of the Department to a research orientation. He also proposed that a true Eye Center be developed, and received encouragement to pursue this idea from Dr. Copping and Dr. Larson.

In pursuing it, he had had experience with a powerful group, the Lions Club in Florida. The Lions had become interested in blindness through contacts developed decades earlier with Helen Keller, a woman who had grown famous by overcoming both blindness and hearing defects. Dr. Kaufmann immediately contacted the Lions Club of Louisiana and eventually persuaded them to donate $20,000,000 to build four floors of the building at 2020 Gravier Street, "The Lions Eye Center."

The faculty group practice provided funds for construction of additional floors so that it could finally have a true group practice home. Additionally, Dr. Kaufmann recruited Drs. Nicolas and Haydee Bazan to his ophthalmology research program. Ultimately, their presence would lead to the development of the Neuroscience Center, a research engine of monumental importance to the School.

Dr. Kaufmann would retire in 2008, having relinquished his Chairmanship several years earlier to Dr. Donald Bergsma, a long-time faculty member.

Many other changes in the school occurred under Dr. Larson's guidance. He worked hard to upgrade the program in Genetics and he merged the Department of

Tropical Medicine and Medical Parasitology with the Department of Microbiology, creating the Department of Microbiology, Immunology, and Parasitology, under Dr. Ronald Luftig. Tropical Medicine had been in decline for several years following the retirement after 38 years of service by Dr. J. Clyde Swartzwelder, an international star in the field.

Dr. Larson also tapped Richard Paddison to head Alumni Affairs and Continuing Education, two long-neglected areas, and Dr. Charles White from the University of West Virginia to Chair Ob/Gyn on the retirement of the legendary Abe Mickal. When **Henry Jolly, MD ('40)** retired as long-time Chair of Dermatology, he was replaced briefly be **Dr. Ricardo Mora ('73)**. Mora would be succeeded by Dr. Lee T. Nesbitt, who would enjoy a long and successful reign.

Another notable addition to the faculty was Dr. Mohammed Naraghi to chair Anesthesiology on the retirement of Dr. John Adriani. For the first time in school history, Anesthesia became a separate department rather than a section of surgery.

Dr. Larson also recruited Dr. Morris Schaffer from Tulane to head up a newly formed Office of Research, and Charles Chapman and Virginia Howard, as editorial writers. This triumvirate helped many fledging research scientists successfully compete for federal grants. Another major accomplishment during Dr. Larson's tenure was the dedication of the Medical Education Building in 1981.

In 1981, Dr. Larson presided over the 50th Anniversary of the founding of the School with a series of events starring a faculty of the past and present. The festivities were recorded in book form as *This I Remember*.

Dr. Larson also worked on revamping the Department of Pediatrics, bringing in Robert Suskind from the University of South Alabama; the Department of Psychiatry, bringing in Dr. William Easson from the University of Aberdeen (Scotland); and the Department of Radiology, by bringing in Dr. Erich Lang from Shreveport to head the Department.

Historically, the Department of Radiology had been a kind of extension of the Charity Hospital Radiology Department, but Lang, a graduate of the University of Vienna, who was gifted with an entrepreneurial spirit, soon turned it into a multifaceted operation providing not only routine x-ray interpretation but international radiology services as well.

Lang would stay for several years, giving way to Dr. Wilfredo Castenada from the University of Minnesota. Dr. Castenada recruited Dr. Janis Letourneau, an outstanding radiologist who ultimately would become the Associate Dean for Faculty Affairs.

In the aftermath of Katrina, the Department would suffer catastrophic losses of residents and faculty, due to the closure of several hospitals. Dr. Castenada would resign and be replaced by Dr. Leonard Bok, who would rebuild the once thriving department.

When Dr. Alan Copping, Chancellor of the Medical Center for 14 years and former Dean of the School of Dentistry, was chosen to become President of the LSU System in

1984, a position he would hold for 14 more years, Dr. Larson briefly considered applying for the Chancellor position. But the search team quickly recommended Dr. Perry Rigby, the then Dean of the School of Medicine in Shreveport, as Chancellor. While Dr. Rigby prepared to leave Shreveport, Dr. Copping appointed **Dr. Donna Ryan, ('70),** who was serving as Professor of Medicine and Vice Chancellor for Clinical Affairs, as Acting Chancellor.

During Dr. Ryan's tenure, Dr. Larson stepped down as Dean, eventually moving to the University of Medicine and Dentistry of New Jersey as Dean. Dr. Ryan appointed Dr. Robert Dyer, Professor of Anatomy and Associate Dean, as Acting Dean. Soon after Dr. Rigby arrived, Dr. Ryan accepted an executive position at the Pennington Biomedical Research Center in Baton Rouge.

ဆာ

Chapter VIII

The Daniels Era
(1986 – 1995)

Dr. Rigby served as Chancellor for 10 years before becoming Director of Health Care Systems for LSU and Chairman of the Medical Education Commission of the State of Louisiana. In the aftermath of Katrina, he would also again become a practicing hematologist/oncologist, providing education and clinical care in an area temporarily depleted by faculty losses.

To replace Dr. Larson as Dean of the School of Medicine, Dr. Rigby opted for a national search, an unusual occurrence in School history. Previously, only Jack Finerty PhD, who served as Dean from 1966-1971, and Vernon Lippard, MD (1946-1948), had come from a national search.

The search committee interviewed many candidates but immediately zeroed in on Dr. Robert Daniels, a nationally known psychiatrist and medical educator who was serving as Dean of the University of Cincinnati School of Medicine. Daniels had been in the running for President of the University of Cincinnati, but did not get the job and elected to move on. Daniels accepted LSU's offer of the position and began serving in 1986. He brought with him his spouse Dr. Vikki Ashley, a PhD psychologist and author, who acted as a vigorous if unpaid advocate for the School of Medicine.

When Dr. Daniels took the reins as the new dean, the School of Medicine was strong in academics, but was hard-pressed to come to grips with Louisiana's financial state. Oil markets, as well as the shipping business, had taken a serious nosedive throughout the first half of the 1980s. Port cities like New Orleans bore the brunt of this downturn's effects. Louisiana had consistently been a cash-poor state since the Civil War, but hard times in important Mississippi River ports such as New Orleans and Baton Rouge made a bad situation worse.

As a result of increasing financial pressures, the state cut back expenditures virtually across the board. The Medical School—like all other state institutions—suffered from these constraints. Not only were its direct appropriations reduced, but the public hospitals that LSU relied on were also fiscally stretched to the limit. This had several immediate effects, all bad. Clinical services were reduced. Funds to pay faculty for resident supervision and administration of hospital services decreased and needed repairs in infrastructure were delayed. Officials had long called for improvements at Charity and University Hospitals, but with little money in the state's coffers, these improvements would also have to wait. Thus, residency programs, clinics, and services were all threatened, with direct implications for the strength of the School of Medicine's medical education program.

All was not lost, however. Dr. Daniels realized that his faculty was dedicated and strong. As an outsider he could bring a fresh perspective to the job, years of experience, and as a psychiatrist he understood motivating people to excel.

One of his first acts was to hold a faculty meeting and propose that the school plan, yes actually plan, for the future. His question was deceptively simple: "Where do we want to be in five years?"

The answer came from a year of work by a 100-person committee that looked at many aspects of the school, and the committee had members, including staff and students, who would bring different points of view to the discussion. Strengths and weaknesses were identified. Everyone could have their say but the final product had to be doable and whining was prohibited.

The result was a 16-page bound document. It consisted of nine major sections, with a total of 28 subparts. It included finance, hospital relationships, education, research, clinical departments, administration, faculty, space and alumni affairs. It was adopted in January 1988. It was not simply placed on a shelf to be forgotten but was referred to often and updated in 1990.

Dr. Daniels used the Medical School's position as leverage for building networks of public and private partnerships to supplement state funding of the School. He early-on made a major decision to appoint Mr. Robert Plaisance, who had a Master of Business Administration degree, as Associate Dean for Fiscal Affairs. This was the first such appointment in the entire LSU System. Mr. Plaisance brought business acumen and a no-nonsense attitude to the office and demanded a heretofore unknown level of financial accountability in the School of Medicine.

Realizing the potential of the School of Medicine's development infrastructure, Daniels requested the LSU Medical Alumni Association to incorporate the LSU Health Sciences Center Foundation. This organization would concentrate on raising capital and forming partnerships between LSU and medical industry companies for investment and development.

Dr. Daniels was a master at planning and implementing both short- and long-range goals for the School of Medicine. To achieve these goals, he continually looked for funding sources and research innovations. He also worked to develop political contacts within the State Legislature and worked with consultants to make sure that the School's representatives were well-equipped for the rough-and-tumble world of state politics. Daniels hired, as one consultant, a former Lieutenant Governor who arranged a legislative reception at a club in Baton Rouge. Before the reception the consultant gathered a representative number of faculty and through role-playing taught them how to talk to legislators and gain support.

The evening was a great success and something of a revelation. At a debriefing session, several faculty pointed out that they had met legislators who did not realize that the School of Medicine was in New Orleans and not Baton Rouge. But all of these efforts bore fruit. The School saw continued growth, and its influence on the state's medical community grew.

In 1987, Daniels received the Daniel Drake medal from his alma mater, the University of Cincinnati, in recognition of his contributions to medical education. The award has been made only 10 times in 168 years.

At the close of the 1980s, Dean Daniels appointed **Warren Plauché** ('57) as Associate Executive Dean, who spearheaded an effort to join the Federal Area Health Education Center (AHEC) program. This little-known initiative was designed to help educational institutions put money and students into rural areas. This fulfilled the dual task of addressing the needs of underserved sectors of the population and exposing students to rural practice in hopes of encouraging them to practice there. No administrator at the LSU School of Medicine had thought to tap into this money, but clearly Louisiana—and LSU—were perfectly suited to the mission of the AHEC program. From 1988 to 1989, four AHECs were established in Louisiana, beginning with Southeast Louisiana and extending across the entire state. They would change the face of rural healthcare and education in dramatic fashion. Plauché, who was also Professor of Ob/Gyn, would serve until 1998 when he retired.

Over their years of existence, the AHECs around Louisiana have provided myriad services throughout the state. Thousands of medical students have practiced with their preceptors—veteran physicians who volunteer their time to teach the students. These students have often sacrificed summer vacations in order to witness the practice of medicine in areas of the state unknown to many of their colleagues. As a result, many have chosen to establish their own practices in these areas after they finish their training, usually in Family Medicine.

The AHECs have also proven to be a fertile training ground for minorities and disadvantaged students. Under AHEC, freshman medical students from LSU visit inner city schools in New Orleans, in an effort to get students to pursue medical careers. In addition to physicians, the AHEC programs also foster recruitment of nurses and other healthcare professionals, and have played an important part in other initiatives by the LSU School of Medicine. It was only one of the many improvements made during Dean Daniels' term at the School of Medicine.

The Neuroscience Center of Excellence had opened in 1989, under the direction of Dr. Nicolas Bazan, but plans were underway to expand it. It moved into two new floors of the

LSU/Lions Clinic Building on Gravier Street, and using it as a model, plans were underway for a number of similar efforts, including the Alcohol Research Center, Center on Aging, the Center for Molecular and Human Genetics, the Stanley S. Scott Cancer Center, and the Cardiovascular Center of Excellence, all of which opened in 1991. These research centers provided countless amounts of knowledge and data in their specialties. The Alcohol Research Center, to name just one example, continues to produce research studies on the effects of alcohol on numerous organ systems.

Under Daniels the library resources of the School of Medicine were also pooled into a single unit. The John P. Isché Memorial Library combined two libraries at the School of Medicine into one sprawling library complex on three floors of the newly built Resource Building at 433 Bolivar Street near University Hospital.

In the fall of 1991, eight hundred and seventy alumni and friends gathered at the Aquarium of the Americas in downtown New Orleans for the School's 60th Anniversary. The past few years had been tough (and the trials were not over yet), but they had much to celebrate. The School had opened a number of Centers of Excellence, a new clinic building and research operations spearheaded by both basic science and clinical departments. Daniels was clearly leaving his mark on the school.

By the time the LSU School of Medicine celebrated its 60 years in existence, its expansion heralded unprecedented growth in its programs and facilities. At the 60th Anniversary Scientific Session, then Louisiana Governor Buddy Roemer noted the thousands who benefited from the care of LSU-trained physicians across the state. In this group he could count himself, given that LSU graduates helped the governor keep his diabetes under control. This anniversary event, staged by the Alumni Association and attended by over 10% of the then living alumni, was a symbol of the continuing effectiveness and influence of the Medical School, and the Medical Center that had grown out of it.

The Neuroscience Center of Excellence (NCE), for instance, received a $14 million grant from the Department of Defense in 1993 to expand the Center by adding three floors to the LSU/Lions Clinic building at 2020 Gravier Street. This was only part of a $25 million grant from the federal government to fund research at the NCE. These floors were added to the building in 1995 and 1996. This expansion produced new faculty positions and seminal research in neurological diseases.

This large grant was quite the turnaround for the Department of Defense (DOD) and can be traced to political folly, public outrage, good science, and cats. Several years earlier a powerful Louisiana congressman, egged on by some constituents who were animal lovers, demanded that the Department of Defense pull a grant from LSU. The grantee, Dr. Michael Carey, Professor of Neurosurgery, had been doing research for several years on penetrating head wounds. Dr. Carey, on the basis of his service as a neurosurgeon in Vietnam, knew that brain wounds were a major cause of death and disability among soldiers.

Under DOD contract, he had perfected an animal model using anesthetized cats, wounding them in the brain with a small pellet, studying the altered physiology and testing various neuroprotective agents to minimize brain damage. That this might actually save the lives or neurological function of American soldiers wounded on a battlefield was irrelevant to the animal rights zealots who appeared to equate the well being of cats at least equal to if not higher than the well being of G.I.s.

Since the congressman apparently had an overabundance of cat lovers among his supporters, he pronounced the research outrageous and the DOD obliged by pulling the contract. The congressman also asked the Government Accounting Office (GAO) to investigate Carey's work. They assembled a team of experts who concluded that Dr. Carey's work was worthwhile science. Inexplicably, the GAO buried the experts' conclusion deep in its eventual 400-page report.

During all of this, Dr. Carey was called to active duty when the U.S launched Operation Desert Storm, the successful U.S. effort to liberate Kuwait from Iraqi invaders. While he was out of the country his actions were vigorously defended by his wife, Dr. Betty Oseid of the Department of Pediatrics.

The congressman's precipitous actions set off howls of protest from many quarters, including research scientists from across the country, the Louisiana State Medical Society, the American Medical Association and most importantly Veterans organizations. Surprisingly, neither the congressman nor the cat people expected this response. They beat a hasty retreat, leaving the congressman to fend for himself.

He maintained that he had acted properly, but he also enthusiastically called for research support for LSU's Neuroscience Center and expressed the thought that a large grant to expand it was in order.

LSU ordered its own faculty review, which supported Dr. Carey's research, and it also supported Carey's work. Dr. Daniels for his part took an active role and met periodically with Dr. Carey and in typical fashion offered both practical advice and strong moral support.

Eventually, Drs. Carey and Oseid would be awarded the "Medal of Valor" by the AMA for demonstrating to the country the value of biomedical research even in the face of death threats from animal rights zealots. Dr. Carey would receive the "Legion of Merit" from the U.S. Army and his story would be featured on the television program "60 Minutes." He would continue brain injury research, using anesthetized rats as the animal model, through yet another DOD contract.

Two other Centers of Excellence opened during Daniel's tenure. In 1991, the Stanley S. Scott Cancer Center opened under the direction of Dr. Merv Trail. It honored an influential citizen who had died of lung cancer and was funded by a large grant from Freeport MacMoRan Corporation.

In 1993, the Alcohol Research Center was developed under John Spitzer, the Chairman of Physiology, and Steve Nelson, who would one day become Dean of the School. Its research productivity has been astounding.

Under Daniels leadership medical students at LSU also worked hard to give of their time and energy in service to the public. In 1993, they founded a community service clinic at the New Orleans Mission. Staffed by student volunteers working under faculty supervision, this clinic offered primary care services to the homeless. Students treated respiratory and gastrointestinal infections, hypertension, and complications from exposure to the elements. The volunteers also helped patients who were trying to overcome drug addiction and alcoholism.

The medical students also established Camp Tiger in 1986. This is an ongoing project of each freshman class. These young students organize and run a week of games, activities, and entertainment for disabled children from the New Orleans area. With financial help from the Medical Alumni Association and others, freshmen run the camp. Overseen by volunteer faculty members, these students embodied the spirit of volunteerism and self-sacrifice that characterized the LSU School of Medicine.

The LSU School of Medicine lost several important faculty members during the late 1980s and early 1990s. Dr. Fred Allison retired on July 1, 1987, after nearly twenty years of faithful service to LSU. He had been very effective in recruitment to the Department of Medicine as well as significantly encouraging the growth of fellowship programs in the department. Dr. Allison had been named to the Edgar Hull, MD, Professorship as well as the Department Chair. He had also served on the editorial boards of the *Annals of Internal Medicine*, *Proceedings of the Society for Experimental Biology and Medicine*, and the journal *Antimicrobial Agents and Chemotherapy*. The LSU School of Medicine lost a valuable member of its faculty when Dr. Allison retired.

On June 14, 1988, Dr. John Adriani died. When he retired in 1975 as professor of anesthesiology at the School of Medicine, he had served LSU well for 31 years. Adriani had spearheaded the creation of the Department of Anesthesiology while he was in the Department of Surgery. World-famous in his field, Adriani taught pharmacology and later served on the faculty of the Loyola (later LSU) School of Dentistry. He was a consultant or member of the boards of directors for many organizations and agencies, including the U.S. Food and Drug Administration and the Federal Trade Commission. Adriani also consulted with the U.S. Attorney's Office on numerous occasions in efforts to stop illegal drug sales. A firm proponent of the use of generic prescriptions and an expert on pharmaceuticals he was president of the Association of University Anesthesiologists in 1955 as well as chairman of the AMA's Council on Drugs from 1967 to 1971. He received numerous awards, including the Distinguished Service Award from the International Anesthesiology Research Society and a Certificate of Honor from the Library of Congress. His contributions to the LSU School of Medicine were abundant and important.

Fortunately, doctors like Fred Allison, John Adriani, and Fred Brazda, the long time Chair of Biochemistry—who would pass away in January 1994—, had left behind a legacy of a new generation of physicians and researchers who carried on their tradition of excellence, including Drs. **Charles "Bo" Sanders** ('64), J. Patrick O'Leary, William Chillian, Nicholas Bazan, Robert D'Ambrosia, and **Charles Hilton** ('76). This new generation of LSU physicians guided the School toward the new millennium.

There were exciting ventures ahead for the School of Medicine. In many cases, LSU administrators and faculty built on the firm foundation of the previous 60 years of the School of Medicine. Since the early 1960s, LSU personnel had established research and teaching facilities in countries abroad, most notably in helping to establish a medical school in Costa Rica. By the early 1990s, some departments had expanded their programs to Ghana, Bangladesh, Thailand, and South Africa. The Class of 1995 formed the International/Public Health Interest Group, a student organization that sponsored an international externship in conjunction with the Pediatrics and Obstetrics departments. Students traveled to a variety of locations, including India, Honduras, Thailand, Chile, and Belize. In these varied locations, students were exposed to a number of clinical and public health issues in some of the poorest or least-developed areas of the world. They treated patients with drug abuse, AIDS, malnutrition, and the diseases related to poor sanitation.

International initiatives mirrored the increasing diversity at the School of Medicine. In the fall of 1994, fifty-one percent of the School's freshman class was female. Additionally, the new class included 29 African-Americans and 25 Asian-Americans. In May 1994 the Medical School began hosting the Women in Medicine Seminar to address various topics facing female doctors, including gender bias and sexism. The Women in Medicine society at LSU presented its first annual award to Dr. Carolyn Duncan, who had served as Professor of Pediatrics and Neurology for 20 years.

On Daniels' retirement from the Deanship in 1995, a Lectureship in Medical Education and an Endowed Professorship of Medical Education were dedicated in his name by the Medical Alumni. He was lionized at the event for a decade of vigorous and innovative leadership. When the Isidore Cohn, Jr., MD, Student Learning Center was built, a major laboratory was named for Dr. Daniels and his wife Dr. Vikki Ashley.

Dr. Daniels continued to offer advice to the Health Sciences Center for several years as an Assistant Vice Chancellor after stepping down as Dean. He lives in retirement in New Orleans.

৪০৫৪

Chapter IX

Dr. Marier Becomes Dean

When Dr. Daniels retired from the deanship in 1995, a successor was quickly named. His successor was Dr. Robert Marier. A Yale Medical School graduate in 1969, Dr. Marier completed his residency in Internal Medicine at Massachusetts General in Boston. He served in the Public Health Service for two years and was trained in Infectious Diseases at Yale soon thereafter. In 1978, Dr. Marier came to LSU as a member of the ID section of the Department of Medicine.

He rose to Professor of Medicine and gradually assumed a greater and greater role in the operation of Charity Hospital, serving as Medical Director from 1985-1993. He obtained a Master's degree in hospital administration and became Administrator of University Hospital when the state acquired it.

In the succeeding years, the School took on an extraordinary level of responsibility in healthcare. On July 1, 1997, the state transferred most of its public hospitals to the control of the LSU System. Dr. Marier headed the newly created LSU Healthcare Services Division in its transition period. The HCSD's immediate concerns centered on infrastructure, physician networking, and financing. Eventually, HCSD and the LSU School of Medicine would form partnerships with doctors and facilities across the state. Under Dr. Marier's leadership, the LSU School of Medicine expanded the faculty group practice to become the LSU Healthcare Network, managing faculty private practice through managed-care agreements at clinics across the state.

One of Dr. Marier's lasting contributions to the School of Medicine was his push to revise the curriculum and create the Student Learning Center.

From time immemorial, men (and, later, women) who wanted to practice medicine congregated around older physicians who would guide them through an apprenticeship of sorts. In the United States this led to the creation of many medical schools of variable quality, often proprietary enterprises and with no consistent curriculum content. The art and science of medical education was transformed by Abraham Flexner, a nonphysician educator. Using private grant funding, he undertook a study of all the medical schools in the United States. After his extensive groundbreaking report in 1910, inferior schools were forced to close and the four-year education model was adopted by those medical schools that survived his inspection.

Since its inception, the LSU School of Medicine had followed the traditional model of medical education: students spent their first two years attending lectures and doing lab exercises, and then emerged for the next two years to learn clinical skills in a hospital setting. For the first half of their medical education, students spent virtually all of their time reading, processing, and memorizing.

It became increasingly difficult to manage the volume of information students had to learn as the pace of scientific discovery quickened throughout the last half of the twentieth century. Eventually, this presented a number of problems. First among them was the sheer volume of information that students had to assimilate. The question was, were students learning or just memorizing?

All indications suggested they were mostly memorizing. Students at LSU created a note-taking service that supplied them with all of the material in lectures if they missed anything the professor said. The resulting stack of paper was usually three feet tall for one year, and students were usually expected to memorize it all.

Additionally, there was no way of assuring that students were relating basic science material to clinical practice. At the end of the day, many doctors who entered clinical practice questioned several aspects of their medical education. Why had they learned the things they did? Were they part of a process of merely being shuffled through a system developed decades before? Could medical education be better?

Medical societies and professional associations began to address these questions. The American Association of Medical Colleges began a special program to study and deal with these challenges in the mid 1990s. The Medical Schools' Objectives Program (MSOP) studied ways to better the curriculum. Ultimately, the AAMC suggested three primary objectives for medical education. First, that medical schools instill in their graduates an appropriate awareness of ethics, altruism, and teamwork. Second, that medical graduates had to have the requisite scientific knowledge with the greatest possible understanding of the human body and its processes. Finally, that medical students had to have comprehensive experiences in clinical practice, in order to know both how to perform procedures and how to interact with patients and their families.

The AAMC also funded a number of initiatives at several American medical schools through the Robert Wood Johnson Foundation. These schools remade their curriculum and provided a road map for other medical schools to follow. In the late 1990s, LSU School of Medicine also began to study how it could incorporate the AAMC's proposals into its own curriculum.

It had been decades since the School had done a major overhaul of its curriculum and it was due for a site visit from the Liaison Committee on Medical Education. Approval of this committee is vital to a School of Medicine. Without its approval graduates cannot sit for licensing examinations or obtain residencies, and the LSU Administration knew that would be hard to retain approval unless the curriculum was modified and modernized.

Dr. Charles Hilton ('76), Associate Dean and Professor of Medicine, took the lead in curriculum update, along with several committees of the faculty. Drs. Richard DiCarlo, Sam McClugage, and Peter DeBlieux assisted Dr. Hilton and Dr. Marier, and provided vital administrative support for the plan. In fact, in the earliest days of deanship, Dr. Marier professed an interest in medical technology, curriculum improvement, and individualized learning. These would become the hallmarks of the plans for LSU's future.

The new programs to be implemented in the first two years at LSU would be named the "Science and Practice of Medicine" (SPM). Additionally, the Medical School studied its current programs extensively, calculating lecture hours, comparing its statistical data relating to student performance to data from other schools, and comparing curriculum to that of other medical schools. The Medical School also began to heavily invest in technology and an educational campaign designed to expand its facilities and scholarly capabilities.

From the outset, the objective of the revamped curriculum was to produce medical graduates who were undifferentiated generalists. That is, medical students would receive the skills necessary to be knowledgeable, compassionate, and skilled, while being able to fit into a residency program and be molded in it into the specialty of their choice. Through the entire process, students would benefit from adult learning principles. They would be actively engaged in their learning and received immediate feedback from their professors. In this way, they would also feel that they were a part of the educational process rather than mechanized learners.

The SPM program would eventually have three components. First, it would take advantage of a computer program named Diagnostic Reasoning (DxR) that presented students with sample cases that could be tailored to what they were learning in their basic science classes. Students could ask questions, order tests, examine parts of the "patient's" body, view x-rays, etc. Dr. Hilton and his colleagues realized in a few short months of using DxR that students were learning to use the traditional conceptual framework of case study as a way to link their clinical reasoning skills with the knowledge they were actively gaining in their first- and second-year classes.

But they noticed something else: the students were advancing leaps and bounds ahead of what their teachers thought they could do. For example, students working up a DxR "patient" who manifested an incidental visual problem had the opportunity to study the eye before officially taking an ophthalmology course. How? When they did not know what they were looking at or why it was important, students went online or in their textbooks and read about it. They became so interested in their "patients" that they investigated more and more about what was needed to diagnose or treat them.

Eventually, the students would take the case studies further than they were intended (or expected) to go. With sophisticated reasoning skills, they began exploring more advanced treatment options and diagnostic tools than they had yet learned about. All of this would eventually prove that the students were advancing in basic knowledge and clinical skill far beyond what the traditional four-year model of medical education had previously allowed them to do. The students achieved a high degree of collateral knowledge and diagnostic reasoning that uniquely prepared them for clinical practice.

This was not the only part of the SPM curriculum, however. Students would also be expected to learn basic procedures that would greatly help them adjust to clinical life later in medical school. In the Procedures Labs, students would learn how to take blood pressure; insert IVs; perform lumbar punctures; conduct prostate, pelvic, and breast examinations; correctly check heart sounds or lung sounds. Through these lab exercises – all conducted on simulators or models – faculty members could ensure that all of their students achieved a basic level of proficiency.

Finally, students would be put into small groups with experienced faculty members. In these Clinical Skills Forums, students and faculty considered ethical, humanistic, and professional attitudes that students would encounter as practicing physicians. From the first year of their medical education, then, students would be instilled with an acute awareness of the issues that every physician has to deal with, from issues of patient confidentiality, to euthanasia, to bedside manner, and on. But this was all in the future.

Dr. Marier and many other faculty members wanted to implement SPM. To be sure, a few traditionalists were opposed to the whole idea. But everyone agreed on one thing: There was no place to teach it. So one Sunday morning, a group of faculty and administrators met at Dr. Marier's condominium and cooked up a pot of spaghetti and much more. They dreamed of a facility that would be the center of learning in the Medical School. They designed it – whatever "it" was, for it was a completely new idea – around the three components of the SPM curriculum. What would eventually be known as the Student Learning Center included eight small group rooms, two simulation labs, and two procedures labs, as well as a large lecture room and a state-of-the-art computer lab in the foyer that allowed students to use wired and wireless access for online resources.

The Student Learning Center (SLC) would be equipped with all the latest technology. Projector systems throughout the small group rooms and the large lecture hall would allow for all types of multimedia presentations. There would be computer connectivity in all areas of the SLC, as well as a broad floor plan that was especially conducive to students gathering throughout the day.

It was one grand pipedream because there was no space to put it and no money to build it. Then serendipity stepped in. The ENT Department was moving from the first floor of 2020 Gravier Street to the Clinical Science Research Building, vacating 14,000 square feet of prime campus real estate. It was every clinical department's second choice as the site of the Learning Center. Each department's first choice, of course, was for Marier to give the proposed site to their own department. Realizing that the school's accreditation might hang in the balance, Marier made a tough decision, and with the blessing of Chancellor Merv Trail, the space was dedicated to the Learning Center.

So the Learning Center would be built using prime clinical space on the first floor of the Lions/LSU Clinic Building. There was only one minor problem. Building this with state funds required the appropriation through the Capital Outlay process. That would take years, and it was years the School didn't have. But a group stepped forward to save the day, and perhaps the school itself. **Dr. Russell Klein ('59)**, Associate Dean for Alumni Affairs and the Alumni Association Board of Directors, agreed to take on the project. Intense fundraising began immediately. Major donors included the James D. Rives Surgical Society and the Committee of 100 – Champions of Excellence; $1,200,000 was raised for construction and more over time for furnishing and equipment. Stryker Corporation and the Bernard and Marie LaHasky Foundation aided greatly here.

The Alumni Board began seeking qualified architects for the project with little success. The initial design suggestions were pedestrian, to put it kindly, and the questions asked by the architects were uninformed.

A major accomplishment was finding Darren Rozas of Rozas-Ward Architects to design the facility.

After several architects had been unimpressive in their interviews, **Earl Rozas ('64)**, a Past President of the LSU Medical Alumni Association, suggested that it was time to interview his architect son, Darren. Since Earl would have no vote and volunteered to absent himself from the discussion, the Board agreed.

Darren presented himself and his impressive record with designing medically related projects. He actually knew how big an operating room, even a fake room, needed to be. No previous firm could answer that sort of basic question. He actually listened to our plans, asked intelligent and probing questions and began to sketch a design on a chalk board. The Board had found its architect. Earl modestly gave all credit for this obvious display of talent to Darren's mother. The Board did too.

The Alumni Association, through its subsidiary, The Institute of Professional Education, took ownership of the space through a cooperative endeavor agreement with the LSU Board of Supervisors in early 2001, built the Center by August 2001, and donated it back to LSU in a grand ceremony.

The Center was named for Dr. Isidore Cohn, Jr., a legend in the LSU School of Medicine and strong advocate of technology and innovation in the advancement of medicine. Formal dedication occurred in April 2002 at the Annual Meeting of the James D. Rives Surgical Society. The SLC, which opened in time for the 2001-2002 school year, began shaping the education of all medical school classes. By every measurable standard, the Learning Center was a categorical success.

The success story could have stopped there, but the leadership of the School of Medicine realized the assets housed in the SLC could be used for a new generation of technological initiatives. The simulation complex could also serve the faculty as a platform for medical research. Dr. Marier embraced that fact by creating the Office of Medical Education Research and Development, headed by Dr. Sheila Chauvin. This office was designed to promote and develop research initiatives by School of Medicine faculty, especially as regards faculty development and evaluation. The SLC thus became a tool for research and clinical practice, benefiting the entire medical center.

Prior to Hurricane Katrina, LSU School of Medicine had one of the most advanced human simulation centers in the United States. And it was poised to go even further. Recognizing that simulation technology could be used to retrain physicians in new procedures through continuing education, train residents and fellows after graduation, and do "team training" for entire groups, the Medical Alumni Association was planning to construct the Center for Advanced Practice, which would also be located at 2020 Gravier and would complement the activities at the Student Learning Center.

Money had been raised, agreements with the LSU System had been confected, and negotiations with a contractor were underway. Construction was planned to start in October 2005.

Katrina struck at the end of August, flooding the city, the School, and the Learning Center. Some equipment was salvaged from the Center but most was lost. The Alumni Association used its construction funds for other more pressing needs, including replacement of Learning Center equipment so student education could continue in Baton Rouge.

FEMA, the much maligned agency charged with recovery of the Crescent City, was required to reimburse LSU for some of the damaged equipment, especially the mannequins, one of which cost $250,000. FEMA demanded proof that the "dummies" were unusable and required that an "autopsy" be performed by the manufacturer, located in Sarasota, Florida.

The School decided to ship them back via UPS and put them in "body bags"; the filled bags were hauled to the street in front of 2020 Gravier Street and awaited the truck.

Before the UPS man arrived, a truckload of National Guard Troops, charged with keeping order in the city, drove by, came to a stop and with guns at the ready demanded to see who was in the bags. They were relieved to discover that it wasn't human remains. The manufacturer would eventually issue "death certificates" for the mannequins – accidental death by drowning. FEMA eventually paid up.

Marier during his deanship would also oversee expanded relationships with Children's Hospital and with the Dental School. He would expand the Dean's staff by adding an Associate Dean for Research and an Associate Dean for Medical Education. Numerous new faculty and Departmental Chairs would be added. A "Rural Pathway" program would be started to encourage students into serving in rural areas of the state.

Another notable accomplishment occurred under Dr. Marier in 1997 when the Ernest N. Morial Asthma, Allergy, and Respiratory Disease Center opened at the LSUHSC. Named in memory of Ernest N. Morial, a late mayor of the New Orleans who died of asthma, it was dedicated to prevention, research and treatment of these respiratory conditions which disproportionately affect urban poor and African Americans.

To direct the Center, Warren Summer, MD, Professor of Medicine and Chief of Pulmonary Disease recruited **Dwayne Thomas, MD ('84)** from the University of Florida. Under Dr. Thomas the Center would receive numerous educational and research grants and be recognized as one of only 20 such centers in the entire United States.

In 1998, Dr. Thomas was also tapped to be Medical Director of the Medical Center of Louisiana, and in 2003 he would be named its Chief Executive Officer. He would hold that position until 2008 when he would be named Associate Dean for Health Quality and Patient Safety. Dr. Summer would become the Morial Center Director.

Marier worked to strengthen LSU's private practice plan with the establishment of the Healthcare Network. In collaboration with the Jazz and Heritage Foundation and the Daughters of Charity, he oversaw the creation of the New Orleans Musicians Clinic to provide care at little or no cost to uninsured area musicians.

In early 2001, Dr. Mervin Trail, long-time Chancellor of the Health Sciences Center, suddenly died. **Dr. Mary Ella Sanders ('75)**, Vice-Chancellor for Clinical Affairs, former Alumni Board President and former Chairman of the Board of Regents for Higher Education of the State of Louisiana, assumed the position of Acting Chancellor.

Dr. Marier applied for the Chancellorship but the LSU System selected **Dr. John Rock ('72)**, a well known Emory University faculty member. Dr. Rock placed Dr. Marier in charge of developing a School of Public Health and named Dr. J. Patrick O'Leary, Associate Dean and Chair of Surgery, as Acting Dean.

The School of Public Health would be established but the LSU System selected Dr. Elizabeth Fontham as its first permanent Dean. Dr. Marier then retired and became Executive Director of the Louisiana State Board of Medical Examiners, succeeding Dr. John Barry Bobear, who had served on the faculty and as Medical Director of Charity before going to the Board position.

Dr. Rock opted for a national search for a new Dean and chose Dr. Sam McClugage, Associate Dean for Admissions and Professor of Anatomy, to lead the search. In short order the committee found its man, an international surgical superstar with deep ties to the school. The man was **Larry Hollier ('68)**.

℘☾☙

Chapter X

Dr. Hollier Takes Over

When **Larry Hollier** ('68) replaced Dr. J. Patrick O'Leary, who had served as Acting Dean since 2002, he began his second stint at the school as a member of the faculty and his third stint as a physician in New Orleans. The date was January 1, 2004.

After graduation, Dr. Hollier had served a residency in General Surgery under Dr. Isidore Cohn and had taken a fellowship in vascular surgery at Baylor University. In between, he had sandwiched in two years in the Air Force. After the vascular training, he served for several years on the LSU faculty, establishing a vascular surgery training program and a separate section of vascular surgery before being tapped to head the newly formed Section of Vascular Surgery at the Mayo Clinic in Rochester, Minnesota.

In 1987, he returned to New Orleans to become Chief of Surgery at Ochsner Medical Institutions, but in 1993 he left to become Executive Director and Chairman of Surgery at Health Care International, a hospital based in Glasgow, Scotland.

In 1996, he returned to the U.S. and became Chairman of Surgery at Mount Sinai Medical Center in New York, where he rose steadily to become President of the Hospital in 2002. In 2004, when the Deanship at LSU became available, he was able to realize a long-cherished dream to finish his career guiding his alma mater.

On arriving, he was impressed by several things. The student body impressed him both individually and as a group. They had an excellent work ethic and commitment. The faculty was dedicated and had a good esprit d'corps but several departments needed to be strengthened from educational and financial standpoints.

He urged targeted faculty recruitment. A major acquisition to the faculty in 2005 was naming Arthur Haas, PhD, as Chair of Biochemistry to replace the newly retired Robert Roskowski. Haas, a Professor at the University of Wisconsin, had studied at Northwestern under Dr. Irwin Rose, a Nobel Laureate in Chemistry.

A major student program, pushed by Dr. Hollier, was the Rural Scholars Program. This involved admitting ten students annually who would commit to practicing in a rural community in exchange for a full four-year tuition waiver.

Revamping departments through a process known as mission-based budgeting was also moving forward. The Alumni Association, buoyed by the success of the Isidore Cohn Jr.,

MD, Student Learning Center, was in the midst of planning to create a Center for Advanced Practice to give residents and practicing physicians a place to learn the latest technology. Funds were being raised, agreements with the LSU System were confected, architects were drawing up plans, and a builder had been selected.

The 75th Anniversary of the founding of the School of Medicine was on the horizon. A yearlong celebration was planned. Things were going well under Dr. Hollier's direction. Then something really bad happened.

෪෬

Chapter XI

Katrina and the Aftermath

On Friday, August 26, 2005, she was a big storm headed toward the Florida panhandle. On Saturday the landfall site had shifted more to the West. New Orleans was now at least in the landfall zone and public officials were beginning to advise evacuation. By Sunday, New Orleans was nearly at ground zero and it was time to get out of Dodge.

LSU, Charity, and the brave individuals working at both, would suddenly face the nation's biggest modern disaster challenge from a storm named Katrina. She was hundreds of miles wide, with winds up to Category Five strength through much of her sojourn through the Gulf of Mexico. As millions of Gulf Coast residents fled for safety, a core group of doctors, nurses, and administrators hunkered down in Charity and University Hospitals with their patients. Some LSU students also stayed in the downtown campus with personnel from the School's physical plant, administration, and campus police departments.

The School of Medicine—along with the rest of the Health Sciences Center—prepared for a few days' evacuation followed by a hurried return to the city in time to start the school year anew and get back to research, teaching, and patient care.

Unfortunately, Katrina did not turn further west, the city was not spared the destructive force of her tidal surge, and LSUHSC ultimately was inundated by the floodwaters that would cover 80% of the city. All of the complex's buildings—75 years in the making—were surrounded by up to eight feet of water. The Dental School, lower to the ground and some miles distant, would fare even worse.

The aftermath of the storm did not immediately appear so dire. The hurricane winds died down around the city by Monday afternoon, August 29, 2005. People from the hospitals and the Health Sciences Center began to walk outside to survey the damage.

There was some wind damage, and electricity was out over a wide area, but the generators at the Health Science Center and the hospitals had plenty of fuel. The Big Easy had dodged the bullet once again. Things would be back to normal soon. . . or so people thought.

Sometime during the middle of the night from August 29 to August 30, however, unseen tons of water coursing through the city's canal system undermined the poorly constructed levee walls and forced open large holes in the New Orleans side of 17th Street

Canal and the London Avenue Canal near Lake Pontchartrain, while high waters pushed a barge through the levee protecting the Industrial Canal at the city's Ninth Ward.

Early on the morning of August 30, Dr. Sam McClugage, Associate Dean for Admissions, who had stayed behind to help with post-storm administration, woke his wife with prophetic words: "The worst case scenario has happened." The city was rapidly flooding.

Approximately 180 people were trapped at the Residence Hall and in the various buildings of the Health Sciences Center complex. All of these people thankfully had enough food and water stored in the cafeteria to keep them alive and well fed. What they would not have, it would turn out, was electricity—and the air conditioning, lighting, and elevator access that went along with it. The generators would eventually run out of fuel. As bad as this would be, the hospital situation would become even worse.

Doctors in the Charity Emergency Room—one of only a handful of Level I Trauma Centers in the Southeastern United States—hurriedly moved their patients up the stairs to the safety of the second-floor auditorium. As the hours wore on, doctors and staff opened windows and tried their best to keep patients cool in the sweltering heat. Many faculty, including Drs. David Kline, **Fred Lopez ('90)**, **Brian Barkemeyer ('87)**, **Cathi Fontenot ('84)**, **Dwayne Thomas ('84)**, **Peter DeBlieux ('88)**, and Keith Van Meter, worked tirelessly.

But the situation continued to get worse as it increasingly became apparent that the crisis would not soon ease. Generators ran out of fuel, despite attempts by the staff to siphon gas from the ambulances parked on Charity's ambulance ramp or from cars in the adjacent garage.

Meanwhile, some of the most critical patients faced great danger. As the days wore on, generators finally sputtered to silence. Patients on ventilators had to be hand-bagged for the duration of their stay. This task was filled round-the-clock by doctors, nurses, attendants and even other patients. For the most critical patients—those in the Neonatal Intensive Care Unit (NICU) at University and those in the ICU's at Charity—time was not just dragging on. It was running out.

On Wednesday, August 31, two days after Katrina, the world woke up to see televised images of a city drowning *and* in the midst of violent anarchy. Canal Street businesses and others around the city were looted, burned, and vandalized. There were reports of violence throughout the area. The flood waters were no deterrent to armed thugs and looters who terrorized the hurricane-ravaged city and posed a serious risk to those left behind.

At Charity Hospital, the violence also touched those trapped inside. Doctors heard sniper fire on Tulane Avenue. Rumors about armed gunmen spread like wildfire. Dead bodies of drowned victims floated down Gravier Street, past the E.R. entrance. All the while, doctors struggled to aid critical patients. They were alone and facing staggering odds.

flooding of the LSU Health Sciences Center after Katrina

Doctors and staff could do only so much with their tragically limited resources. No help had yet arrived, however, and, in the post-storm maelstrom of downed cell phone towers and interrupted communications, there was no indication that rescuers were coming any time soon. Early on Wednesday morning, then, doctors were amazed to see a CNN report on a battery-powered television that Charity Hospital had been evacuated. A resourceful resident with a working cell phone then reached Wolf Blitzer of CNN, and begged for help in evacuating the hospital. CNN sent out a crew, including medical reporter Sanjay Gupta, MD, which documented for the entire world the miseries and hardships present at Charity Hospital. Help began to make its way, however slowly, to the stricken "Big Free."

Some of the help that Charity would get came through the good offices of former Vice President, Al Gore. Several years earlier, Dr. David Kline, Chairman of Neurosurgery at LSU, had successfully repaired a peripheral nerve injury that had been sustained by Gore's son.

A friendship then developed between Gore and Dr. Kline and they kept in touch. Kline's daughter-in-law, living in San Francisco, made a personal appeal to the former Vice President to use his influence to help New Orleans and her father-in-law; Gore's staff sprang into action, helping to greatly speed the evacuation.

By Wednesday night, August 31, 2005, four of about 40 critically ill patients had been able to leave the crippled hospital. This was brought about because the owner of an out-of-state ambulance company saw the CNN reports and donated the services of four of his helicopters.

The "heliport" was the roof of the Tulane Medical Center garage. Transport of the four desperately ill patients was difficult in the flooded streets. Fortunately hospital personnel were able to flag down a National Guard truck tall enough to make it through the waters.

Dr. Ben deBoisblanc ('81), the LSU faculty member in charge of the Charity ICU, supervised the transport, packing a bag of emergency supplies including drugs and medical devices "just in case." "Just in case" became a reality about a block away from Charity when one of the patients developed a tension pneumothorax.

Ben had thought of everything, including bringing a chest tube, everything except a bottle of Xylocaine, so he inserted the tube without anesthetic, relieving the pressure on the man's lung and saving his life. A year later Ben attended the man's wedding.

Dr. Brian Barkemeyer ('87), a neonatologist with the Department of Pediatrics, evacuated several premature and severely weakened babies from University Hospital on canoes and flatboats to Children's Hospital personnel, who were waiting on the Claiborne Avenue off ramp a few blocks from University Hospital.

The doctors at LSU made these evacuations happen without much help from anyone but each other. In an unprecedented time of teamwork, solidarity, and commitment to patients, these staff members endured the worst conditions imaginable in the midst of the worst natural disaster ever to befall the United States.

Still, the ordeal was far from over. Those still trapped at the Health Sciences Center were also trying to survive in increasingly desperate circumstances. In all of these downtown locations, there was no functioning sewage system, running water or electricity. Toilets backed up and did not flush, filling the air with a stench augmented by the intense heat. Electricity had long since disappeared, as generator after generator ran out of fuel. There was also the increasing fear about the high level of unrest in New Orleans. Clearly, a great portion of the city was out of control. Gun shots were heard around the Health Sciences Center, especially at night. Sniping at rescue helicopters became something of a sport for some of the populace. This would go on for several days until some specially trained military units arrived from out of state. According to some sources these units began going out at night to return sniper fire and promptly the random gunfire ceased.

All of these safety concerns wore on the minds of LSUHSC staff who had evacuated to Baton Rouge and, of course, on the minds of the family and friends of those stranded at LSU and New Orleans-area hospitals. Very quickly after the storm hit, LSUHSC administrators set up temporary headquarters at the LSU Systems Building in Baton Rouge. Greatly aided by Dr. William Jenkins, the LSU System president, a round-the-clock team of officials, staff members, and even students began fielding phone calls from employees, family members, and those in New Orleans themselves.

Doctors and nurses at the hospital fed themselves sparingly and gave themselves IV fluids to keep up their strength. For five days, they endured the heat, humidity, stress, and trauma of the Katrina aftermath. They braved failures in communication, inadequate federal response, and slow uncoordinated rescue. They lost only eight patients.

Most of the most critical Charity patients were not helicoptered out until one p.m. on Friday, September 2. One of them died in the concrete garage of Tulane University. The rest of the complex was not rescued until three p.m. on Friday afternoon.

It became increasingly clear to LSU officials in Baton Rouge, that evacuating the Health Sciences Center itself would be challenging and potentially dangerous. The School appealed to several state agencies for help. By Friday afternoon, the time, method, and point of departure for the evacuation had changed several times. The nearly 200 people still in the Medical Science Center had scurried to the top of the parking garage, then to the second-floor landing at the Residence Hall, and back again. By Friday, September 2, they were exhausted. Then, Ronald Smith and Ronald Gardner, Vice Chancellors of the Health Sciences Center, were notified that the personnel at the HSC would be evacuated that night. They could be picked up at the Louis Armstrong New Orleans International Airport, where they were being ferried in National Guard trucks.

Smith and Dr. James Cairo, Dean of the School of Allied Health, boarded two 55-seat buses and headed for New Orleans. They were not aware of what they would find or whether they would be turned back. They were told to call for an escort when they reached Laplace but their cell phones went dead and so they decided to push on unescorted. Eventually, they made their way to Armstrong International after midnight on Saturday morning. They did not know how they were going to fit all of the people at the HSC into the two buses. That would not be their only worry. The scene they encountered was surreal and chaotic. The airport, although lit by generators, was teeming with desperate evacuees, many of whom began to beat on the side of the buses demanding a ride.

Finally, Mr. Smith spotted some State Troopers and convinced them to clear a path. Campus Police, meanwhile, formed a security perimeter around the LSU group near the airport's ground floor. This is where the Baton Rouge-bound buses met the evacuees and left under State Police escort, one hundred and eighty people crammed on two 55-seat buses. Finally, by Saturday morning, LSU had all of its own out of New Orleans.

The medical school's staff also offered a special contribution to relief statewide efforts by treating patients that had been evacuated from the city of New Orleans. Perhaps the most impressive display of medical cooperation after the hurricane was the makeshift hospital set up at the Pete Maravich Assembly Center on the LSU campus. Another similar effort would take place at the Lafayette Cajundome supervised by **Dr. Paul Azar ('70),** who through sheer force of personality brought order to a scene of complete chaos.

As soon as immediate needs were satisfied, students, faculty and staff at the medical school turned their energies to help reestablish their school. They manned phones in the improvised medical school headquarters in the System Office. Although HSC Chancellor

Motorboats wending down Tulane Avenue (St. Joseph Church in foreground, right)

Dr. John Rock ('72) had been out of the state on vacation when Katrina struck and unable to reach Baton Rouge, he was able to provide some direction via the Internet. The leaders able to make it to Baton Rouge, most notably **Dr. Larry Hollier ('68),** Dean of the School of Medicine; **Dr. Charles Hilton ('76),** Associate Dean for Graduate and Undergraduate Affairs; Dr. Sam McClugage, Associate Dean of Admissions; and **Dr. Russell Klein ('59),** Associate Dean for Alumni Affairs and Development, were able to immediately begin resurrecting the School of Medicine.

The Alumni Association played a unique role because as a 501 (c) 3 charity it was able to immediately reestablish its bank account in Baton Rouge, begin to process thousands of dollars of donations that poured in, and most importantly disburse it to needy residents, students, and staff. The response from alumni, medical industry, and medical organizations was immediate, massive, and heartening.

The Office of Alumni Affairs would quickly produce a "Katrina Edition" of LSU Medicinews, which not only chronicled the destruction sustained by the school but also its successful resurrection.

Even after patients and staff were evacuated from New Orleans, the work facing LSU staff and faculty was just beginning. Most other New Orleans-based schools were busy taking stock of their losses and placing students in out-of-state locations. Under the guidance of then LSUHSC Chancellor **John A. Rock ('72)** and a cadre of dedicated administrators and students, LSU established emergency communications systems to bring together the LSU family. They also sought alternative classroom space, as well as finding placements for more than 700 residents in hospitals around the state. LSU School of Medicine was going to stay in Louisiana.

Serendipity played a vital role in this. Before the hurricane struck Mr. Smith decided to evacuate some payroll and information technology staff and computerized payroll, personnel and other records. This was crucial to the recreation of the HSC in Baton Rouge. For his work Mr. Smith would be named an Honorary Alumnus of the School of Medicine.

By September 26, 2005, LSUHSC administrators, faculty and staff had pulled off a miracle. That day, students reentered classes on the campuses of the Pennington Biomedical Research Center and the LSU main campus in Baton Rouge. Departments were scattered across numerous hospitals in Baton Rouge and Lafayette, tending to their students and residents, but they were mostly intact. Virtually all of the computer systems of the Health Sciences Center were up and ready for use. Students and faculty who had not been able to find housing were housed aboard the Finnjet, an ocean-going ferry from Finland leased to accommodate more than 1,000 LSUHSC personnel and students.

The plan was to anchor the ferry at the port of Baton Rouge. The local port authority balked at accommodating this monster vessel. They then received a call from the governor's office. *Force majeure* was in effect in the state. It gave the governor immense temporary power, including the ability to assume control of the port of Baton Rouge. The boat was allowed to dock. The boat was a fully functional home away from home, with meals three times a day, regular shuttles to class, and wireless Internet access, provided by the Alumni Association.

The cabins each accommodated two persons. The plan was to offer a cabin to a faculty member, student, resident or staff member and their significant other. For a brief moment the administrators discussed a response if requests came from unmarried or same-sex couples, then wisely they decided not to inquire about marital status or gender preferences. For nearly ten months, the Finnjet, which acquired the nickname "Loveboat," housed the bulk of the LSUHSC student body and enabled them to continue their studies with the least number of interruptions possible. As soon as the boat docked in Baton Rouge students began to board her. Some were hungry and asked to be fed. As the Finnjet crew had not had time to acquire any local food they defrosted and served the only large quantity of food they had in the ship's freezer – reindeer stew.

As testimony to the faith and dedication of the LSUHSC student body, more than 92% of School of Medicine students returned to LSU to continue their studies. It was a staggering achievement for a school and city that some may have left for dead. **Dr. John**

Rock ('72) accepted a special award from the Association of Academic Health Centers, which recognized "the heroic efforts, outstanding accomplishments, and the immense compassion of the Louisiana State University Health Sciences Center family in response to the catastrophic events surrounding Hurricane Katrina."

Three months after the storm, the School of Medicine's accreditation in both undergraduate and graduate medical education was reaffirmed by the American Association of Medical Colleges and the Accreditation Council for Graduate Medical Education. This official recognition solidified the confidence of patients, faculty, and students in the ability of the School of Medicine to continue to give their students a valuable educational experience. This was an amazing feat. Accrediting agencies began clamoring to inspect the state of the School before the flood waters began to recede. Immediate inspection would have been a disaster so **Dr. Charles Hilton** ('76) and **Dr. Richard DiCarlo** ('87), Assistant Dean for Undergraduate Curriculum, devised a plan to send daily email updates on our progress to everyone who was inquiring, buying valuable time for the school to resurrect.

Work with contractors and remediation specialists began in October 2005, with primary attention given to making sure that all water and water-damaged goods were removed from buildings and their surroundings. The first priority was given to supporting the efforts of researchers, who needed to get back on campus as soon as possible to salvage their research and begin new work. To this end, liquid nitrogen was delivered to the Health Sciences Center regularly as early as October 2005 to preserve research samples. Since there was no regular transportation, Mr. Smith, et al, became fast friends with the Oklahoma National Guard, who obligingly transported precious cargo to New Orleans. And since there were no elevators, brute force moved the huge tanks up flights of stairs, and since there wasn't any electricity "glow-sticks" marked the way. The Clinical Science Research Building, the primary building for clinical research at LSUHSC, was officially reopened to researchers and staff in January 2006.

The Alumni Association began to meet via teleconference before the flood waters had receded, and on October 29, 2005, they met in person in Baton Rouge in the headquarters of the Louisiana State Medical Society.

Plans to celebrate the 75th Anniversary of the School of Medicine in 2006 had been in the works for some time. The first event scheduled for January was to be an elegant black tie event at the Fairmont Hotel, the site (as the Roosevelt Hotel) where the School was actually formed in January 1931.

The Fairmont, flooded by Katrina, was unavailable, but the Hilton was open, requiring only a 100-guest minimum, and the members of the Alumni Board immediately and individually underwrote the event.

Four hundred guests would eventually attend, and Governor Huey Long, in the person of a Baton Rouge actor, would enter the ballroom in a white linen suit and Panama hat

(Huey's trademark outfit) and appoint everyone in the room to the Board of Supervisors. He proposed re-creation of the School of Medicine, which was unanimously approved.

It was a glorious if symbolic return to New Orleans.

The Health Sciences Center staged an actual triumphant return of the students to the New Orleans campus in July and August of 2006, after months of hard work in rebuilding and reconfiguring the HSC campus.

The Dental School, its New Orleans campus completely flooded, would remain on the Baton Rouge campus for a considerably longer period.

Dr. John Rock, who had lost his home in New Orleans, stepped down as Chancellor in November 2005, ultimately moving to Miami to found a new medical school under the auspices of Florida Atlantic University. Associate Dean and Chair of Surgery, Dr. J. Patrick O'Leary, accompanied Dr. Rock to serve him as Associate Dean. **Dr. Chapman Lee ('69)** assumed the role of Acting Chair of Surgery. Dr. Hollier was named to replace Dr. Rock as Chancellor and also continued to serve as Dean.

Dr. Hollier immediately faced a financial crisis. The Health Sciences Center had been burning through its financial reserves at an alarming rate despite every effort to cut expenses and raise funds. Bankruptcy loomed by the end of February 2006.

With the help of many people Dr. Hollier was able to get Louisiana Governor Katherine Blanco to give the Health Sciences Center seventy million dollars from the Louisiana Recovery Authority. The Health Sciences Center would survive.

In the aftermath of Katrina, the public hospital situation was not nearly as rosy as the situation at the School of Medicine. In early 2005, Dr. Rock decided to bring in as Vice Chancellor a hospital administrator, Mr. Donald Smithburg, to oversee the Healthcare Services Division. This entity was responsible for running the public hospital system under the aegis of the LSU System. LSUHSC had been given this responsibility some years earlier when Dr. Trail was Chancellor. The LSU System soon decided to move the administration to Baton Rouge. Mr. Smithburg became a System Vice President and the Chancellor lost effective control of the hospitals. This would cause no end of problems after the hurricane. The Hospital Services Division under the leadership of Mr. Smithburg declared that Charity Hospital was total loss and could not reopen. Controversy swirled around that decision for many months. Protest rallies were staged and Smithburg threatened retaliation to anyone – student, resident or faculty member – who participated. They participated anyway.

A tent hospital was set up near the shuttered University Hospital and a clinic opened in a vacant downtown department store. A temporary hospital was opened in Jefferson Parish to accommodate trauma. Pointless foot-dragging delayed for months any attempt to reopen University Hospital. Many blamed Smithburg for the delay. While he was no doubt correct in his assessment that the Charity Hospital building could never reopen as a full-service hospital, the same was not true for University and many were put off by his manner of handling the entire situation.

To make matters more complicated there was no agreement on how much FEMA owed the state for damage to the hospital complex, especially the shuttered Charity building.

It would be 14 months from the storm before University Hospital was reopened, and then only partially. With 75 medical/surgical beds and 10 ICU beds, it lacked room for psychiatric services; the de facto psychiatric hospital for New Orleans continued to be the cells in Orleans Parish Prison.

Finally, and over the objections of neighbors, the state reopened the site of De Paul Hospital, in Uptown New Orleans, as a psychiatric facility. The objections of the neighbors to having psychiatric patients in their midst seemed more than a little contrived since De Paul from its founding many decades earlier had been a mental hospital.

Mr. Smithburg eventually left his position in the LSU System in 2007 and was replaced by Dr. Michael Butler. Few tears were shed at his departure. **Dr. Fred Cerise ('88),** who had served as Secretary of the Department of Health and Hospitals, was named Vice President of the LSU System in charge of all hospitals and both Health Sciences Centers. University Hospital now renamed LSU Interim Hospital, at the insistence of FEMA, would continue to slowly open more beds.

Numerous proposals for a permanent downtown hospital to replace Charity and University were studied. FEMA refused to declare that Charity was more than 50% damaged by the hurricane and offered modest damage payments that they increased modestly over time. A proposal to link an LSU hospital with a new VA Hospital (the old one having permanently closed) bogged down over size, cost, and location. Proposals surfaced and sank regularly. The new Governor, Bobby Jindal, and the new Secretary of DHH, Dr. Alan Levine, authorized a new study of the problem. In June 2008, Secretary Levine announced support for a 424-bed LSU Hospital adjacent to and perhaps sharing services with a new VA Hospital. The two facilities would be located on a sparsely populated plot bounded by Tulane Avenue, Canal Street, Claiborne Avenue and Rocheblave Street. Although slightly smaller than the original proposal for the LSU Hospital, shell space would allow for future expansion. "Preservationists" fought the proposals tooth and nail, arguing that Charity should be renovated as a hospital.

In the alternative, they argued for three other nearby sites, all judged unsuitable by the state or the VA. Their proposals met with stiff resistance from the State Office of Facility Planning and Control and outside consultants not hired by LSU, who argued for the original downtown site. The idea of retrofitting Charity as a modern hospital was dismissed out of hand.

Fallout from Katrina touched LSUSOM in another, tragic way. **Dr. Anna Pou ('90),** a brilliant head and neck surgeon on the faculty of the Department of Otolaryngology, volunteered to help staff the Tenet Hospital (Memorial Hospital) on Napoleon Avenue, the old Baptist Hospital, as Katrina bore down on the city.

There were 200 patients in Memorial when the hurricane flooded the area and 52 others on an upper floor leased to American LifeCare a separate organization that provided long-term care and rehabilitation services. It was not a hospice but many of its patients had DNR orders on their charts and some were ventilator-dependent. Dr. Pou began to provide care to them also.

Attempts to rescue family members, patients, staff and neighbors who had sought refuge in the building, some 2,000 people in all, were slow, uncoordinated, and hampered by the chaos gripping the city. Ultimately corpses of 45 Tenet or LifeCare patients would be left in the building. Rumors that some had been euthanized began to circulate and an investigation involving 17 Memorial and LifeCare patients was conducted.

Louisiana Attorney General Charles Foti, reeking of political ambition, pushed himself into the investigation. He, it is said, immediately saw this case and the drowning death of some elderly patients in a St. Bernard Parish nursing home as his ticket to the Governor's Mansion. He launched his own investigations, marshaled "experts," leveled murder charges against Dr. Pou and two Tenet nurses, and separately against the owners of the nursing home.

Backlash from the public immediately set in. Foti's "facts" and "experts" came under intense scrutiny in both cases. The Orleans Parish Coroner, after much consultation and soul-searching, refused to declare any of the deaths as homicides. Foti had to pass off the Pou case to the Orleans District Attorney, Eddie Jordan. Jordan, clearly in over his head, offered immunity to the nurses in exchange for testimony against Dr. Pou. They turned his offer down.

Foti reexamined his political situation and decided that he didn't need to be Governor after all and that he'd be satisfied with continuing as Attorney General.

The Orleans Parish Grand Jury examined the "evidence" presented by Jordan and refused to indict Dr. Pou. The criminal case against her was finished. LSU, which had supported her throughout her ordeal, welcomed her back.

Eddie Jordan, after several miscues unrelated to the Pou case, was forced to resign. A jury found the St. Bernard Nursing Home operators innocent. Foti made a run for reelection against two relative unknowns. He was eliminated in the primary, finishing a poor third.

Goaded by public outcry and intense lobbying efforts by physicians the 2008, the Louisiana legislature passed a series of laws designed to protect healthcare workers from certain civil liabilities when care is rendered during emergency situations. The legislature also created a mechanism to provide expert opinions to police and district attorneys before any criminal charges could be brought against healthcare workers serving in a disaster. The events at Memorial would generate several civil lawsuits and also many discussions about the ethical implications of managing mass disasters with limited resources and be rehashed for years in public forums and in books and magazine articles.

In the aftermath of the storm, many faculty changes took place. Some chose to retire and some moved to other medical schools or entered private practice. In a few cases, Dr. Hollier had to make the heart-wrenching decision to terminate their employment because of financial exigency.

As soon as he was able, he began to rebuild the faculty. He brought in Dr. Leonard Bok, who had previously served on the faculty to be Chairman of Radiology. **J. Christian Winters ('88)** was named Chairman of Urology; Roberto Quintal, MD, Chief of Cardiology at Touro Infirmary, assumed that post at LSU. Dr. Frank Culicchia, a long-time faculty member at Tulane and Chief of Neurosurgery at West Jefferson Hospital, replaced the retiring Dr. David Kline.

In 2007 Christopher "Chip" Baker, Professor of Surgery at Harvard, was named the Isidore Cohn, Jr., MD, Professor of Surgery and Chairman, and John England, MD, Chairman of Neurology at the Deaconess Clinic in Billings, Montana, became Chairman of Neurology, replacing the retiring Austin Sumner.

Dr. Augusto Ochoa of the Department of Medicine was named Director of the Stanley Scott Cancer Center in early 2007. But an even bigger administration appointment would come out of that department a few months later.

Dr. Hollier, who had been functioning as both Chancellor of the Health Sciences Center and Dean of the School of Medicine for over 18 months, initiated a search for his replacement as Dean. After a national search the committee unanimously recommended Dr. Steve Nelson, Vice Chair of Medicine, Chief of Pulmonary Disease and Director of the Alcohol and Drug Abuse Research Center, as Dean.

Dr. Nelson, a faculty member since 1984 and the John H. Seabury Professor of Medicine, was also Director of the General Clinical Research Center, a joint LSU-Tulane project, and a consultant to Ochsner for 13 years.

Immediately confirmed by the LSU Board of Supervisors, Dr. Nelson began a multifaceted program to improve the School. He immediately began to push the recruitment of faculty in many departments, especially Surgery and Neurology.

He convened a cross-section of students, faculty, residents and staff and asked for their advice in planning for the future of the school. They responded with gusto and with detailed suggestions.

The Alumni Association stepped up to the plate, dusted off the plans it had formulated pre-Katrina, and underwrote the construction of a Center for Advanced Practice on the fifth floor of 2020 Gravier Street. Designed to train residents and physicians in practice, it would complement the Isidore Cohn, Jr., MD, Student Learning Center, which FEMA had agreed to reconstruct on the sixth floor.

The Center for Advanced Practice would be formally donated to the LSU System in 2008 and the Board of Supervisors approved that it be named in honor of **Russell Klein, MD ('59)**, the retiring Associate Dean for Alumni Affairs who had served in that position for 24 years.

Under Dr. Nelson's guidance, Dr. Jay Kolls, a former faculty member, was recruited from the University of Pittsburg to Chair the Department of Genetics; Dr. Patricia Molina was named Chairman of the Department of Physiology; Dr. Jean Jacob was named Director of Research Development, and search committees began to look for Departmental Chairs for Pathology and Ophthalmology. **Dr. Cathi Fontenot ('84),** who had served for years to University Hospital as Medical Director, took the reins of Alumni Affairs from **Dr. Russell Klein ('59).**

As 2008 drew to a close, three and a half years after Katrina and two years after the Diamond Jubilee year ended, there were many unanswered questions. The funding of the new LSU Hospital had yet to be finalized, but newly elected Louisiana Governor Bobby Jindal had pledged his support and the future of the School of Medicine looked bright indeed.

As 2009 dawned things took an ugly turn. The plan put forward by LSU to govern the new hospital came under increasing criticism, especially from Tulane. Tulane proposed a governance system composed of LSU, Dillard, Xavier, and Tulane, with all decisions requiring unanimous approval. In other words, Tulane would have effective veto power over the hospital operation while staffing two competing institutions and having no financial responsibility for the new hospital or its success.

The LSU plan envisioned some involvement by other educational entities but the financial responsibility would be vested in a board controlled by LSU, which would be empowered to sell revenue bonds to help fund construction of the facility. No entity such as Xavier, Tulane, or Dillard would be on the hook financially for the success of the venture, but that didn't stop them from demanding a large decision-making role in its operation.

The President of Xavier was offered up as a mediator in the dispute, but the effort went nowhere, especially since Xavier wanted a say in the running of the operation. Preservationists demanded again and again that the old Charity facility be reopened as a hospital. They proved to their own satisfaction that it could be done better, faster, and cheaper than the LSU plan and touted it at every opportunity.

Outside consultants hired by the state, not by LSU, said their plan was flawed, the State Office of Facility Planning and Control said it wouldn't work, and Director of the Louisiana Recovery Authority said he would absolutely not support the idea. Other critics pointed out that the Preservationists hadn't factored equipment, parking, outpatient clinics and sufficient operating rooms into their grand plan or budget.

It seemed that when all was said and done remodeling the old hospital to meet current needs or building a new one was going to cost about the same. This made little difference to the Preservationists, who were more interested in old buildings than healthcare or regional economics. They refused to consider any adaptive use of the building.

Things then became even more surreal. The Speaker of the Louisiana House of Representatives, Jim Tucker of Algiers, authored a bill to place the governance of the hospital in the hands of a citizens' board, some members to be named by the Governor and some separately by the legislature, which conjured up visions of political governance at its worst. It unanimously passed the House of Representatives, but bogged down in the Senate.

LSU, which from the System level on down had been mostly quiet, tried to rally some public support and offered a Memorandum of Understanding on hospital governance to the Department of Hospitals and the Governor and held several meetings with Tulane brokered by the Secretary of Hospitals, Alan Levine. LSU Vice President, **Dr. Fred Cerise ('88)**, got into a very public fight with State Treasurer John Kennedy over the hospital business plan and the Governor asked for more information without publicly addressing what concerns he might have.

LSU President Dr. John Lombardi tried to explain the situation and publicly defend LSU's position, but LSU was criticized for arrogance and secrecy, and it was time to pile on the big bad Bayou Bengals. A clear LSU game plan was slow to emerge. Faculty and alumni and community leaders tried their best to help. Rumors, although groundless, that the School of Medicine planned to move to Baton Rouge did not improve the situation.

Two other innocent-sounding bills were also introduced into the Legislature. One, authored by a North Louisiana Republican, would delay expropriation of land needed for the hospital until all funding to build was in hand. It was sailing along until the preservationist began to tout it as an eminently sensible plan. That was its kiss of death and it died in committee.

Another sought to enlarge the size of an entity known as the Louisiana Workforce Commission and also enlarge its powers. The commission as originally constituted, years ago, was made up of representatives from Tulane, Ochsner, LSU (N.O.), and LSU (Shreveport). It kept tabs on and reported publicly on residency positions available in the state and other information related to Graduate Medical Education. It was not a policy-making body.

Under the proposed law, its size would be drastically increased with the addition of several nonphysicians, and it would suddenly gain the power to move residency slots from institution to institution. Few wondered who would benefit under that arrangement. It died too.

Marathon meetings were held and a document was prepared for the approval of the Board of Supervisors of LSU and the Board of Administrators of Tulane regarding hospital governance. Scott Cowen, President of Tulane, then asked Tucker to pull his bill, which he did.

Finally, the Memorandum of Understanding was discussed by the Tulane Board of Administrators and the LSU Board of Supervisors. Tulane approved it as presented but the Supervisors made several significant amendments. Many criticized their unwillingness to sign the original agreement but no one successfully criticized their amendments, which were designed to give LSU more control over the hospital governance.

Abruptly Angèle Davis, Commissioner of Administration for Governor Jindal, announced that the state was suspending acquisition of land for the hospital pending resolution of the governance issue. Many believed that this was designed to force LSU to make concessions.

At the same time, the Federal Government indicated a strong willingness or at least an intention to resolve favorably the longstanding dispute over how much the state was owed by FEMA for storm damage to Charity Hospital through either arbitration or civil suit.

This spurred intense behind-the-scenes negotiations to move forward on the new hospital and a plan emerged that gave LSU an acceptable level of control over the hospital while allowing input into its governance from the community and other entities, including Tulane and Xavier University.

In August 2009, the Governor, DHH Secretary Levine, Tulane President Cowan, and many dignitaries gathered on the LSU Health Sciences Center Campus to join LSU President, Dr. John Lombardi, in signing the Memorandum of Understanding that would govern operation of the new facility.

Although many financial and logistic details remained to be worked out, the construction of a new hospital looked more and more certain, and as 2009 began drawing to a close the future of the School of Medicine looked bright indeed.

In accordance with federal law, the State of Louisiana and FEMA entered into binding arbitration to determine whether Charity Hospital was over 50% damaged by Katrina and if so, how much was owed to the State.

In early January 2010, a three-judge panel ruled in favor of the State of Louisiana and ordered FEMA to pay over $474 million dollars to replace the hospital. According to an announcement from the Office of Governor Bobby Jindal, groundbreaking would occur in August 2010.

ഇരു

FACULTY

VIGNETTES

*Groundbreaking for the original Student Learning Center, 2001 – Prepared to swing the symbolic sledgehammer are, left to right: Isidore Cohn, Jr., MD; **Chapman Lee** ('69), President of the James D. Rives Surgical Society; **Ken Adatto** ('68), Former President of the Medical Alumni Association; and Dean Rob Marier*

Fred Allison, Jr., MD

When Fred Allison came to LSU from the University of Mississippi in 1968 to become Head of the Department of Medicine and eventually the first Edgar Hull Professor of Medicine, it was really his second tour of duty in New Orleans.

A 1946 graduate of Vanderbilt, he trained in internal medicine there as well as in Boston at Peter Bent Brigham Hospital and in Saint Louis at Barnes Hospital. Having known, as a student, the then-Head of the Department of Microbiology at LSU, the legendary G. John Buddingh, he accepted a position in that department in 1950. In 1951, at the urging of Dr. Harry Dascomb, he transferred to the Department of Medicine but left LSU in 1952 for additional training in infectious diseases at Washington University in St. Louis. In 1955 he joined the faculty of the Department of Medicine as Chief of Infectious Diseases at the University of Mississippi's new four-year School of Medicine in Jackson.

He remained there, rising through the ranks to full professor and attained national status for studies of the cellular response to inflammation, before accepting the Headship at LSU. He secured funding from then Dean John Finnerty to expand the Department of Medicine faculty and began immediately to improve both student and resident education.

One of his first moves was to institute "Morning Report," a valuable clinical teaching exercise for residents in training. He also revived the Department of Medicine's weekly Death Conference at Charity Hospital, another valuable experience in quality control of health care.

Fred improved the format of Grand Rounds with the help of Dr. George Davis, PhD, Coordinator of Learning Resources, by telecasting the conferences to distant sites.

He added many new faculty members to the departmental roster. To mention a few, there were Fred Hunter in Gastroenterology, Luke Glancy and Pramilla Subramanian in Cardiology, Charles V. Sanders, David Martin, George Karam and Rob Marier in Infectious Diseases. Others were Joe Biundo and Eve Scopolitis in Rheumatology; Howard Buechner, Warren Summer and Steve Nelson in Pulmonary Medicine and Critical Care; Alfredo Lopez in Nutrition and Metabolism; Efrain Reisen in Nephrology and Hypertension; Stephen Leach and Prem Kumar in Allergy; Jack Wilber, Frank Svec and Charles Hilton in Endocrinology, and Henry Rothschild in Genetics.

In order to improve student education as well as clinical conferences in general, he inaugurated a "Teaching Teachers to Teach" program using an education specialist, Janine Edwards, PhD, to coordinate the program. Faculty with special skills in this respect, namely Jorge Martinez, Frank Svec and Frank Gonzalez, served as role models.

As an outgrowth of this effort Dr. Rob Marier and Dr. Edwards would author a book, *Clinical Teaching for Medical Residents*, based on the LSU experience. The methods they outlined would be widely adopted by training programs across the country.

During his tenure as the first Edgar Hull Professor of Medicine, off-campus training sites were established in New Orleans for both students and residents at Southern Baptist Hospital, the New Orleans Veterans Hospital, Hotel Dieu Hospital, and the Touro Infirmary. Likewise, programs at the Earl K. Long Hospital in Baton Rouge and the University Hospital in Lafayette were transformed into major training sites for students and residents. While at LSU, fifteen separate sections were established within the Department of Medicine with strong programs in clinical and basic research generously funded by the National Institutes of Health as well as other sources.

Many of his protégés, among them Ben deBoisblanc and Cathi Fontenot, would rise to prominence in the School of Medicine.

Allison retired from LSU in 1987 as Professor of Medicine Emeritus to assume the Chief of Medicine position at the Metropolitan Nashville General Hospital as a full-time member of the Department of Medicine at Vanderbilt University School of Medicine. In this capacity, he also interdigitated closely with the Meharry College of Medicine training programs in Nashville. From 1993 to 1996 he served as interim Director of the Division of General Internal Medicine for Vanderbilt's Department of Medicine. He retired from Vanderbilt as Professor Emeritus in 1999. In 1999 he was appointed to the Board of Trustees of the Metropolitan Nashville and Davidson County Hospital Authority and currently serves as that group's Vice Chairman. Retirement years have been devoted to the writing of personal memoirs, gardening, fishing, and tennis.

෪෬

Richard F. Ashman, PhD

Born in 1890 in Philipsburg, Pennsylvania, and a graduate of Tulane University, Dr. Richard F. Ashman was hired in 1931 as a faculty member in the Department of Physiology by Dr. Clyde Brooks, who was serving as Chair of both Pharmacology and Physiology. Dr. Ashman, described by a colleague as a tall, thin, quiet man who subsisted on mints and cigars, soon established himself as an authority in electrocardiography. Renowned for his academic and clinical work, Dr. Ashman was named head of the Physiology Department in 1932, when Pharmacology and Physiology were split apart and he was also named Director of the Heart Station at Charity Hospital, a remarkable feat for a nonphysician.

In 1937, Dr. Ashman published *Essentials of Electrocardiography* with Dr. Edgar Hull. This important textbook, a hallmark in the development of clinical electrocardiography, was widely respected, drawing praise from Dr. Paul Dudley White, the leading American cardiologist of the day. The text was even translated into Spanish for use in Latin America.

Richard Ashman lecturing on cardiology

Drawing from his clinical experience as head of Charity Hospital's Heart Station, Dr. Ashman developed a technique for detecting aberrant heartbeats in atrial fibrillation. This pattern came to be known as the Ashman Phenomenon and is still recognized by cardiologists.

As head of Physiology, Dr. Ashman recruited several faculty members. Among them were A. Guy Eaton, PhD, from the University of Rochester and J. Roy Doty, PhD, a pupil of Andrew C. Ivy, PhD, who at the time America's best known physiologist. At the end of the Second World War he added Dr. Louis Toth and Dr. Leon Churney.

After 19 years as Head of Physiology, Dr. Ashman retired from LSU and became an energetic promoter of the arts. He published *The New Orleans Poetry Journal* during the 1950s, a small poetry magazine that printed works from aspiring poets from around the country, including Phillip Levine, a future Pulitzer Prize winner. Dr. Ashman was also an avid follower of the national political and economic issues, questions that were the subjects of raucous debates between Dr. Ashman and his longtime friend, Edgar Hull. Of course, he remained close to the School of Medicine, especially through his son, Hubert C. Ashman, who graduated from LSU in 1943.

He was succeeded as Director of the Heart Station by Dr. Louis Levy II, an outstanding clinical cardiologist who also graduated in 1943 and became equally well known as an electrocardiographer.

Dr. Ashman died in 1970, but not before securing his legacy as an important contributor to our understanding of the heart and one of the most important professors in the history of the School of Medicine. A Professorship in Physiology was funded by the Alumni Association in his name in 1993. Dr. Levy would be similarly honored with the endowment of a Professorship of Cardiology in his name.

₧ʣ

Drs. Nicolas G. and Haydee E. P. Bazan

South America delivered a one-two punch to LSU in 1981 the day that Nic and Haydee landed on its doorstep. Because they were internationally known research scientists they were being recruited by Dr. Herb Kaufmann, Chairman of Ophthalmology and Head of the Eye Center, to direct the center's research enterprise.

At that time Nic was Chairman of the Biochemistry Institute at the National University in Bahia Blanca, Argentina. Nic, who boasted both an MD and a PhD, had gained international recognition for his studies in neuroprotection and neurodegeneration and Haydee had become famous for her work on wound healing and inflammation of the eye.

Deeply religious, and well known, they were recognized human rights advocates. Argentina's military junta became increasingly upset with them. Nic attended a scientific conference in Virginia in 1981 and when he returned to Argentina was informed that his job had been abolished.

The outcry from the international scientific community was intense and there was wide coverage in the Argentina press. Despite this, Nic was told that his job was gone forever. Nic fought a heroic battle not only trying to regain his job and stay in his country, but also because he opposed the dictatorial regime. He was supported by his peers and by the Argentine press. There were hundreds of editorials and newspapers articles supporting his plight. This did not sit well with military junta. Moreover he was being followed and was receiving threatening phone calls.

Fearing that his telephone was tapped, he called a powerful friend in Houston from a pay phone. That friend contacted the "Argentine Desk" at the U. S. State Department. Nic and his family were told to flee to Buenos Aires, leaving all their belongings behind.

In Buenos Aires, staff from the U. S. Embassy picked them up, escorted them onto a plane for the USA. The escape probably saved their lives. In those days many who opposed the junta simply disappeared.

They immediately began work at the LSU Eye Center. But Nic had a dream which he patiently nurtured, the formation of a Neuroscience Center of Excellence, which came into being in 1987.

Led by Nic, whose work has included studies of stroke and cerebral ischemia, epilepsy and Alzheimer's disease, the members of the Center have received over $100 million in grants. Nic has authored over 350 papers and book chapters.

He is the Editor-in-Chief and Founder of the *Journal of Molecular Neurobiology* and Past President of the American Society of Neurochemistry. He has delivered the William Harvey Lecture in London; received the Jacob Javits Award from the National Institute of Neurological Diseases and Stroke of the NIH, and is a member of numerous academies including the Royal Academy of Medicine and the Royal Academy of Sciences of Spain. He has received the Proctor Medal, the highest honor of the Association for Research in Vision and Ophthalmology, was named Boyd Professor by LSU, its highest academic honor, and was honored belatedly by the President of Argentina, after the ouster of the junta.

Haydee has also received numerous honors and currently serves as Professor of Ophthalmology, Biochemistry and Molecular Biology and Neuroscience at the School of Medicine.

A special issue of Neurochemical Research was dedicated to him and the Nicolas Bazan Professorship of Emergency Medicine was dedicated during the 75th Anniversary rededication of the School of Medicine.

The Bazan Chair in Prostate Cancer Research (Nic is a survivor) is also under development.

The Neuroscience Center of Excellence sponsors an interdisciplinary graduate program that awards Master of Science and PhD degrees. Discoveries at the Center have resulted in twenty patent applications. Each year it stages an annual retreat to plan for the future. That future is bright indeed.

ഇ‍ൽ

Gerald Berenson, MD, FACC

A 1945 graduate of Tulane University School of Medicine, Gerald Berenson joined the Medicine Department in 1954, after a residency at Tulane and a fellowship in pediatric cardiology at the University of Chicago.

Before coming to LSU, Dr. Berenson had studied the impact of climate on heart disease. In 1955, and now at LSU, he was awarded his first grant to study heart disease in adults and worked in this area for many years. His research convinced him of two things. First, that cardiovascular disease treatment at Charity Hospital could be improved greatly by establishing a modern Coronary Care Unit, which after much effort was accomplished.

His second—and more important—idea was that most adult heart disease had its origins in childhood. To prove this hypothesis, Berenson proposed to study children hospitalized for other illnesses. Since he was not a pediatrician, granting agencies turned him down. These rejections were a blessing in disguise because studying hospitalized children would likely not yield long-term data. One grant consultant suggested that Dr. Berenson develop a long-term community-based study instead.

Dr. Berenson had historic ties to Bogalusa, Louisiana, a small community with a stable population. And so in 1972 the incredibly productive Bogalusa Heart Study began. In the coming decades, the study produced reams of data on the evolution of heart disease. It would continue as an LSU program until 1991, when Dr. Berenson answered the siren call of his alma mater and moved to Tulane.

Even after moving across the street, he continued cordial relations with LSU and remains one of the most important clinical research scientists in the history of the School of Medicine. In 2007, in recognition of his long and illustrious career, the Medical Alumni Association named him an Honorary Alumnus.

&)(%

John Barry Bobear, MD

A native of Baltimore, Maryland, and a 1950 graduate of Albany Medical College, John Bobear journeyed to New Orleans for his training in Internal Medicine and Pulmonary Disease at LSU. His training was interrupted by a two-year stint at Brooke Army Medical Field Service School, where he learned outpatient psychiatry, which he subsequently practiced at Fitzsimmons Army Hospital.

In 1956 he joined the LSU faculty, rose to the rank of Professor, a position he held until retiring in 1990. During the years 1962-1978 he served as pulmonary consultant at Southern Baptist Hospital before relinquishing that duty to his protégé Dr. **Ewing W. Cook ('69)**.

From 1977-1985 Dr. Bobear served as either Associate Medical Director or Medical Director of Charity Hospital, initially replacing his close friend Dr. Harry Dascomb when the latter became ill. John was President of the Charity staff at that time.

A member of Alpha Omega Alpha, Dr. Bobear received the "Breath of Life Award" from the American Lung Association in recognition of his accomplishments. For many years he served as Editor of the Orleans Parish Medical Society Bulletin and often produced editorials on the social, economic or humanistic aspects of medical care that were widely quoted in the lay or medical press.

In 1990, he was recruited to become Director of Investigations for the Louisiana State Board of Medical Examiners, investigating complaints against physicians who were accused of violating the Medical Practice act. He did this with such fairness and such excellent results that he was ultimately named Executive Director of the LSBME, a position he held for many years.

He lives in well-deserved retirement in New Orleans with his wife Valerie.

৪০০৪

Fred Brazda, PhD

In a 1944 profile of Dr. Fred Brazda published in *The Tiger*, the newspaper of the LSU School of Medicine, he was described as "a gentleman and a teacher." Truer words are rarely spoken.

Fred George Brazda is another example of medical talent from around the country that came to the LSU School of Medicine in the early years. Brazda received his PhD from Northwestern University in 1937 and taught at Creighton University before joining the Department of Biochemistry in 1938 as an instructor.

He had a lifelong love of chemistry inspired, he said, by the influence of his chemistry teacher when he was a sophomore in high school. Eventually, his biochemical research

Fred Brazda, PhD

spanned a wide range of interests. He was especially renowned for his work on vitamins and in intermediary metabolism. As he once put it, he "had a life-long love affair with the liver."

Appointed to the Chair of Biochemistry in 1946 and to a full professorship in 1949, when he was just 40 years old, Dr. Brazda took charge of an extremely heavy teaching load. During World War II, he routinely handled a teaching load meant for a contingent of instructors, but many thought he single-handedly improved the quality of teaching in the basic sciences during that time. He was also instrumental in elevating the Department's research enterprise, recruiting such notables as Richard Reeves, PhD, who would determine the three-dimensional structure of the glucose molecule and also become an expert on the metabolism of the amoeba. Until his retirement in 1977, Dr. Brazda was beloved by generations of LSU students. As other schools were added to the Medical Center, Brazda acquired responsibility for their education also. He taught the vast majority of the medical center's students in biochemistry between 1939 and 1977.

Dr. Brazda extended his personal influence abroad when he spearheaded the Biochemistry Department's efforts at the University of Costa Rica's Medical School, the first School of Medicine in that country. He was known as the finest lecturer at the LSU School of Medicine and certainly that talent translated well in his time abroad, no matter the language barriers that stood in between.

A leader of the School in every sense of the word, he provided unsurpassed medical education and helped guide medical students throughout their years in medical school. He strongly supported the efforts of Dr. Roland Coulson to establish a Graduate School and when it produced its first graduate in Biochemistry, Dr. Herbert Dessaur, Brazda brought him onto the faculty. He also served local and national societies with distinction, acting as an advisor with the Lucile Reid Cancer Institute in Bakersfield, California. Additionally, he trained dozens of technicians for laboratories around the city and provided help and guidance for lab directors at the Charity and Veterans Affairs Hospitals in New Orleans. In recognition of his immense popularity and skill, Brazda also served as Acting Head of LSU's Department of Pharmacology from 1950 to 1952 and was also tapped to stand in for Dr. William Frey as Acting Dean on several occasions when the latter was serving in medical communities abroad in the 1960s. His son, Frederick W. Brazda, graduated from the School of Medicine in 1970.

In 1990 the Medical Alumni Association funded the first basic science professorship in the history of the school. The honoree was Fred Brazda. In accepting the honor Fred said that he wished to thank LSU by paraphrasing Julius Caesar "I came, I saw, I loved." LSU loved him back. He died in 1994 at the age of 85.

ഇൗരു

G. John Buddingh, MD

As a faculty member he made a long trip to get to the School of Medicine, but once he arrived, his impact on the School was crucial and lasting. G. John Buddingh was born in the Netherlands and received his MD degree from Vanderbilt University in 1929. An infectious disease consultant for the armed services during World War II, Dr. Buddingh became head of the LSU Department of Microbiology in 1948 and served in that position until his retirement in 1974.

Buddingh's research work was important and voluminous. He was an authority on polio, smallpox, and herpes virus infection. Dr. Buddingh's work also examined various dermatropic viruses, meningitis, influenza, and pneumonia. His research made Dr. Buddingh an internationally known microbiologist. His presence at LSU was a principal reason why Dr. Fred Allison took the position of Chairman of the Department of Medicine in 1968. Allison, who would hold that position until his retirement in 1987, had trained in infectious disease under Buddingh at Vanderbilt in 1946 and 1947.

The laboratory was not the only place in which John Buddingh displayed his great talents. He was also a beloved teacher within the School of Medicine. His dedication was impressive. He traveled to England, France, Germany, and Japan for educational and research visits and conferences throughout his career, proudly and capably bearing the name and reputation of his home school.

Every morning, Dr. Buddingh could be found at the Contagion Building at Charity Hospital, examining bacterial cultures and providing advice to the residents and interns. Additionally, Dr. Buddingh played a critical role in the development of the LSU-International Center for Medical Research and Training (ICMRT) in Costa Rica during the early 1960s. This program, now considered to be an international medical mission in partnership with the Costa Rican Ministry of Health, was one of five centers established by American medical schools from around the country. LSU's program is the only center still open today and has provided millions of dollars for infectious disease research and therapy, including screening and treatment programs for AIDS, hepatitis, diarrheal diseases, and other bacterial and parasitic conditions. This program has been one of the School's Medicine most important international outreach projects.

A Professorship of Micro-biology was established in Dr. Buddingh's name by the Medical Alumni Association in 2006 to honor the accomplishments of G. John Buddingh, the researcher and the man. Part of the citation read, "He went out of his way for students and was loved by all of them." As always, the ability of a faculty member to be a good teacher is paramount to all of his other accomplishments. In the case of Dr. Buddingh, students were attracted to his warm personality and strong talent. He invited small groups of students to his home every Sunday afternoon for coffee and camaraderie. Dr. Buddingh was a man with diverse interests, including music and art, which rounded out his personality and allowed him to be down-to-earth and approachable.

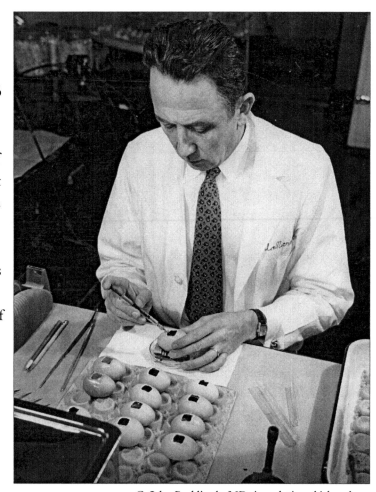

G. John Buddingh, MD, inoculating chick embryos

He commanded the respect of students and colleagues alike through his excellence in research, his profound skill for teaching, and his exceptional disposition. For all of these reasons, he is warmly remembered as an important asset to the LSU School of Medicine. He died in 1979 of emphysema. He was 72 years old.

ଋଷଓ

Irvin Cahen, MD

Many considered Irvin Cahen a genius. He certainly was a trailblazer if nothing else and a premier orthopaedist. Born in New Orleans in 1915, he graduated from high school at 13 and earned his medical degree from Tulane in 1937, when he was just 21. After training in Orthopaedics, he entered the Army and served with the 64th General Hospital in Europe. In this he was able to study and master the techniques that German orthopaedists had developed to treat fractures in battlefield conditions. They had also applied these techniques to American airmen shot down over Germany. Initially, American Army doctors who examined freed prisoners of war believed that the nails, pins, rods, and screws used by the Germans were torture devices. Dr. Cahen realized that this was not the case.

He mastered some of the German technology before returning to New Orleans. Preparing to open his private practice, he was contacted by a local veterinarian. A valuable racehorse had broken his leg. Instead of destroying the animal, the vet wanted to try a surgical repair using internal fixation. He asked Dr. Cahen to lend the expertise he had gleaned in Europe. Dr. Cahen agreed, the operation was a success, and the horse lived out his life at stud. The vet ultimately handed Dr. Cahen a check for $10,000, an unheard of sum in the late 1940s, for his part in the successful operation.

The vet explained that it was customary to charge 10% of the value of such an animal, if the lifesaving surgery was a success. The animal was valued at $200,000, and the vet gave Dr. Cahen half of the fee. He used it to open his office. So, you could say he owed his initial success to his single foray into veterinary medicine.

In 1947, he joined the faculty of the newly reorganized Department of Orthopaedic Surgery at LSU under its chair, Dr. Henry Simon. In 1959, Dr. Cahen was named Chair to replace Dr. Simon. He remained in that position until 1976, when he was succeeded by Dr. Robert D'Ambrosia. So beloved in the community was Dr. Cahen that, when the Alumni planned to dedicate a chair worth $1,000,000 to the School in his name, even Tulane-trained orthopaedists contributed.

He retired to Sun Valley, Idaho, where he played golf in the daytime and relaxed at night with a Dewar's Scotch on the rocks.

He died in 1993 at the age of 78.

છાજ

Isidore Cohn, Jr., MD

Isidore Cohn, Jr., MD

Dr. Isidore Cohn, Jr., led the Department of Surgery for twenty-seven years. He carried on the grand tradition of his predecessors Urban Maes and James Rives as an effective and impeccable chairman of one of the most visible departments in the School of Medicine.

When he assumed the Chairmanship he quickly began to improve it, both in the clinical and research arena. He had gone outside the state for his medical education, earning an MD and PhD from the University of Pennsylvania and serving his residency there. He was planning to join his famous father, Dr. Cohn, Sr., in practice when he was recruited by Dr. Rives to join the surgical department in 1952 and was appointed to head it just ten years later. His duties included not only administration but also research, teaching, and patient rounds at Charity, as well as numerous and varied leadership positions around the city and country. Student teaching, already strong under Dr. Rives, soared to new heights under Dr. Cohn. On twelve occasions his department was voted best clinical department by students.

Dr. Cohn inherited a department staffed principally by part-time clinical faculty. To be sure, many of these were giants in the region. They included the legendary Dr. "Septic Sam" Romano; William Leon; Walter Becker; Charles Miangolara, a hero of the Second World War; Larry Strug, a splendid lung surgeon; Howard Mahorner, who would go on to become President of the American College of Surgeons; and the well-loved **Claude Craighead ('40)**.

But they were part-time and clinicians who specialized for the most part in general and thoracic surgery. Dr. Cohn wanted two things, a more diverse program and a surgical research program. To do that he needed full-time faculty and he needed the help of basic science faculty, especially in the areas of physiology, biochemistry and microbiology. He would establish strong relationships with all of these departments. Over a thousand articles would come out of the Department during his tenure.

As a gastrointestinal surgeon, Dr. Cohn focused on intestinal obstruction and ways to reduce morbidity and mortality from this complication. His research focused on the use of antibiotics to reduce the possibility of sepsis or peritonitis. To this end, Dr. Cohn worked tirelessly to improve research conditions at the School of Medicine, helping to establish germfree research facilities at the school in order to study the effects of bacterial agents in animal—and potentially human—subjects. Dr. Cohn was a recognized leader in cancer of the gastrointestinal tract, particularly pancreatic and colon cancer, and also researched better ways of diagnosing cancer, including the use of nuclear magnetic resonance, an exciting new tool in the 1970s. He served as President of the Society for Surgery of the Alimentary Tract in 1976 to 1977.

Dr. Cohn has also served as director, chairman, or member of the board of directors of the New Orleans Surgical Society, the American College of Surgeons, the American Board of Surgery, and the Southern Surgical Association, among many others. He has served as a member of the Surgical Research Review Committee for Veterans Affairs, as well as holding a position on the National Taskforce on Colon and Rectal Cancer in the American Cancer Society. He was also named a visiting professor at the Medical University of South Carolina and an honorary member of the Colombian Society of General Surgeons and served on the editorial boards of several journals, including *The American Surgeon, The Review of Surgery, and The American Journal of Surgery*.

He was also a pioneer in cultivating professional relationships with minority physicians and medical professionals. He recruited one of the first black laboratory technicians in the School of Medicine and, later, Dr. Cohn invited black surgeons at New Orleans' Flint Goodrich Hospital to the Surgery Department's regular Saturday conferences. Thus, he provided a courageous and beneficial example to the School of Medicine in accepting minority physicians as equal partners in medicine and education.

Even before he retired as head of the Department of Surgery in 1989, the affection felt for Dr. Cohn was abundantly evident. In 1987 the Isidore Cohn Jr., MD, Chair of Surgery, the first million-dollar chair in school history, was dedicated. But recognition for him was far from finished. When the Alumni Association began a fund-raising campaign for a "Student Learning Center," the James D. Rives Surgical Society became the largest single donor. The Learning Center naming rights went to that donor, and they unhesitatingly chose to name it the Isidore Cohn, Jr., MD, Student Learning Center. The Center opened in 2001, and stood as a tribute to Dr. Cohn's more than fifty years of affiliation with LSU until, heavily damaged by Katrina, it was temporarily closed.

Beginning in early 2008, the Isidore Cohn, Jr., MD, Student Learning Center would be rebuilt higher and better. A rededication took place in 2009, coinciding with the start of the academic year.

ᏽᏅᏥ

Roland Coulson, PhD

It is doubtful if many faculty members in the history of LSU School of Medicine will surpass Roland Coulson, PhD, Professor of Biochemistry, for length of active service. Sixty years (1944 – 2004) is a long time. It was a career at least initially based more on accident than design.

A native of Rolla, Kansas, Coulson had received a Master's Degree in Biochemistry from LSU (BR) and then went to the University of London to pursue his PhD. This occurred in the late 1930s. War clouds were gathering and registration for the military draft was taking place. Coulson registered in Baton Rouge before departing for England.

As he completed the requirements for his PhD, war in Europe broke out and Coulson abruptly found himself in the Royal Air Force (RAF), not as a combatant but as a research scientist. Posted to Canada in November 1944, he applied for leave to visit his family in Kansas. He traveled by train and as soon as he crossed the border at Detroit, he was detained by FBI agents, who boarded the train and ordered him not to leave the country and to report immediately to Draft Board #2 in Baton Rouge.

He did as directed, immediately creating a quandary in Baton Rouge. He stood before the Board in British uniform, his only clothes, and with a history of service in England, Egypt and Canada to a foreign but allied power. That made it hard to charge him with any crime such as draft dodging.

He was told not to return to Canada and to await further word. Further word never came and apparently the British never again showed a speck of interest in him either, so Coulson took a bus to New Orleans looking for, as he put it, a strong drink and good food. Having that drink in a bar, he met an old friend from his days on the Baton Rouge campus who was now a second-year medical student at LSU.

The student, Pete Temple, offered to introduce him to the Dean because faculty were in short supply and Temple assured him he could have a job immediately. Introductions took place, the next day a position in Biochemistry was offered and Coulson accepted. LSU did this on faith that he was what he said he was because Coulson would not actually pick up his PhD in London until 1958. Such was faculty recruitment during WWII.

It became immediately obvious to Coulson why the Dean, Beryl Burns, was so interested in hiring him. There were only two faculty in the Department, the splendid Fred

Brazda, and charter faculty member and Department Chair, Howard Beard, clearly now incompetent probably from dementia and soon to retire. Actually this was not the worst faculty situation. Pharmacology had only Chapman Reynolds, a 1935 graduate on its faculty, and he suffered from cancer. Reynolds would pass away in 1950.

Coulson immediately began teaching and doing research, and became a favorite of the students and a leader of the faculty.

Coulson had a dream, early on, to develop a program capable of awarding master's and doctorate degrees in the basic sciences. He pushed this, often with little support, until 1947 when a fledging program began to take root in the basic science departments. His principal opposition to doing this came from Dr. **Robert Simmons ('36)**, Associate Dean and Registrar of the School, who believed that the School should award only the MD degree and leave Master's and PhD programs to the departments on the Baton Rouge campus. Simmons conveniently ignored the fact that the School of Medicine was part of the Baton Rouge campus and put in road blocks when he could. This did not deter Coulson, and a graduate program began to take shape. The situation would not be resolved completely until 1965 when New Orleans would be recognized for what it really was, a campus separate from Baton Rouge and with its own Chancellor.

In 1965 an administrative reorganization would be completed with Dean William Frye being promoted to the post of Chancellor and a separate Graduate School created under its first Dean, Roland Coulson. He would serve in that capacity until 1974, when to his relief, as he put it, he was allowed to return to teaching and research. He continued his work until 2004, when illness forced his retirement. He passed away soon after, the then-longest serving faculty member in school history, and one of the most beloved.

ℰↄ⚫ↄ

Claude Craighead, Jr. ('39)

The son of a prominent physician in North Louisiana, Claude Craighead was born in 1914 in Shreveport, La. His father initially discouraged his interest in a career in medicine, and in college he did not initially pursue a pre-med program. During his third year at Centenary College he switched from a liberal arts curriculum to pre-med and entered the School of Medicine in 1935.

Always at the top of his class, he graduated in 1939, served an internship and part of a residency in surgery before being called to active duty in the Army. Originally he was scheduled to join LSU's military unit, the 64th but he was called to duty before it was activated and although Dr. Maes tried to arrange transfer orders it was not to be. He served in Ireland and England, performing an amazing amount of surgery and orthopaedics until discharge, returning to finish his residency in 1949.

Although he considered taking a practice offer in Shreveport, he joined the staff of Brown-McHardy Clinic in New Orleans on the recommendation of Dr. Rives. McHardy, a nationally known figure in medical gastroenterology, was head of the section in the Department of Medicine and would serve as President of the American College of Gastroenterology. Dr. Craighead would become the Chief of Surgery at the clinic and become widely known for his skill as a thoracic and gastrointestinal surgeon, operating on many notable patients.

Claude joined the part-time clinical faculty in 1949 and the full-time faculty in 1984. He was a founding member and early President of the James D. Rives Surgical Society and was active in Medical Alumni Affairs, serving as President of the modern Association in 1987 - 1988.

The Claude C. Craighead Chair in Thoracic Surgery was established in 1994. Dr. Craighead passed away in 2005.

80CR

Joseph Rigney D'Aunoy, MD

Joseph Rigney D'Aunoy, MD

Described by a contemporary as a man with more enemies than Huey Long, Dr. D'Aunoy served as first Chairman of Pathology from 1931 to 1939 and as the second Dean of the School from 1937 to 1939. He also served as "Secretary of the Faculty," an ill-defined but apparently powerful position, and was the "chief planner," as a colleague described him, for the school in its infancy.

He was nationally known in his field, an important characteristic because it gave the school immediate legitimacy in the eyes of accrediting agencies. He was also a hard and demanding task master given to snap judgment. Many recounted that D'Aunoy would, on the first day of class, address the incoming freshmen with the advice to look at the man on your left and on your right because one of you three would be gone by Christmas.

He had a key role in the early days of the school, but his treatment of students and faculty was the stuff of legend and most were terrified of him. He was known to expel students for what many considered trivial reasons, such as attending class without a tie, and there was no appeal of his decisions. One expelled student challenged him to a fist fight but Dr. D'Aunoy declined.

Clearly D'Aunoy helped the school in many ways but two stories, both perhaps apocryphal, tell much about the man. A student was called to D'Aunoy's office. This usually meant expulsion and his friends gathered around the office to offer their support. The student emerged smiling. They asked if he was expelled but he said no. They couldn't believe it but the student explained that he told D'Aunoy that if he was expelled from medical school he planned to kill D'Aunoy.

In the second story D'Aunoy, after he stepped down as Dean, was taken gravely ill and was hospitalized at Hotel Dieu Hospital with bleeding from a renal tumor. A call went out to faculty for blood donations. It is said that no one responded.

ഔ

George Davis, PhD

Armed with a newly conferred degree from Yale University, George Davis migrated south to join the faculty of the Department of Physiology in 1951. He would remain on campus until 1985, a 34-year run that would affect more than just the Physiology Department.

As a neurophysiologist, Dr. Davis' research centered on the understanding the neural basis of locomotor hyperactivity and various problems of peripheral nerve function. An equally important effort for Dr. Davis was assisting in the improvement in the medical teaching programs, from a pedagogical viewpoint and a technological basis.

In 1966 there had been no significant change in the medical curriculum since the founding of the school! Chancellor Bill Frye asked newly installed Dean John C. Finerty to see what can be done to improve the situation. Dr. Finerty appointed Dr. Davis chairman of a group to make recommendations on the curriculum. The group helped the faculty understand the problems and possible solutions. They had great support from Drs. Frye and Finerty. After several weeks the group had a revised curriculum to propose and it was adopted by the faculty almost unanimously. The same approach produced a modernized grading system the next year.

The new curriculum included first-year Neuroscience, including anatomy, physiology and related clinical specialties. As director of this course, Dr. Davis enlisted faculty members from all neurological disciplines to form teaching teams. This was the start of integrative medical education. For many years all residents in Neurology and Neurosurgery spent one semester in intensive study of neurophysiology.

The Medical School had long enjoyed many ties with the Republic of Costa Rica. In the late 1950s, Costa Rica asked for help in starting a medical school. Some Costa Rican prospective faculty were brought to New Orleans for special training while the new building was erected on the campus in San Jose. Dr. Frye then designated Dr. Davis as "Chief of Party"; he moved to Costa Rica for two years (1961-63) and assisted both the new faculty and many short-term visitors from LSU.

Medical education also needed improvements in physical facilities and technical support. In the 1960s Dr. **Jack Strong ('51)** was charged with long-range planning for the LSU Medical Center. Dr. Strong asked Dr. Davis to chair the subcommittee on building requirements. The main accomplishment of this group was the design and completion of the Medical Education Building.

Among other applications of technology to medical education was the use of television. In 1953, following a couple of demonstrations of equipment, Dean Frye provided money for a TV camera and two TV sets. These were used to show various physiological demonstrations, sending pictures and narration from the laboratory to the first-year classroom.

In 1965, the Louisiana Department of Hospitals, with much help from Dr. **Ralph Sanchez ('50)**, head of LSU Continuing Education, established the Louisiana Hospital Television Network. LHTN assisted in providing LSUMS with upgraded cameras and other equipment, which were used to generate as many as a dozen hours of conferences per week to the network. The improved television capability was also used in many other ways, including student examinations, patient interviews, and basic and clinical research.

In 1968, the Division of Learning Resources was formed, combining sections of Medical Illustration, Photography, Television and Classroom Services. Dr. Davis was named the initial Coordinator. The division space, which had been unchanged since it was built in 1932, was completely redone. A program enabling continuous modernization of equipment and techniques was established under Dr. Davis.

Dr. Davis retired from the LSU Medical Center in 1985.

&)C&

Cathi Fontenot, MD ('84)

Cathi Fontenot, MD ('84)

Because she has left her mark in so many areas it is difficult to select a single one to highlight. A specialist in Internal Medicine and Geriatrics, she is a sought-after bedside clinician in both the public and private sectors. As Director of Wellness and Screening for the New Orleans Police Department she has coordinated the screening of over 1,000 officers and coordinates the administration of flu vaccine to all active New Orleans Police.

As Medical Director for ten years of the New Orleans Musicians Clinic, she has helped provide access to health care to some of our most important and most vulnerable citizens.

As Section Chief of Comprehensive Medicine from 1988 to 2003, a 15-year run, she guided that Section with grace and skill and in recognition she was named Medical Director of the Medical Center of Louisiana, a post she held for five more years. As Medical Director in August 2005, she was at the University Hospital Campus of the Medical Center of Louisiana during Katrina, directing disaster management, patient care, employee survival and ultimately (after five days without water or power) evacuation of the hospital. She played a major role in the rebuilding of healthcare in New Orleans post-Katrina, overseeing the recovery process first in tents and department stores, ultimately in community primary care clinics and the Interim LSU Hospital (University). That was followed by a six-month stint as Interim CEO of the Medical Center of Louisiana.

She was elected in 1995 to Alpha Omega Alpha National Honor Medical Society, received the Pfizer Award of Excellence in 1996, honored in 2000 by the Orleans Parish Medical Society as Distinguished Woman in Medicine, and featured in *Glamour Magazine* in December 2005 for her work during and after Hurricane Katrina.

A Past President of the Medical Alumni Association and long-time Board Member, she was recognized as Alumnus of the Year in 2007. And on January 1, 2009, she assumed the role of Associate Dean for Alumnus Affairs, all the while continuing to serve as a consultant to those charged with planning the new hospital.

෨෬

Charles Mayo Goss, MD

Dr. Charles Mayo Goss, the foremost American anatomist of his day, served as Chairman of the Department of Anatomy at LSU from 1947 until 1965. He replaced Donald Duncan, who had served as Acting Chairman after Beryl Burns, the second Chair of Anatomy and Dean, resigned in 1945. Goss served as editor on three occasions for *Gray's Anatomy* and on two occasions for *Bailey's Textbook of Histology*; Dr. Goss also served as managing editor of *The Anatomical Record*.

A 1924 graduate of Yale University School of Medicine, Dr. Goss taught at his alma mater before moving to Columbia, then to the University of Alabama, before coming to LSU.

He inherited a small department whose most notable member was George W. D. Hamlett. Called Delay (his third name) by friends, he was an accomplished lecturer and a brilliant embryologist, but he was a really odd duck. Sporting a huge walrus moustache, he boasted that he never brushed his teeth and regularly brought live grub worms to his lectures, which he would eat in front of the students. His

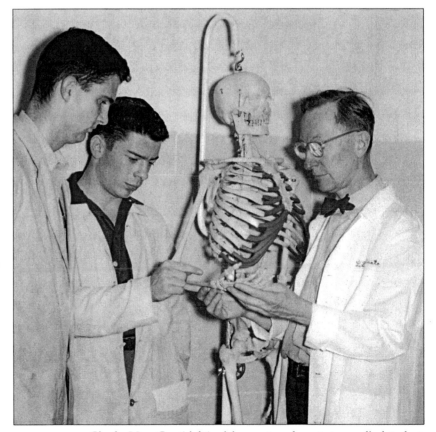

Charles Mayo Goss (right), giving anatomy lesson to two medical students

social life was said to be limited. Delay had another oddity. In his office he kept a large pet snake variously described as a python or a boa constrictor. He was in the habit of feeding it white mice in front of visitors and occasionally throwing it to people.

A new member of the faculty was warned about Delay's habit and paid him a "preemptive" visit to advise Dr. Hamlett that he didn't like snakes and that if he caught the snake, both the snake and Dr. Hamlett would be the worse for the encounter.

The other noteworthy faculty member was Dr. George Ronstrom, who came to LSU in 1933 from the University of Illinois. His major claim to fame was being married to Maude O'Bryan, a well-known reporter for the *New Orleans Times Picayune*.

Dr. Goss was an expert on cardiac embryology and developed techniques for growing cardiac muscle cells in tissue cultures. He persuaded Dr. Ruth Miller, a noted anatomist on the faculty of Johns Hopkins, to join his department, immediately strengthening the teaching of Gross Anatomy. He recruited the legendary Dr. Marilyn Zimny to join his department in 1955 and the equally well-known Frank N. Lowe in 1949. Dr. Lowe was internationally known for his work in electron microscopy. Dr. Zimny would eventually lead the department, becoming the first female department head in the history of the school.

Dr. Goss' immediate successor was Dr. Melvin Hess of the University of Pittsburg. Hess had been a graduate student in Texas under Jack Finnerty, PhD, Dean of the School of Medicine. He worked hard to build up the Department, recruiting Sam McClugage, John Ruby, Robert Dyer and Richard Peppler. Peppler would go on to become Vice-President at the University of Tennessee. The others would serve eventually as Associate Deans at the School of Medicine. Hess also helped recruit Bob D'Ambrosia from Pittsburg to become Orthopaedics Chair.

In 1975, Hess suffered a debilitating stroke and stepped down as Chair in favor of Dr. Marilyn Zimny. He died a few months later.

80CR

A. Sidney Harris, PhD

When Richard Ashman, PhD, Chairman of Physiology reached retirement age in 1951, a search was conducted for his successor, and Dr. A. Sidney Harris came over from Baylor University. Harris had earned his PhD from Washington University and spent many years working under the legendary C. J. Wiggers at Western Reserve University.

Harris inherited a tiny staff. Louis Toth, PhD, a man of remarkable compassion and a favorite of students had come to LSU in 1946 from the University of Rochester. Leon Churney had joined the faculty in 1947 from the University of Pennsylvania. Harris immediately added two more faculty members: Raymond Russell, PhD, newly minted from the University of Rochester, and the remarkable neurophysiologist, George Davis, PhD, from Yale.

Harris changed the department curriculum, making each faculty member responsible for his area of special expertise and adding a number of new laboratory exercises. He began the custom of extending joint appointments to faculty in clinical departments—particularly medicine, neurology and surgery—selecting those who had a particular interest in physiology. No other faculty additions were made until 1965 when Dr. Howard Randall, an outstanding renal physiologist, joined the faculty.

During Dr. Harris' tenure, the department was also given responsibility for teaching in the new additions to the Medical Center—the Dental School, School of Nursing, and Graduate School. Ultimately, responsibility for teaching in the School of Allied Health was added as well.

Harris proved to be a remarkable leader in two other areas. In 1954, he experienced increasing difficulty in recruiting qualified technicians to work in his department. He noted that New Orleans had a cadre of well-educated African-Americans. Because of prevailing social conditions, they were confined to mostly menial occupations. Although some faculty had reservations, he hired James Hawkins, a qualified and able black technician who was an immediate hit with faculty and students alike and served the school with skill and integrity for many years. Only those who lived through that era can appreciate the courage shown by Dr. Harris in hiring a black man for a responsible technical position.

Harris would take integration another giant step forward when he succeeded in having another black technician admitted to the graduate school. This was accomplished before the first minority student was admitted to the School of Medicine. Albert Bocage, who would receive his PhD in 1968, joined the faculty and serve until the end of his life in 1975. He was also the first black faculty member in the School of Medicine.

Beginning in 1955, Harris pioneered the use of the then-new medium of closed circuit television as a student teaching aid. In 1966 videotape was added both to preserve important presentations and to compress lengthy procedures through judicious editing. Dr. George Davis later became the guru of this technological enterprise, and it eventually evolved under his leadership into the full-fledged Division of Learning Resources.

In 1973, Dr. Harris retired leaving a strong department to his successor, Dr. John Spitzer of Hanemann Medical College. For twenty years, A. Sidney Harris shaped his department into a renowned group of researchers and educators who dedicated their lives to enhancing the quality of basic science education at the School of Medicine. Dr. Harris is one example—albeit a very crucial one—of the caliber of department leadership that has distinguished the history of the LSU School of Medicine. He was a man of vision, skill, integrity and remarkable courage.

He moved to Carmel, California, after retiring and passed away in 1995 at the age of 92.

෨෬

Thomas Hernandez, PhD, MD ('47)

The decidedly Cajun accent fooled a lot of people. It was not immediately obvious that you were dealing with a man who had received a PhD in Biochemistry from the University of Iowa in 1942 and an MD in 1947 from LSU, who had served two stints in the military, and who had been written up in *Newsweek* for his ground-breaking research.

Dr. Hernandez, who would Chair the Department of Pharmacology from 1960 to 1977, was not a classically trained pharmacologist but rather a biochemist who became more and more interested in pharmacology over time and eventually switched departments. He replaced Dr. Ernest Beuding, a product of the Pasteur Institute, who had become departmental head in 1955.

Dr. Hernandez always retained an abiding interest in the study of metabolism, and collaborated for 35 years with his good friend Dr. Roland Coulson studying the metabolism of compounds using a most unique research animal, the Louisiana alligator.

At one time he and Coulson had 110 alligators at the school and co-authored two books: *Biochemistry of the Alligator* and *Alligator Metabolism*. Their research included studies of insulin metabolism and neurotransmitters, among others. He often said that the alligator was a most misunderstood creature. How it was misunderstood was not clear to most observers.

Drs. Hernandez and Coulson received extensive national attention when they were highlighted in *Newsweek* in 1963. Dr. Hernandez also wrote a well received layman's guides to pharmacology: *Know Your Medicine*.

He was also a great storyteller, recounting his adventures with fellow Cajun, Dudley LeBlanc, an entrepreneurial patent medicine salesman of the 1950s and 60s who made millions selling the "tonic" Hadacol. He also told of the welcome he received when his military service took him to the federal

Thomas Hernandez, PhD, MD ('47)

penitentiary in Atlanta, where the prison librarian greeted him warmly. They recognized each other from Tom's undergraduate days in Baton Rouge. The librarian was James Monroe Smith, the imprisoned former President of LSU, serving time for embezzlement of federal funds.

He was also able to reconnect there with Dr. **Harold Janney ('35)** who was the Chief of Medicine at the prison. Janney would ultimately become Chief Medical Officer for the entire Federal Prison System.

In retirement, Dr. Hernandez became a Champion of French language and culture. He passed away in 2007.

ℰⓞℭ

Charles W. Hilton, MD ('76)

After graduating from the School of Medicine in 1976, Dr. Hilton trained in internal medicine and endocrinology in the Jacksonville campus of the University of Florida. He then went into private practice in Pensacola but continued to teach part-time. In 1986, he joined the LSU faculty, rising to Professor of Medicine in 1996. He had not planned on moving to New Orleans or going full time into academic medicine until by chance he met Dr. John Wilbur, LSU's Chief of Endocrinology, at a medical meeting in New Orleans. There was an immediate rapport and he accepted a faculty position soon thereafter. LSU would owe Dr. Wilbur a debt of gratitude for his find. In short order Hilton would be named program director for internal medicine residency training and then Vice Chairman of the Department.

In 1998, Dr. Hilton was named Assistant Dean for Academic Affairs, and in 2000, he was promoted to Associate Dean, with responsibility for undergraduate and graduate medical education, as well as oversight of all the Area Health Education Centers in South Louisiana.

Charles became the prime mover behind the redesign of the undergraduate curriculum for the School of Medicine, which was first put to use in August 2001. He then developed the Office of Medical Education Research and Design (OMERAD), which is designed to help teachers teach and learners learn.

In the aftermath of Katrina he was instrumental in reestablishing both undergraduate and graduate medical education programs, helping to relocate 1,400 students and residents and led the School through more than 25 accreditation site visits. More than any other individual, he was responsible for both the School and its programs maintaining accreditation in the months following Katrina.

Charles is the author of 50 scientific papers, is a Fellow of the American College of Physicians and a Laureate of the Louisiana Chapter. The LSU School of Medicine Alumnus of the Year Award in 2002, the Allen A. Copping Award for Teaching Excellence, and the Robert S. Daniels Professorship of Medical Education are only three of his many honors.

He and his wife, **Deborah Caruso Hilton, MD ('98)**, have two sons, Charles, and Taylor. Taylor is attending LSU School of Medicine.

ଓଋ

Edgar Hull, MD

Dr. Edgar Hull was born in Pascagoula, Mississippi, in 1904, the son of elementary school teachers in small-town America of the late nineteenth and early twentieth century.

He graduated from high school at 16 and enrolled at LSU Baton Rouge in pre-medicine. Upon completing the two-year program, he was anxious to enroll at Tulane University School of Medicine, but the state of his finances forced him to take a job teaching all classes in a public grammar school in Bayou Casotte, Mississippi.

After school let out, he worked as a clerk in a local paper mill and then entered Tulane in 1923. Upon graduation in 1927, he interned at Highland Hospital in Shreveport and then stayed on for six months of advanced training at Highland Clinic.

In 1929, he opened his office in Pleasant Hill, Louisiana, and did well until early 1931, when the depression caused the bottom to drop out of the cotton market, the area's main industry. Faced with an impending financial disaster, he applied for a faculty position at the newly formed LSU School of Medicine in New Orleans. He expected this to be short sojourn, but it would stretch into decades.

Recommended by Dr. Richard Ashman, a professor of physiology who had known Dr. Hull from his student days at Tulane, he was hired and promptly established himself as an important young instructor. Well-known for his bedside manner and diagnostic ability, he began teaching generations of doctors how to examine patients and to make an accurate diagnosis of even the most complex problems. He consistently reiterated to his students, "If a physician listens to the patient long enough, he or she will tell you the diagnosis." He was quiet and unassuming, but Dr. Hull made his presence known by his meticulous clinical excellence and kindness towards all.

A consummate professional, he cared for his patients, coworkers, and students with all of his heart and energy. An internist who was famous for being "a doctor's doctor," Dr. Hull shaped the lives of hundreds of physicians who graduated from, or trained at, the medical school. His legacy lives on in the high standard of patient care, medical humanism, and personal attention that is taught to LSU medical students today.

Dr. Hull had a special affection for rural patients and their physicians. Reared in a rural area, and having begun his career as a country doctor, Hull recognized the importance of rural medicine. In a state where so many patients did not have access to urban hospitals,

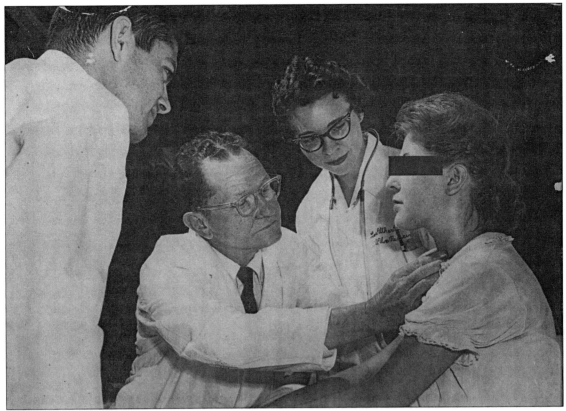

Dr. Edgar Hull, ceneter, examining a patient

local physicians were the first line of defense against injury and disease. Hull was fully committed to LSU's mission of training physicians for all areas of Louisiana, especially those areas that had inadequate medical care available to the general population.

He was more than a teacher and clinician. His varied research and published work are a testaments to his wide range of skills. He wrote with Dr. Richard Ashman a textbook of electrocardiography in 1937, which was the "bible" of that part of cardiovascular disease and earned Hull an international reputation. One story attests to this. When President Dwight Eisenhower was hospitalized for a myocardial infarction, Paul Dudley White, a Boston cardiologist, consulted on his case. He asked two other physicians for their opinion on his electrocardiogram. One was Dr. Edgar Hull.

But heart disease was not his only forte. His published articles, books and presentations covered such topics as syphilis, mercury poisoning, tuberculosis, medical nursing, conditions of the thyroid, and medical education. Dr. Hull was invited to share his talents across the country and the world, serving visiting professorships in Italy as a Fulbright Scholar, in Costa Rica as a Markle Fellow, and as a visiting faculty member at Yale University.

Dr. Hull served as Chairman of the Department of Medicine from 1939 until 1954. At that time he was succeeded by Dr. **Walton Ramsey Akenhead ('39)**, a brilliant fellow cardiologist who had trained in Seattle, Washington, and had been on the faculty for several years. Dr. Hull once said that he realized Dr. Akenhead's potential when Akenhead was only a second-year medical student. Akenhead, an excellent athlete, probably could have been a major league baseball player. He had been a star in high school and had been scouted by the pros but opted for medicine. As he once observed with a gravel-voiced chuckle "Major league baseball lost a hell of a fastball pitcher when I went into medicine."

Unfortunately, Dr. Akenhead would develop lung cancer and die prematurely in 1960. Dr. Hull would reassume the Chairmanship until 1966 when he moved to Shreveport. Dr. John H. Seabury would serve as Acting Chairman until 1969, when Dr. Fred Allison would become Chairman.

Seabury, an outstanding specialist in pulmonary and infectious disease, built an international reputation at LSU for expertise in fungal infections of the lungs. He once noted that a principal reason why he chose LSU over Tulane, which also wanted to hire him, was because Dr. Hull treated him with so much kindness and respect when he interviewed for a position at the School.

Dr. Hull's gentlemanly demeanor concealed a powerful persona and great influence. His influence stemmed from his clinical skill. Each weekday morning he would see one or two private consultations in an examining room adjacent to his office. These were patients referred to him by physicians across the state and were often people of great influence. Dr. Hull would order labs, x-rays and cardiograms and send a written report within a day. Many people felt they were in his debt.

He rarely used his influence but when he used it he used it forcefully. At one time he had a protégé on the faculty, a young cardiologist who was asked by a resident to see a patient at Charity that the resident had diagnosed with rheumatic carditis.

In the company of the resident, a nurse, and several students, the faculty member examined the patient and, with that retinue in tow, took her to the Charity Heart Station, performed cardiac fluoroscopy, returned her to her bed, and gave her advice.

Later that day, the patient reported to another nurse that the faculty member had raped her during the exam. That nurse reported the complaint to her supervisor, who reported it to an Associate Director at Charity, who reported it the Director. No one bothered to investigate further and the police were called. They immediately arrested the hapless cardiologist.

In police custody and allowed one phone call, he placed it not to a lawyer or a family member. He called Edgar Hull, who did some telephoning of his own. In short order, the complaint was investigated; the doctor was exonerated, and released. The Associate

Director and Director at Charity were promptly terminated. The fate of the nurses was not noted.

As the population of Louisiana expanded, it became obvious to Dr. Hull that a second public medical school was needed and that Shreveport was the obvious place. He used his influence to make that happen too.

Dr. Hull would be named the first Dean of the LSU School in Medicine in Shreveport in 1966. He supervised the opening of the school, the completion of the school's campus, and he saw the school's first medical school class through their four years in medical school. After he retired as Dean in 1973, he moved back to Pascagoula, and practiced medicine for several years.

The first endowed Chair established by the Alumni Association, the first ever created in the school, was named for Edgar Hull, in 1984, shortly before he passed away. Dr. Fred Allison would be named the first Edgar Hull Professor of Medicine.

Dr. Hull's daughter, **Alice Louise Maier ('62)** graduated from the School of Medicine and practices in Mississippi. Her late husband was also a graduate of the School of Medicine.

ഇൻ

Henry Jolly, MD ('41)

Few faculty members in the history of the School of Medicine were more beloved or served with more distinction than Dr. Jolly. Following an abbreviated internship he served for four years in armed forces, returning in 1946 to begin a residency in Dermatology at LSU under the tutelage of its then Chairman, Dr. James K. Howles, a world authority on syphilis. He then did a fellowship at Tulane before opening his private practice in Baton Rouge in 1950.

In 1954 he joined the LSU faculty, living part time in New Orleans and maintaining a residence and practice in Baton Rouge. He served on the faculty until 1987, when he retired. From 1974 – 1985 he was Chairman of Dermatology at LSU. He was named Alumnus of the Year in 1985 upon his retirement as Chairman.

But retirement was something Dr. Jolly did in name only. In 1987, he became the second president of the modern Medical Alumni Association while at the same time serving as President of the American Dermatological Association. In 1988, he served as Founding President of the LSU Medical Center Foundation.

A Professorship of Dermatology was dedicated in his honor by the Committee of 100 – Champions of Excellence in 1991. At the event he was lionized not only for his administrative skill and medical acumen but more importantly for his generous and thoughtful nature. A Professorship was also created to honor Dr. Jolly's mentor, Dr. Howles. Dr. Jolly lived in retirement in Baton Rouge until his death in 2004.

ෂാൽ

Frederick H. Kasten, PhD

A self-described "poor boy," Fred Kasten, a New York native, aspired to nothing more that being a radio repairman when he grew up. As a 15-year-old in 1942 he volunteered to work in the War Emergency Radio Service, and when he was old enough in 1944 he joined the Merchant Marine as a radio operator serving in the North African Theater. Subsequently, he served in the Navy as an electronics technician. On discharge, he recognized that he was destined for more than radio repairs, and started by going back to finish high school.

After graduating from the prestigious Bronx High School of Science he enrolled at the University of Houston, aiming at becoming a high-school science teacher. Again recognizing that he had talent, he went on to obtain a PhD at the University of Texas and then conduct research at Roswell Park Memorial Institute. He then taught at the University of Southern California and Loma Linda School of Medicine before beginning a 27-year career at LSU School of Medicine, Department of Anatomy, where he rose to international prominence for his work in biologic staining, histochemistry, tissue culture and the history of medicine.

During that time he received a Fogarty Fellowship that allowed him to do research in Russia and in Communist East Germany becoming the first American Scientist to do any extensive research in East Germany. His proficiency in German (he also speaks French) led him to write *One Hundred Years of Histochemistry in Germany* as well as *The History of Staining*. Additionally, he was twice called on to write the "Dyes and Biological Stains" section of *Stedman's Medical Dictionary* as well as 25 book chapters, 70 research publications, and 35 reviews of books.

His interest in history led him to serve as faculty advisor for the History of Medicine Club at the School of Medicine for nine years. Underwritten by the Alumni Association but the brainchild of Dr. Kasten, it staged a total of 56 events that included lectures by eminent physicians and notable historians and an end-of-the-year banquet.

A long-time advocate for the poor, the helpless and the forgotten, he has worked to provide free dental services to children and mental healthcare for teens and adults, and has written extensively on Nazi War Crimes that involved German physicians.

He lives in retirement in Tennessee, as a gentleman farmer and ham radio operator.

80CR

David G. Kline, MD

Neurosurgery had a presence at LSUSoM from its beginning in 1931 when Dr. Gilbert Anderson, a 1917 graduate from Columbia University School of Medicine who had trained at the University of Minnesota and who was a founding member of the Harvey Cushing Society, was appointed to the faculty. He served until his death in 1948, when he was succeeded first by Dr. Guy Odom, who would leave to become Professor of Neurosurgery at Duke University, and then by Dr. Richard Levey, Chief of Neurosurgery at Touro Infirmary.

Eventually Dr. Charles Wilson came in to head the Section of Neurosurgery and would remain until 1965, when he became Head of the Department of Neurosurgery at the University of Kentucky.

In 1967, Dr. Isidore Cohn, Jr., Chairman of Surgery, brought in Dr. Peter Jannetta and Dr. David Kline. Jannetta ultimately moved to the University of Pittsburgh in 1971, but Dr. Kline remained as Division Head, and became the first Chairman of the newly recognized Department of Neurosurgery in 1976.

Dr. Kline's standing in the field is clear, having served in important positions with the American Board of Neurological Surgery, the American Association of Neurological Surgeons (AANS), the Society of Neurologic Surgeons and the Southern Neurosurgical Society. He founded the Louisiana Society of Neurological Surgeons in the late 1970s.

One of Dr. Kline's other talents lay undiscovered for decades and surfaced only by accident. Summoned from his office to see an emergency consult at Charity Hospital, he forgot his Charity ID badge. He was stopped from boarding the elevator by a security guard, who informed him none too politely that he would have to go get his ID.

Dr. Kline was grabbed by the guard when he, very much in a hurry, attempted to walk past him; he was restrained, but only for a second. The next thing the guard knew, he found himself on the ground, being restrained by Dr. Kline. Among his many other accomplishments, Dr. Kline had been an outstanding intercollegiate wrestler.

Dr. Kline has served as a visiting professor at other institutions on 45 occasions and has been lauded as the world's leading authority on peripheral nerve injury. One well-known case confirms his position. When the son of then-Senator Al Gore sustained a peripheral nerve injury and the Senator could have chosen any physician in the world, his choice was David Kline. The operation was a success.

In recognition of his standing in the field, the LSU Board of Supervisors named him a Boyd Professor, the highest academic distinction in the LSU System. In 2005 a Chair in Neurosurgery was dedicated in his honor, and in 2006 he was awarded the Cushing Medal, the highest honor granted by the American Association of Neurological Surgeons. It is named for Dr. Harvey Cushing the "father" of the specialty. It has been awarded on only 17 occasions. In 2008 he received, the Founders Laurel of the Congress of Neurologic Surgeons for "outstanding and sustained contributions to Neurosurgery." Since 1951 this award has been made only five times.

In 2006, Dr. Kline stepped down from the Chairmanship and was succeeded by Dr. Frank Culicchia, the Chairman of Neurosurgery at West Jefferson General Hospital and a long-time faculty member at Tulane. In 2008, Dr. Cuclicchia and Dr. Nicholas Bazan, Chair of the Neurosciences Center of Excellence, organized a David Kline Festschrift, bringing together 100 internationally known physicians and research scientist to honor Dr. Kline.

Dr. Kline, having served LSU for 35 years, retains the rank of Emeritus Professor and Chairman while enjoying retirement in North Carolina.

ഇറ

Kim Edward LeBlanc, MD, PhD

Family Medicine had its beginnings at LSU School of Medicine as a Section of the Department of Medicine in 1969 under the direction of **Ralph Sanchez ('50)**, a nationally known figure in that nascent discipline.

In 1976 it would evolve into a full fledged department under the equally well-known **Gerald Gehringer ('52)**, who would not only lead the department until 1986 but also serve as President of the American Academy of Family Physicians. Sanchez would continue to serve as Coordinator of Continuing Medical Education for many years at the School after Gehringer's arrival.

In 1986, Robin J. O. Catlin, a British physician, came to LSU from the University of Massachusetts to lead the department until 1995. He was succeeded by Russell Anderson, a University of Kentucky graduate who had taught for years at the University of Alabama.

Anderson was succeeded in 2002 by Dr. Kim Edward LeBlanc, who boasted not only an MD from Shreveport but a PhD in Exercise Physiology from Baton Rouge. LeBlanc had previously served as Head of Family Medicine at University Medical Center in Lafayette, La. He had been associated in one way or another with programs of the School of Medicine since 1981, had been appointed to the State Board of Medical Examiners in 2000, and had served as coroner of St. Martin Parish for 12 years.

Aside from establishing a strong Family Practice Residency Program, LeBlanc took a concept originally devised by **Warren Plauché ('57)** when Plauché was Associate Dean to new and undreamed of heights. The concept was a Rural Scholars Program. The program is designed to seek out applicants to the School of Medicine who indicate a desire to practice in rural or underserved areas of Louisiana and to nurture that desire through scholarships and undergraduate training opportunities, particularly in Lafayette, so that physicians would be attracted to primary care in rural areas of the state.

Under his direction the program has grown greatly in size and received national recognition for its success. LeBlanc has been named to the Marie Lahasky Professorship at the School of Medicine and has authored 21 journal articles and eight book chapters. In his spare time he acted as team physician for the U.S. Women's Olympic Basketball Team and has completed 32 marathons and 130 other races. By one estimate he has run 75,000 miles in total, all the while running an extremely productive Department of Family Medicine.

ℰᏨ

Ralph D. Lillie, MD

Described by one colleague as a "master magician of histochemistry," Ralph D. Lillie served on the faculty in the department of pathology for 19 years. While this time spot of service is by no means unique, what is amazing is that Dr. Lillie did not begin to serve until he was 64 years of age and had just retired from the NIH.

A 1920 graduate of Stanford University School of Medicine, who trained in pathology at San Francisco General Hospital, he started with the NIH in 1925 before it was ever called the NIH. In its early incarnation it was known as the Hygienic Laboratory. When it became the NIH he worked his way up to become Chief of the Laboratory of Pathology and Histochemistry.

He had had an abiding interest in staining technology that served him, and medicine everywhere, well during WWII. Historically, the raw material for stains was manufactured in Germany, raw materials that suddenly became unavailable. It was Lillie who developed acceptable substitutes manufactured in the United States.

A prolific author, with 339 publications and two text books of Histopathology and Stains to his credit, he worked vigorously at LSU until a stroke ended his life at the age of 83. In his honor the Histochemical Society held its next annual meeting in New Orleans and dedicated it to his memory.

౸౸

Ronald Luftig, PhD

When Marilyn Zimny, PhD, headed the search committee to select a Chairman of Microbiology to replace Calderone Howe, PhD, who was retiring in 1982, she took on a formidable responsibility. The Department had not progressed under Howe's leadership as it had during the tenure of his predecessor, Dr. G. John Buddingh, and an infusion of new blood was needed.

Ronald Luftig, PhD

Also, the institution was wrestling with the issue of what to do with the Department of Tropical Medicine and Parasitology, a department that had been in decline for several years. In recruiting Dr. Ron Luftig from the University of South Carolina School of Medicine, it found answers to both questions. A graduate of the University of Chicago who had served on the faculty of Cal-Tech and Duke University before moving to Carolina, Dr. Luftig brought with him a wealth of research and teaching experience and a deft touch.

This allowed the eventual merger of Tropical Medicine and Parasitology into the Department of Microbiology. More importantly, Dr. Luftig made certain that Parasitology would not whither on the vine. It had been in decline under its Chair, Dr. David Clyde, who had succeeded the great J. Clyde Swartzwelder, PhD, who had brought it to fame during a 38-year run.

In 1988 Luftig was named Director of the LSU International Center for Medical Research and Training, a position he continues to hold to this day in addition to his Departmental Chair. For many years at the ICMRT he was greatly assisted by the late Dr. William Pelon, a long time faculty member.

Dr. Luftig has been a frequent site visitor for the National Institutes of Health and a visiting professor at many universities but continues a heavy teaching and research load at the School of Medicine. He is known as a person of integrity and rare good sense and a leading basic scientist at the School of Medicine.

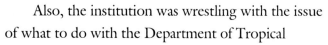

George Lyons, Jr., MD ('54)

In 1970, a search committee recommended that George Lyons, Jr., a faculty member since 1958, be named Department Chair of Otolaryngology, to succeed Dr. Irving Blatt, who had served in that capacity since 1960, after being recruited from the University of Michigan. Dr. Blatt had decided to enter private practice.

This was an exciting time in Otolaryngology in New Orleans and at the School of Medicine. Four MDs, including Dr. Blatt, had preceded Dr. Lyons as Department Chair. The first was Dr. Homer Dupuy, Jr., who led the department from its inception in 1931 until his death in 1936 from a bleeding ulcer. Dupuy had been nationally known as a pioneer in ENT cancer surgery and was the inventor of several surgical instruments.

George Lyons, Jr., MD ('54)

Dupuy was succeeded by Dr. George Taquino, Sr., a 1911 graduate of Tulane, who would serve until 1953 when he would be succeeded by Dr. Valentine Fuchs. Fuchs, a decorated veteran of World War II and an excellent teacher, would take over at a chaotic time for his specialty in New Orleans. Seven different ENT training programs, most of poor quality, existed in New Orleans.

The President of the American Board of Otolaryngology, Dean Lierle, MD, stepped in, proposing that only two programs, the one at Tulane and the one at LSU, continue to offer training. Dr. Fuchs would eventually retire because of severe peripheral vascular disease, which necessitated the amputation of both legs, but not before helping secure LSU's place as a premier ENT training program.

Under Dr. Blatt, who succeeded Fuchs, things would continue to improve dramatically. The length of training and the number of residents were increased and Dr. Mervin Trail, who had come to New Orleans in 1968 from Baltimore, was added to the geographic full-time faculty. This would prove to be a remarkable addition for many reasons.

Audiology, which became important under Dr. Blatt, took on even greater stature under the charismatic Dr. Lyons. Dr. Blatt had had a strong interest in audiology research going back to his residency days at the University of Michigan; he looked for someone to do the research and recruited Charles Berlin, PhD, from Johns Hopkins University. The Kresge Hearing Research Laboratory, founded in 1967 under Dr. Charles Berlin, blossomed under Dr. Lyons. Also under Dr. Lyons, a cochlear implant program, one of only five in the United States, began. Designed to treat nerve deafness, it proved to be extremely successful.

Strong relationships with the Ear, Eye, Nose and Throat Hospital were forged under Dr. Lyons. Postgraduate programs in head and neck cancer, facial plastic surgery and laryngology were also added under him before he stepped down as Chairman in 1993 in favor of Dr. Merv Trail. He remained on the part-time faculty until 2004, when he retired.

ᎦᎠ

Urban Maes, MD

No faculty member was more important than Urban Maes in the early years of the School of Medicine. For fifteen years, as Chairman of Surgery he was a guiding force in the medical school. In the process, he helped shape the image and direction of the School of Medicine, and made it a leader for clinical excellence in surgery.

Dr. Maes, born in 1878, began his medical career at the Tulane University School of Medicine, graduating in 1900. He served with the Public Health Service during New Orleans' last yellow fever epidemic in 1905 and as a battlefield surgeon in France during World War I. Maes achieved the rank of full colonel by the time he was discharged in 1919, and was a consultant to the Army for the base hospital at Fort Sam Houston, Texas, and to the U. S. Marine Hospital at New Orleans (a part of the Public Health service) until 1922.

Urban Maes, MD

A recognized national leader in surgical practice and education, he came from Tulane to the LSU faculty in 1932. While at LSU, Maes continued his service to the military. In 1940, before the United States was attacked at Pearl Harbor, Dr. Maes headed the formation of the 64th General Hospital. This unit was sponsored by the School of Medicine, but was clearly the brainchild of Urban Maes, who served as a planning consultant for the Army throughout the Second World War.

He was one of the most important surgeons in the city of New Orleans, renowned for his dexterity and diagnostic skill. He was on the staff of Touro Infirmary for more than 45 years, and he held important surgical consulting positions at Charity Hospital. Together with his teaching position with the Department of Surgery, Maes was a busy man.

He authored 95 papers on all phases of surgery, a prodigious feat for the time.

He served as president of the Orleans Parish Medical Society, vice president of the American Surgical Association, first vice president of the Southern Surgical Association, member of the board of governors of the American College of Surgeons from 1928 to 1932, chairman of the AMA's surgical section, member of the American Association of Military Surgeons until 1943, and chairman of the medical advisory board of the Selective Service office in New Orleans.

As a school leader, Maes was unparalleled. He was chairman of the Faculty Council of the medical school for a number of years, and his leadership played an important role in shaping the course of the medical school during critical times. When a large number of faculty members resigned in late 1945 following the summary dismissal of the medical school's dean, it was Maes' resignation that had galvanized the others to act. When the dispute was resolved, it was Maes who led the charge for faculty members to rescind their resignations.

He served as Departmental Chair until 1947, when he passed the torch to his protégé and long-time associate, Dr. James D. Rives.

ℰᏩ

Jorge I. Martinez-Lopez, MD ('50)

Jorge I. Martinez-Lopez didn't give himself much of a chance of being accepted to LSU School of Medicine in 1946. Although he had an outstanding academic record as an LSU undergrad, he was up against many returning military veterans and was a native of Puerto Rico. So he was both pleased and surprised when the acceptance letter arrived.

The government of Puerto Rico, equally pleased, provided him a scholarship, stipulating only that he intern at a hospital on the island. That he did after graduation in 1950, at the Arecibo District Hospital on the northern coast of Puerto Rico.

It was there that he had his first brush with fame. The date was November 1, 1950, and he was the only physician on duty in the ER when vehicles began to arrive full of seriously wounded people. A Puerto Rican nationalist group, in attempting a coup on the island, was shooting civilians and police alike in an attempt to topple the government. Although the attempt failed, Jorge was called upon to initiate what was called a "prompt and phenomenal" response at the hospital to the disaster.

Becoming a cardiologist was an accident. Originally intending to become an obstetrician and accepted to a program, he was called to active duty by the army after volunteering to serve when the Korean War broke out. During his army service he decided to pursue a career in Internal Medicine and ultimately cardiology. In this he was strongly influenced by Dr. Walton Akenhead, Chair of Medicine at LSU, who convinced him ultimately to join the full-time faculty of the School after he finished his training. He would remain on the full time faculty for nearly 30 years, being responsible for among other things, the courses in "Physical Diagnosis" and "Introduction to Clinical Medicine," and the majority of adult cardiac caths. He served as Director of the Cardiology Department at Charity for 11 years (1975-1986).

So effective was he as a cardiologist that he, an LSU trainee and faculty member, was asked to join the Musser-Burch Society of Tulane School of Medicine, which had hitherto limited membership to Tulane Medicine trainees or faculty. Eventually he served as its president.

After retiring from LSU and having served in the army reserve for many years he went back on active duty at William Beaumont Army Medical Center in El Paso, Texas.

Ultimately, this would lead to his becoming a faculty member at Texas Tech University School of Medicine in El Paso, where he continues to serve for the past 21 years.

Three of his children followed him into medicine: **Jorge ('76), Anthony ('78)** and **Ricardo ('80)**. Jorge serves on the faculty. A grandson, Benjamin, currently is enrolled at the School.

൭ൟ

Samuel G. McClugage, Jr., PhD

It took a long time but finally in 2008 Sam McClugage agreed to become the permanent Chair of the Department of Cell Biology and Anatomy. He had held acting or interim appointments as head on three occasions since coming to LSU in 1971 from the University of Cincinnati. He succeeded Dr. Ranney Mize, who had served as Chairman of Anatomy since 1992.

He added the Chairmanship to his already full plate as Associate Dean for Admissions and Professor of Anatomy. As Professor of Anatomy he has also had significant teaching responsibilities in the Schools of Medicine, Dentistry and Allied Health.

A favorite of students, he was twice named Best Preclinical Professor. He was also elected to Alpha Omega Alpha Honor Medical Society and named an Honorary Alumnus of the School of Medicine, among many other awards. He recently was also awarded the Robert Sabalis Exemplary Service Award by the American Association of Medical Colleges, a rare and prestigious honor.

He would mentor many medical and dental students. Perhaps the most important mentoring was to a young medical student, Charles Hilton. Dr. Hilton was the first medical student to work in his research laboratory in the summer of 1972. He would go on to become a notable endocrinologist and ultimately Associate Dean for Undergraduate and Graduate Medical Education.

Sam served as the first faculty advisor to Camp Tiger. This freshman medical student project has provided a week-long day camp for handicapped and disabled children annually since 1983. He also served as faculty advisor to the Phoenix Society, an organization devoted to helping impaired students. This organization ultimately led to the development of the Campus Assistance Program, offering aid to faculty, staff and students across the entire campus.

So great was the LSU System's confidence in Dr. McClugage's ability and judgment that in 2001 he was chosen to Chair the Health Sciences Center Chancellor Search Committee when a replacement for the late Dr. Merv Trail was sought. He was then asked to also Chair the Search Committee for a new Dean for the School of Medicine, which resulted in Dr. **Larry Hollier** ('68) joining our ranks.

In addition, to his activities within the Health Sciences Center, Dr. McClugage has been active with Habitat for Humanity and the St. Charles Avenue Presbyterian Church. He has been active in the American Association of Medical Colleges and the New Orleans Mayor's Task Force on Crime. He was very instrumental in starting the Weed and Seed Program in the City of New Orleans under the auspices of the US Justice Department.

Married to **Katherine St. Amant** ('77) he is the father of "Trey" McClugage, a pre-med major at the University of Virginia.

A Professorship of Cell Biology and Anatomy was dedicated in Dr. McClugage's honor by the Alumni Association in 2008.

ဆဝ

Abe Mickal, MD ('40)

Born in Lebanon in 1912 and an émigré to Mississippi at an early age, Abe Mickal was an unlikely candidate for the LSU Medical School. Nevertheless, Mickal had many talents—and one was football. After entering LSU in Baton Rouge in 1932, Mickal became an All-American and one of the finest football players in LSU history. He also excelled academically, was commandant of the Corps of Cadets, and attracted the attention of Governor Huey P. Long.

Huey was a legendary admirer of his beloved Tigers. He even offered his services routinely to the team, suggesting plays, cheering from the sidelines, and visiting the team's practice sessions. Abe was one of Huey's favorites, and Mickal respected Huey's vision and programs directed toward the poor of Louisiana during the Great Depression, especially the children of the state.

Dr. Mickal came to the medical school at LSU in 1936, where his strong academic work stood him in good stead. While at the medical school, Mickal admired the closeness of the classes and the collegial atmosphere of the School of Medicine and her personnel.

Despite this familial atmosphere, Dr. Mickal knew much was going to be expected of him. Several departments and staff members rigorously tested the former football star. It was very clear that faculty members at the School of Medicine did not want people to think that they were giving the legendary Abe Mickal a free ride. Dr. Mickal admitted that it was not a malicious process and called his medical school years "delightful."

Having graduated in 1940, Dr. Mickal entered the Army after internship and served as a Major in the Medical Corps. The war ended, and he completed a residency in Obstetrics and Gynecology in 1949, and he was named to the LSU faculty soon thereafter. Just ten years later, Dr. Mickal was named head of the Department of OB/GYN, succeeding Dr. Milton McCall. McCall, who succeeded Curtis Lund, MD, who had served less than two years, had accepted the Chairmanship of the Department of OB/GYN at the University of Pittsburgh. He died soon after leaving LSU of metastatic colon cancer.

Dr. Mickal distinguished himself as a gynecologic surgeon, and, in 1981, was named president of the Society of Gynecologic Surgeons. This, after serving as president of the New Orleans OB/GYN Society and helping found the Society of Gynecologic Oncologists and the Infectious Disease Society for Obstetrics and Gynecology.

For many years Dr. Mickal would be assisted by Dr. **James G. "Jake" Mulé** ('47), who passed away in 1978. Like Mickal, Jake Mulé was famed as a bedside teacher and, like Abe, a favorite of students and residents.

Dr. Mickal exemplified the best values in medical education and clinical skill. His dedication, hard work, and outstanding character made him a beloved figure at the School of Medicine. The Abe Mickal Chair of Obstetrics and Gynecology was dedicated by the Medical Alumni Association in 1985 to honor his contributions to the School.

Abe retired in 1980 as Departmental Chair. He would be succeeded by Dr. Charles White, who came to LSU from the University of West Virginia. Dr. White would serve for 12 years in that position.

Abe Mickal, MD ('40)

℘℃

Joseph Miller, PhD

When Dr. Joseph Miller passed away in 2009 at the age of 85 it marked the end of a life filled with both scientific achievement and remarkable adventure. A World War II draftee, he would serve three tours of duty in Europe as a combat medic. He went ashore in Normandy on D-Day, removing the wounded from the battleground, and evacuating them to safety.

At one time when his unit was placed under the command of Lt. General George S. Patton, Dr. Miller for a time served as his Jeep driver and personal caretaker for the General's bull terrier, "Willie." He also participated in the rescue of the world famous Lipizzan Stallions from Vienna, Austria, transporting them across enemy territory to safety in Czechoslovakia. He also was assigned, because of his musical ability, to play the clarinet for the USO shows staged by the famous entertainer Bob Hope.

On discharge, he completed his education, receiving a PhD in Tropical Medicine from New York University. On graduation in 1953, he accepted an invitation to join the faculty of LSU, where he would serve with distinction for 31 years.

He did studies in Mexico, Costa Rica and Kenya. In Kenya he barely escaped with his life during the Mau Mau uprising that swept through that country. He served as an advisor on Medical Parasitology to the government of Saudi Arabia and remained in the Army Reserve until 1984, retiring as a colonel. He was the author of 80 scientific articles and book chapters. In retirement he moved to Windsor, Colorado, where he was active in civic affairs.

ഓരേ

R. Ranney Mize, PhD, and
Emel Songu-Mize, PhD

Before coming to LSU in 1992 to Chair the Department of Anatomy and Cell Biology, Ranney received his PhD from Northwestern University and then did postgraduate work at the University of Pennsylvania. Here he met and married Emel Songu, a native of Ankara, Turkey, who was completing her PhD degree in Pharmacology.

Together they took positions at the University of Tennessee – College of Medicine (Memphis), and in 1992 moved to New Orleans. She became Professor of Pharmacology. Together they would become both outstanding assets to the School of Medicine as well as to the New Orleans community.

Emel authored 41 articles and book chapters and gave many invited lectureships. Ranney authored 80 articles and served for six months as Visiting Professor, Institute of Ophthalmology, at the University of London England.

Both passionate music lovers, they were active in the Symphony and the Philharmonic Orchestra as well as the Musical Arts Society of New Orleans and the Loyola University School of Music.

In 2003, Ranney stepped down as Chair of the Department to devote himself to teaching and research. Emel continues to serve the School as Professor of Pharmacology.

৪৩

Joseph M. Moerschbaecher III, PhD

Dr. Moerschbaecher earned his PhD at the American University in Washington, DC, and was a postdoctoral research associate in the Department of Behavioral Sciences at the Naval Medical Research Institute. He also completed a postdoctoral fellowship in the Department of Pharmacology at the Georgetown University Schools of Medicine and Dentistry, where he was appointed a Research Assistant Professor of Pharmacology. He joined the LSU Health Sciences Center faculty in 1983. From 1989 through 1998, he served as Professor and Head of the Department of Pharmacology and Experimental Therapeutics, succeeding Dr. **Lee Roy Morgan** ('71), who had become head in 1978. He also served as Co-Director of the LSU Alcohol and Drug Abuse Center. In October 1998, Dr. Moerschbaecher was formally appointed Vice Chancellor for Academic Affairs and Dean of the School of Graduate Studies at the LSU Health Sciences Center. He was succeeded by Dr. Steven Lanier as Department Head.

Dr. Moerschbaecher has been awarded nearly $4.2 million in research funding by the National Institutes on Drug Abuse and Mental Health and others. His research interests included alcohol and substance abuse, and drug effects on learning and memory. Dr. Moerschbaecher has served on research review committees for the National Institutes of Health and other organizations, as well as on the Board of Editors of the *Journal of Experimental Analysis of Behavior* and is a guest reviewer for *Psychopharmacology*, *Physiology and Behavior*, *Pharmacology, Biochemistry and Behavior*, *Journal of Pharmacology and Experimental Therapeutics*, *Journal of Pharmaceutical Sciences*, *Molecular and Chemical Neuropathology*, and *Journal of Medicinal Chemistry*.

He is a member of the Behavioral Pharmacology Society, the American Society for Pharmacology and Experimental Therapeutics, the Association for Medical School Pharmacology, the European Behavioral Pharmacology Society, and the College on Problems of Drug Dependence.

In the aftermath of Katrina he was instrumental in salvaging the library collection of the Health Sciences Center; he oversaw its decontamination and the restoration of the library itself.

80CR

Emma Sadler Moss, MD ('35)

Emma Sadler Moss was born in Pearlington, Mississippi, on September 19, 1898. She survived an illness-filled childhood to attend the Mississippi State College for Women. She originally intended to become an elementary school teacher, but she opted to pursue science. She graduated in 1919 with a Bachelor of Science degree in Bacteriology, and she began her career as a medical technologist. She worked for ten years "at the bench." When her husband John Moss died a painful death from tuberculosis in 1929, Emma was determined to dedicate herself to medicine with the goal to "help prevent and cure disease." She never remarried, and had no children.

She began her medical education in 1930 at the University of Alabama School of Medicine, a two-year program, and subsequently transferred to Louisiana State University School of Medicine in New Orleans, and received her MD degree in 1935. She interned and completed her residency in pathology at Charity Hospital in New Orleans in 1939 and was certified by the American Board of Pathology in Anatomic and Clinical Pathology, and Clinical Microbiology.

In 1939, with the departure of Dr. Rigney D'Aunoy and within less than one year of completing her residency, she was appointed the Acting Director of the Department of Pathology at Charity Hospital, and concurrently she was also appointed to the faculty of the LSU School of Medicine. In 1940, she was named the Director of Pathology at Charity Hospital, and she held that

Emma Sadler Moss, MD
Director, Department of Pathology
Charity Hospital, New Orleans, LA

position for the next 30 years. She was named Clinical Professor of Pathology at the LSU School of Medicine in 1951 and served as Acting Head of the LSU School of Medicine Department of Pathology from December 1945 to July 1946.

During her brief tenure as the acting head of the LSU School of Medicine Department of Pathology, the faculty of the school was in turmoil. To provide the medical students with an appropriate course in pathology, Dr. Moss called on many of her pathology colleagues. The pathology course that year was presented by nationally renowned and distinguished pathologists from across the country; they presented lectures in their particular areas of expertise. No medical school pathology course, before or since, has probably had such an exemplary faculty. No one, other than Dr. Moss, could have organized such a course in such a short time.

Dr. Moss had many scholarly achievements and awards including Gold Medals from the American Society of Clinical Pathologists (ASCP) for exhibits on tropical diseases, mycotic infections and parasitology. She received the Billings Gold Medal in 1954 from the American Medical Association for her exhibit on "Fungous Diseases." She was also the author or co-author of numerous peer-reviewed scientific articles, book chapters, and books relating to her interests in tropical, parasitic, and mycotic diseases. She was also selected as the 1954 Medical Woman of the Year by the New Orleans Branch of the American Medical Woman's Association, and she received the Silver Distaff Award in 1955 from *Woman's Home Companion Magazine*.

Dr. Moss left a significant legacy in medical education. She was particularly proud to have mentored and personally supervised the training of over 150 pathology residents and exactly 578 medical technologists during her career. Few program directors can match (or even approach) such a legacy. In 1941 it was Dr. Moss who established the first medical technology training program to require a baccalaureate degree.

Dr. Moss joined the ASCP in 1938, and served on countless ASCP committees, the Board of Directors, and was elected as President for the 1955-1956 term. In becoming the first woman president of the ASCP, she was also the first woman president of any major medical association in the United States.

Dr. Moss continued her work at Charity and LSU until her death on April 30, 1970. It was the day she was to have retired after 36 years of service. The Department of Pathology ultimately funded creation of the Emma Moss, MD ('35), Professorship of Pathology in June 2003. **Fred Rodriguez, MD ('75),** holds the appointment.

ℰℭ

Lee T. Nesbitt, MD

On April 1, 1988, Dr. Nesbitt became Head of the Department of Dermatology at LSUHSC. He succeeded Dr. **Ricardo Mora** ('73), an LSU faculty member, who had briefly been Interim Head following Dr. Henry Jolly's retirement.

Dr. Nesbitt, a 1966 graduate of Tulane University School of Medicine, had trained in Dermatology at Charity Hospital on the Tulane service before becoming Interim Chief of the Division of Dermatology at Tulane from 1977 to 1981. He had also been appointed to the faculty at LSUHSC in 1972 after his residency, and he did research at LSU, Tulane, and the VA Hospital in immunodermatological diseases. He has certification in both dermatology and dermatopathology.

Dr. Nesbitt is nationally recognized in immunodermatology, bullous and connective tissue diseases. In 2007, he received the Lifetime Achievement Award from the Medical Dermatology Society for contributions to severe medical dermatological diseases. He has served as President of the American Board of Dermatology after being a member of that board for nine years. He has also been president of the American Dermatological Association, the country's oldest and most prestigious dermatological honorary society, and the only two-time president of the Louisiana Dermatological Society. He served on the ACGME Residency Review Committee for Dermatology nationally for nine years, from 2000 to 2009. He has written two textbooks, nine book chapters and over 50 medical articles. He has been the Henry Jolly, MD, Professor of Dermatology at LSUHSC since 1990.

ဆဝ

Thomas Nolan, MD

In 1992, Dr. Charles White stepped down as Chair of the Department of Obstetrics and Gynecology in favor of Dr. Ron Elkins of the University of Michigan. Dr. Elkins would last only four years, retiring because of ill health.

Despite his short tenure, Dr. Elkins accomplished two things of major importance: elevating Dr. Harvey Gabert to Vice Chairman of the Department and recruiting Dr. Tom Nolan from the University of Georgia in 1993 to initiate a new section "General Obstetrics and Gynecology." Nolan had previously had a long career in the Medical Corps of the U.S. Navy and had been on the Georgia faculty for five years.

Dr. Gabert succeeded Dr. Elkins and served for six years. At that time health concerns forced his retirement and Dr. Nolan was chosen to succeed him. Dr. Nolan had already distinguished himself in a number of areas of education and clinical care, including the establishment of several community outreach clinics, which greatly strengthened resident education.

This area of service had been suffering; the number of deliveries had been dropping at MCLANO and Earl K. Long and University Hospital in Lafayette because state reimbursement increases in Medicaid payments had caused the migration of many poor pregnant women to the private community for delivery. Dr. Nolan's efforts greatly improved the situation.

The Department was severely hurt by Hurricane Katrina, with a total of eight faculty members choosing either to retire or to accept other academic positions. This caused severe disruptions in resident education for nearly a year and a number of residents were placed in other programs.

Despite this, Dr. Nolan has continued to provide strong leadership, recruiting new faculty and establishing strong academic relationships with Woman's Hospital of Baton Rouge and Woman's and Children's Hospital in Lafayette.

In 2007, Dr. Nolan was also named Associate Dean for Clinical Affairs.

෨෬

Daniel Nuss, MD ('81)

When Merv Trail was named Chancellor of the Health Sciences Center in 1994, he gave up his Chairmanship of the Department of Otolaryngology, and his Vice-Chairman, Dr. Nuss, was named Acting Chairman. After a year-long national search, Dr. Nuss would be named Chairman permanently.

A 1981 graduate, he joined the faculty in otolaryngology in 1987, after General Surgery and ENT training at Charity and a fellowship in Head and Neck Oncology at MD Anderson in Houston. In 1989 he took a two-year sabbatical and journeyed to the Center for Cranial Base Surgery at the University of Pittsburgh.

On his return, he established himself as an expert on surgery of the base of the skull and head and neck oncology, and in 1993 become residency training program director. In 1994 he was named Vice Chairman of the Department.

Because of his wide range of interests he would also be named to the faculty of the Neuroscience Center and the Department of Neurosurgery.

A member of many professional societies he has played major roles in the North American Skull Base Society (President, 2009) and the World Federation of Skull Base Societies.

The author of 80+ publications and many abstracts, he has served as Visiting Professor at the University of Texas in Dallas, University of California at San Francisco, and University of Tennessee in Memphis, and has been an invited speaker at universities in Australia, the Philippines, Canada, Brazil and Austria.

Perhaps his most notable accomplishment was overseeing the resurrection of his department and its training programs in the aftermath of Katrina. He speedily set up both undergraduate and graduate programs in Baton Rouge, both of which immediately flourished. His wise advice and leadership helped the entire school survive its greatest threat in decades.

෨෨

James Patrick O'Leary, MD

In 1989 Dr. Isidore Cohn, Jr., stepped down as Chairman of the Department of Surgery after 27 years of service in that position. He was succeeded by Dr. James Patrick O'Leary, who was named departmental chair and the Isidore Cohn Jr., MD, Professor of Surgery.

O'Leary had graduated in 1967 from the University of Florida School of Medicine and had trained in Boston and Gainesville. He remained on the faculty in Florida until 1978 when he became Professor of Surgery at Vanderbilt University and Chief of Surgery at the VA Hospital in Nashville.

In 1984 he accepted the Seeger Endowed Chair of Surgery at Baylor University Medical Center in Dallas and Clinical Professor at the University of Texas, Dallas. In 1989 he came to LSU.

Dr. O'Leary also served since 2001 as Associate Dean for Clinical Affairs. In 2004 he served as Interim Dean after Robert Marier stepped down and before Dr. **Larry Hollier ('68)** was appointed to the position. He also served for two years as chief executive officer of the LSU Healthcare Network.

Dr. O'Leary has 176 peer reviewed publications, 5 books, 22 book chapters and has been an invited lecturer on 300 occasions. He has received teaching awards at LSU on three occasions.

Under Dr. O'Leary the department continued its emphasis on research, averaging 85 peer reviewed publications annually. Individual sections of cardiovascular, vascular, pediatric, bariatric, transplant, plastic and oncology have been formed in the department. In addition, fellowships in cardiothoracic surgery and trauma/critical care have been developed.

Dr. O'Leary worked diligently to reinvigorate the Department of Surgery and the entire School of Medicine in the aftermath of Katrina. He retired in June 2007 as Emeritus Professor and Emeritus Chairman to accept a position at the newly formed Florida International University College of Medicine in Miami, fulfilling a long-held desire to return to his native Florida.

හ⊗ల

Howard J. Osofsky, MD, PhD

Although a Department of Neuropsychiatry existed at LSU School of Medicine since its inception, most Chairmen stayed for only brief periods of time and left little mark on the history of the School.

That all changed in 1986 with the arrival of Dr. Osofsky, who had been serving as Chief of Psychiatry at the Menninger Foundation and Visiting Scientist at the Weizman Institute in Rehovot, Israel.

Originally trained as an Obstetrician Gynecologist and after rising to become Professor of Ob/Gyn at the Temple University School of Medicine in Philadelphia, he made a career switch of major proportions and soon returned to the top of his field in another specialty.

His 20-plus years of service as Chair of Psychiatry has included active involvement in the Neuroscience Center of Excellence and his being named to the John and Kathleen Bricker Chair of Psychiatry at LSUHSC. He also served as Chairman of Psychiatry at Touro Infirmary from 1987 – 2001 and Director of the Woldenberg Center for Gerontological Studies in New Orleans.

In 1999 he was chosen to be the first recipient of the National Recognition Award for Best Chair of a Department of Psychiatry from the American Academy of Child and Adolescent Psychiatry in appreciation of his outstanding support and promotion of Child and Adolescent Psychiatry. And in the aftermath of Hurricane Katrina he worked tirelessly to restore and provide mental health services to the citizens of New Orleans. He was recognized for that work on the one-year anniversary of the storm – August 29, 2006, by the New Orleans City Council.

In recruiting Dr. Osofsky, LSUHSC was equally blessed to recruit his wife, Dr. Joy Osofsky. An outstanding Psychologist who trained at Syracuse University she has served as Professor of Pediatrics and Psychiatry at LSUHSC since 1986.

She has served also on the faculty of the University of New Orleans and the University of London as a visiting professor. Internationally recognized for her work as an advocate for children and in violence prevention, she served for four years as President of the World Association for Infant Mental Health and for three years as President of Zero to Three/National Center for Infants, Families and Children, and has co-chaired the Louisiana Violence Prevention Task Force.

ΩCR

Richard M. Paddison, MD

Born in Rochester, New York, Dr. Richard M. Paddison grew up in Savannah, Georgia, cultivating a love for the southern United States. He went to medical school at Duke and trained in Neurology in Philadelphia under Bernard Alpers, the leading neurologist of the era. He came to LSU in 1955 and began shaping generations of students into strong clinicians and later into dedicated alumni. In his thirty years with the LSU School of Medicine, Dr. Paddison made numerous contributions to the strength of the school through his medical work and his commitment to institutional development. He was unfailingly polite and kind, but he was big and loud and usually scared the pants off the students. His attire was often unusual. One colleague remembers him owning a pair of pants decorated with whales and another pair covered in French horns. He owned a bright yellow suit which earned him the nickname of the "Worlds Largest Canary." This was of course never mentioned to his face.

His professional accomplishments are easy to enumerate. He was a full professor five years after his coming to the medical school and he became the first chairman of Neurology in 1965, the year that department became independent from Psychiatry. He served in that capacity until 1975 when he was succeeded by Dr. Earl Hackett and became the organizer and first director of LSU's physician group practice, the LSU Medical and Surgical Clinic. In this way, he brought his fellow faculty members into a single private practice initiative in a single location.

In 1980, Dr. Paddison also coordinated the beginnings of a modern Medical Alumni Association and was ultimately named an honorary alumnus of the School for his efforts. In June 1984, he oversaw the founding of the Committee of 100 - Champions of Excellence, a group of core supporters of the School of Medicine who have pioneered efforts to

Richard M. Paddison, MD

provide funding for professorships in the School. In this early effort, he was aided by **Dr. Cecil C. "Cy" Vaughn ('58)** and **Dr. Bernard Samuels** of the Class of 1957. This group would honor Dr. Paddison himself in 1989.

In addition, the alumni established the Richard M. Paddison Medical Alumni Association Award to honor Dr. Paddison's core values. It is awarded to a graduating senior at pre-commencement. The recipient is selected by his/her classmates as the graduate that they would choose as their personal physician. For this reason, the recipient of the Paddison Award must have developed qualities such as compassion, integrity, sincerity, and personal care of patients throughout their years in medical school. More than that, however, this student must also embody the spirit of Dr. Paddison, a man who never tolerated substandard medical care but who always strove to provide only the best for his patients.

Dr. Paddison became seriously ill in 1984 and retired, leaving to his successor, **Dr. Russell Klein ('59)**, a firm foundation on which to build the modern Medical Alumni Association. Dr. Paddison died in 2000, serving LSU as a volunteer for the last 16 years of his life. At his funeral service he was eulogized by Dr. Klein as "a physician's physician, a man of candor and conviction, loving, giving and reliable." He was all that and more.

ഇൻ

Warren C. Plauché, MD ('57)

It takes some people a long time before they decide to pursue their dream but at age 43 and after years of private practice as an Ob/Gyn, Warren Plauché yielded to a long suppressed wish for a role in academic medicine. In doing this he was guided by Abe Mickal, the Chairman at LSU, an old friend, who had done the same thing years earlier. As Warren later said "the fates had spoken" and he accepted a position on the faculty in 1977.

He threw himself into all aspects of academic life, including research, writing, teaching and patient care. He did ground-breaking research in amniotic fluid analysis and in this, he mentored Dr. Sebastian Faro. Faro ultimately became Chairman of Ob/Gyn at the University of Chicago.

Warren did research on numerous medical diseases in the pregnant patient, including myasthenia gravis in pregnancy, and helped to shape the concept of Maternal Fetal Medicine as an Ob/Gyn subspecialty.

As a joke for his retirement from LSU, Dr. Plauché, a prolific artist, was presented with a composite picture featuring the artist posing with his artwork displayed on a French Quarter fence... his next career, perhaps?

photo montage by Virginia Howard

Warren was also lead editor and lead author of the well-received text *Surgical Obstetrics*, and he served as an examiner for the Ob/Gyn Boards for ten consecutive years.

When Paul Larson stepped down as Dean and was replaced by Robert Dyer as Interim Dean, it created a problem. Although Dyer was Associate Dean at the time, he was principally a PhD anatomist who knew little about clinical medicine. To fill the gap, he asked Warren to serve as Associate Dean for Clinical Affairs, which both gave Dyer credibility and good advice, and allowed Warren to supervise and improve the Office of Graduate Medical Education.

Soon after Bob Daniels became Dean, Warren became the Executive Associate Dean, supervising development of the AHEC program and overseeing the reaccreditation of the Medical School and several departments. So impressive was his work that the Liaison Committee of Medical Education asked him to lend his expertise to other medical schools.

After 21 years at the School, Warren elected to retire, but not before the Alumni Association dedicated the **Warren C. Plauché, MD ('57)**, Professorship of Maternal Fetal Medicine.

In retirement Warren threw himself full time into a hobby he had had for many years, painting, principally in watercolor. He has exhibited in the U.S and Europe and collectors in both places have praised and acquired his work. In the U.S., he divides his time between Georgia and Louisiana, but travels the world as well.

Howard Randall, PhD

An outstanding renal physiologist who trained at the University of Rochester, Dr. Randall came to the School of Medicine in 1965 as instructor of Physiology. He was a strong addition to the Department that A. Sidney Harris had developed, but his major contribution to the School of Medicine started in 1977 when he was named Associate Dean for Student Affairs succeeding Dr. Paul Larson, who had been named Dean.

An advisor to literally thousands of students, he helped guide career choices and residency site selections. He combined knowledge with compassion, integrity and approachability.

In the aftermath of Hurricane Katrina he moved from his destroyed home in New Orleans to Birmingham, Alabama, to be near family. He retired in November 2005 after helping the Class of 2006 to select residency positions.

He fell ill soon after from carcinoma of the colon, which had metastasized to the liver. Opting for comfort care only, he passed away in May 2006. He is fondly remembered for his generous nature, wit and dedication to students.

Dr. Joseph DelCarpio succeeded him as Associate Dean for Student Affairs.

ഇറ

James D. Rives, MD

Dr. James D. Rives served as Surgery Department Chair from 1947 until 1962. He had been a member of the Department since 1932, when he accompanied Dr. Urban Maes to LSU from Tulane. Renowned for his dexterity and diagnostic skill, he was a sought-after consultant.

The Department expanded under Rives, both in number of trainees and the scope of their training. He encouraged both basic and clinical research among the faculty and helped them gain membership in many major surgical societies. He brought many important surgeons into the Department, including Dr. Howard Mahorner, who would one day be elected President of the American College of Surgeons; Charles Miangolarra, who had been Chief of Surgery for the 64th General Hospital; Walter Becker and "Septic Sam" Romano.

Jimmy Rives in coat and tie conducting the "Surgery Pit" in the Amphitheater on the 12th floor at Charity Hosspital circa 1959

Rives was beloved by those who trained under him, and led by **Dr. Donald B. Williams ('37)**, a prominent Lafayette surgeon, they formed the James D. Rives Surgical Society in 1964 and initiated the Rives Visiting Lectureship. The Rives Society remains the oldest continually active organization at LSU Medical School. It and the Medical Alumni Association dedicated the James D. Rives MD Professorship of Surgery in 1994.

Upon his retirement in 1962 the students staged their own version of a popular television program of the era, "This Is Your Life," bringing together many of his friends and colleagues to honor him. Dr. Rives passed away in 1975 at the age of 82.

The Rives Society renamed itself in 2007. In recognition of the service of Dr. Rives' successor, Dr. Isidore Cohn, Jr., it became the Isidore Cohn, Jr. – James D. Rives Surgical Society.

80CB

John Salvaggio, MD ('57)

After graduation from the School of Medicine, Dr. Salvaggio did an internship and residency on the LSU Medicine Service at Charity. He then journeyed to Boston taking a fellowship in Allergy and Immunology at Massachusetts General Hospital.

For two years he studied under Dr. Francis Lowell, the foremost allergist of the day, and then returned to the School of Medicine to set up the Section of Allergy and Immunology in the Department of Medicine.

Two health problems would help catapult Salvaggio to international fame. The first was the problem of "epidemic asthma" in New Orleans. For years and on numerous occasions hundreds of asthmatic patients would turn up in the Charity E.R. and then as suddenly the epidemic would abate. With the help of his associate, **Dr. Russell Klein ('59)**, Salvaggio was able to investigate the epidemics and help bring them to an end.

Dr. Salvaggio's second big break came when he along with John Seabury, MD, Chief of Pulmonary at LSU, and **Howard Buechner, MD ('43)**, Chief of Medicine at the VA Hospital, solved the mystery of bagassosis. First described in the 1930s by two LSU faculty, Drs. Louis Monte and Oscar Blitz, the disease occurred among sugar-cane workers exposed to bagasse, the refuse of sugar cane after the juice was extracted. Others who lived or worked nearby were also affected.

Workers often suffered from severe respiratory problems, especially when they were exposed to bagasse that had been dried in the sun. Dr. Salvaggio and his coworkers showed that the patients were having allergic reactions from exposure to dust containing thermaphilic fungi that grew in the heat on the bagasse. Better storage practices and dust control eliminated the disease.

Dr. Salvaggio would later become president of the American Academy of Allergy and would then move to Tulane as Chairman of Medicine. This move was prompted by the selection of Dr. Calderone Howe to succeed the retiring Dr. G. John Buddingh as Chairman of Microbiology. Buddingh and Salvaggio had shared a close working relationship but this did not continue under Howe's administration.

Eventually Dr. Salvaggio would become Vice Chancellor of Research at Tulane, and serve as head of the combined LSU-Tulane Clinical Research Center at Charity Hospital for several years. In 1992 he would author the definitive history of Charity Hospital. He would die from cardiac disease in 1999 at the age of 66.

ႸჂᏆᎸ

Charles "Bo" Sanders, MD ('64)

Charles Van Sanders, MD ('64), never planned to spend his professional career in New Orleans. A Leesville, Louisiana, native, he took his internal medicine training in Shreveport under **Dr. Ike Muslow ('48)**, Chief of Medicine at Confederate Memorial Medical Center, who had served for many years on the faculty of the School of Medicine in New Orleans. Originally Dr. Sanders considered a residency in Ob/Gyn, but two months with Dr. Muslow turned him permanently toward Internal Medicine.

Early on, he became fascinated by infectious diseases, and urged on by Dr. Muslow, he trained for two years in the subspecialty under Dr. Jay Sanford in Dallas.

He decided on a career in academic medicine and hoped to secure a position at the new School of Medicine in Shreveport, but construction was lagging, and no position was available. Dr. Muslow, who would ultimately serve as Dean in Shreveport, offered to make a call to Dr. Fred Allison, then Chairman of Medicine in New Orleans, and in short order Dr. Sanders joined Dr. Harry Dascomb in the Section of Infectious Diseases. It was July 1, 1970.

Dr. Sanders found the first months difficult. Charity was a much more primitive facility than the Medical Center in Dallas or even Confederate in Shreveport. Research was possible but not easy, and the clinical workload was heavy. Buoyed by Dr. Dascomb's encouragement as well as the addition to the faculty of two classmates, Drs. Joseph Biundo in Rheumatology and Tom McCaffrey in Gastroenterology, he decided to stay rather than take a position in Dallas. It was a decision that would benefit LSU for decades.

Dr. Sanders would work his way up through the ranks, and when Dr. Harry Dascomb was named Medical Director of Charity Hospital, Dr. Sanders was appointed Section Chief of Infectious Diseases. He would serve in that capacity for 13 years. In an odd turn of fate, Dr. Dascomb would retire in a year, after contracting bacterial endocarditis, a condition he had studied for his entire career. Dr. Dascomb would be succeeded as Charity Medical Director by Dr. John Barry Bobear, an expert on pulmonary tuberculosis, Section Head of Pulmonary Disease, and President of the Charity Hospital Medical Staff.

As Section Chief, Dr. Sanders immediately recruited to strengthen the Section of Infectious Diseases' teaching, research and clinical care. Robert Marier, MD, would join him from Yale, ultimately becoming Medical Director of University Hospital, then Dean of the Medical School. Two other noteworthy recruits were **George Karam ('77)**, who would become Chief of Medicine at Earl K. Long Hospital, and David Martin from the U.S. Public Health Service, who would eventually succeed him as Section Chief.

In order to strengthen the teaching of Infectious Diseases citywide, Dr. Sanders reached out to George "Kin" Pankey, Chief of ID at Ochsner, and William Mogabgab, Chief of ID at Tulane, to develop a citywide infectious-diseases conference. Started in 1975, this conference, which was the brainchild of Dr. Sanders, is still going strong today. Dr. Sanders also helped set up an NIH-sponsored AIDS Clinical Trial Unit.

In 1987, Dr. Fred Allison, Department of Medicine Chair for 19 years, retired to his native Tennessee. John Wilbur, MD, longtime Chief of Endocrinology, was appointed Acting Chair. Wilbur coveted the permanent position, but he was solely a research scientist in a department with heavy clinical responsibilities. This put him at a distinct disadvantage as Dean Daniels wanted to strengthen the clinical enterprise. Dr. Wilbur would leave within a year of Dr. Allison's retirement.

Dean Robert Daniels then approached Dr. Sanders for advice about a new Acting Chairman. Dr. Sanders suggested that Dr. Daniels name a topnotch clinician. Since there wasn't a better one in the place, Dr. Sanders got the "Acting Head" designation, and after a national search, he got the job on a permanent basis.

A skilled negotiator, he convinced the Dean to fund 20 new faculty positions in the Department. At the suggestion of Dr. Sanders, the Section of Emergency Medicine, led by **Dr. Albert Lauro ('54)**, a towering figure in the subspecialty nationally, brought in Dr. Keith Van Meter and several other faculty, including **Dr. Peter DeBlieux ('88)**, to elevate the section to national stature. Dr. Luke Glancy was brought in to lead Cardiology; Rheumatology and Physical Medicine were split into separate sections, and the newly recruited Dr. Warren Summer, made Pulmonary into an incredibly productive section. **Cathi Fontenot, MD ('84)**, led the Section of Comprehensive Medicine until called to be Medical Director at Charity Hospital. Although Dr. Sanders is currently the longest serving Chair of Medicine at any School of Medicine, he acknowledges the contributions of his vice chairs, **Dr. Fred Lopez ('90)**, Dr. Juzar Ali, Dr. Carol Mason, and Dr. Judd Shellito, for the success of the department.

In 2008, Dr. Sanders received the Founders' Medal from the Southern Society for Clinical Investigation. Given annually to only one person, the medal recognizes the accomplishments of a national leader in medicine.

☙❧

John Seabury, MD, and Harry Dascomb, MD

In many ways they were an unlikely duo. They both arrived at LSU in the mid 1940s, Harry from the University of Rochester (NY) and John from the University of Michigan. Harry, Hollywood-handsome (a daughter would become Miss USA), and so fashionable a dresser that he was nicknamed "The Cat," was outgoing.

John, who often dressed as if he shopped at Goodwill, was quiet and did not say three words if two would suffice. But both were brilliant and kind. The lead author who worked with Dr. Seabury for years recalls working late one Saturday afternoon in the office adjacent to Dr. Seabury's lab and noticed the unmistakable aroma of seafood gumbo. In the lab Dr. Seabury was using Bunsen burners and labware to heat the gumbo. Asked why, he said that a patient from "bayou country" being treated for pulmonary histoplasmosis was so homesick and despondent that he was threatening to desert. John thought a bowl of gumbo would cheer him up. He did not desert.

John was one of the most widely educated physicians ever to serve on the faculty. The son of a well known Detroit urologist who also practiced dermatology, he worked in his father's office from early teenage.

Before going to medical school he received a master's degree in tropical medicine in California. Between his first and second year of medical school he spent a year as a graduate assistant in anatomy and pharmacology. During his residency at the University of Michigan he also did cardiac and pulmonary research.

Before coming to New Orleans he had been a Markle Scholar in Medicine serving a fellowship in Tropical Medicine under the auspices of the U.S. Army.

Both Dascomb and Seabury would become internationally known for work in the diagnosis and management of mycotic infections especially of the lung and nervous system. Harry would become the first "Medical Director" at Charity Hospital. John would also serve as Acting Chairman of Medicine after the departure of Dr. Edgar Hull, to Shreveport and before the arrival of Dr. Fred Allison, from the University of Mississippi. Harry's son, Alan, would graduate from the School of Medicine in 1968 and carve out a brilliant career as a pathologist.

Each would retire after 30 years of service, John to Mamou, Louisiana, and Harry to North Carolina. John would return to New Orleans after 10 years, only to die in Tomball,

Texas, after Katrina forced his evacuation. He was 90. Dr. Dascomb would live until 2008, dying in North Carolina at age 91.

Grateful faculty members and alumni established Professorships of Medicine in honor of each upon their retirement. John Bobear, a longtime colleague of Dr. Seabury, led the effort for his Professorship and **Ralph Lupin ('56)** and **Arnold Lupin ('59)** of the Lupin Foundation led the effort for Dr. Dascomb.

In an odd twist of fate Dr. Bobear, a Seabury protégé, would succeed Dr. Dascomb as Medical Director at Charity after Dascomb, who suffered from mitral valve prolapse, contracted bacterial endocarditis, a disease he had studied all his life, and was forced to retire. Dr. Bobear would subsequently serve for many years as Executive Director of the Louisiana State Board of Medical Examiners.

ഇരു

John Spitzer, MD

The successor to Dr. A. Sidney Harris Head of the Department of Physiology, John J. Spitzer, MD, came to the LSU Medical Center in 1973. He was accompanied by his wife Judy A. Spitzer, PhD, an outstanding scientist who accepted an appointment in the LSU Department of Medicine with a joint appointment in Physiology.

Spitzer bolstered the teaching, research and graduate programs of the already active department by adding new faculty and attracting substantial outside research and training support from national funding agencies. The early addition of new faculty included Johnny Porter, who received his PhD from the Medical Center; Dr. Harvey I. Miller, a former graduate student of Dr. Spitzer's who previously held appointments at Jefferson and Hahnemann Medical Colleges; and John Little, MD, PhD, a New Zealander coming from the Medical School of the University of Rochester. The various academic functions of the department were further strengthened by the appointments of Dr. Michael Levitzky from Albany, an enthusiastic and effective teacher who also lent invaluable assistance to the Medical Center concerning accreditation and other administrative matters, and Paul S. Roheim, MD, from the Albert Einstein Medical Center, whose research group helped significantly to promote interdisciplinary research activities.

Dr. Spitzer's emphasis on collaborative and interdisciplinary research and training efforts were strongly supported by national funding agencies resulting in two multi-year NIH Program Project Grants (one under Dr. Spitzer's, the other under Dr. Roheim's direction), two multi-year NIH Training Grants (supporting both PhD candidates and postdoctoral fellows), an NIH Alcohol Research Center Grant (that continues to be successful after the retirement of Dr. Spitzer, its first Director) in addition to a variety of individual research grants from several national granting agencies. Thus, the Department at the LSU Medical Center became one of the very few Physiology Departments housing two Program Projects and two NIH Training Grants at the same time and later also serving as the home of an NIH Research Center Grant.

Because of the expanded research funding, the appointment of several strong new faculty members and the productive collaborative efforts of a number of senior faculty members (e.g. John Spitzer, Paul Roheim, Judy Spitzer, Gregory Bagby, Charles Lang and others), as well as numerous other faculty, the Department was also able to mentor junior faculty members by involving them in collaborative research up to the point where a number of them were successful in achieving complete independence, including their own NIH research funding.

The Department was also proud of its teaching efforts as well as its endeavor focused on graduate students to help them become good teachers. It is also worth mentioning that the Department of Physiology "produced" several notable administrators, e. g., a Dean of the School of Allied Health (Jimmy Cairo), two Associate Deans (Howard Randall and Kathleen McDonough), a Department Head (Patricia Molina), a Department Co-Chair (Charles Lang) and a Basic Science Curriculum Coordinator (Michael Levitzky).

Several members of the Department also represented LSUHSC on numerous nationwide and international educational and research forums and served in leadership roles.

In recognition of Dr. Spitzer's outstanding achievements, the LSU System designated him a Boyd Professor in 1991, the highest academic honor it can bestow. The LSU School of Medicine named him the Richard C. Ashman, PhD, Professor in 1996.

In 2001, Dr Spitzer announced his retirement. Dr. Kathleen McDonough was appointed Interim Head and a national search was conducted. Dr. William Chilian from the University of Wisconsin took over as Head of the Department. He relinquished the position in the aftermath of Hurricane Katrina and Dr. Michael Levitzky was named Acting Head. After a national search, Dr. Patricia Molina became the new Head of the Department in 2008.

৪০০৪

William H. Stewart, MD ('45)

One of the most honored and respected of alumni, Dr. Stewart was the son of the School's second and long-serving Chairman of Pediatrics, Dr. Chester Stewart, who came to LSU from Minnesota in 1941 with an MD and two PhDs. After serving in the Army and training in Pediatrics, Dr. Stewart entered the United States Public Health Service in 1951. Initially Dr. Stewart worked with Dr. Alexander Langmuir, a world famous epidemiologist with the Communicable Disease Center in Atlanta, Georgia, preparing the United States for "germ warfare," as the Korean War was then raging. Subsequently, Dr. Stewart moved to Washington, DC, and worked with the NIH on heart disease prevention, ultimately becoming Director of the National Heart Institute. He would rise steadily through the ranks, and in 1965 he would be named by then-President, Lyndon B. Johnson, as Surgeon General of the United States. He would be the youngest person ever appointed to that post. He was 44 at the time of his appointment.

He served as Surgeon General for four years, pushing the use of warning labels on cigarette packs and implementing the Civil Rights Act of 1964 as it applied to hospitals receiving Medicaid and Medicare funding.

In 1969, he declined reappointment as Surgeon General to become Chancellor of the Medical Center, a post that he would hold until 1974. In that year he was appointed Secretary of the Department of Health and Human Resources for the State of Louisiana.

He would be succeeded as Chancellor by Dr. Allen Copping, Dean of the School of Dentistry, and would serve as DHH Secretary for three years. He would then return to LSU, serving as the Chairman of the Department of Public Health and Preventive Medicine until 1986, when he retired.

During Dr. Stewart's tenure as Chancellor of the Medical Center the School of Allied Health was founded under its first dean, Dr. Stanley Abadie. The Bogalusa Heart Study also began during Dr. Stewart's tenure. For his life's work, Dr. Stewart received honorary degrees from seven different universities and served a term as President of the Association of Military Surgeons. He would be named Alumnus of the Year by the School of Medicine in 1999.

The Committee of 100 – Champions of Excellence honored Dr. Stewart in 2002 by dedicating a Chair in the Department of Pediatrics in his name. Dr. Stewart passed away in 2008.

ℰℭℛ

Jack Perry Strong, MD ('51)

Some faculty members in the history of the School of Medicine tower above their contemporaries, and Dr. Jack Perry Strong most definitely fits in this category. He brought strength of character, personality, medical skill, a potent intellect and personal dedication to the LSU School of Medicine, as the longest serving Departmental Chair in School history.

Interestingly, Dr. Strong did not always believe that LSU would be his permanent professional home. After graduating in 1951, and interning in Alabama, Dr. Strong was recruited to the Pathology Department in 1952 as an assistant. (See photograph on page 172 of the Department of Pathology team at work during the 1950s.) He believed he would stay at LSU for a few years and then not necessarily remain even in the field of pathology. Instead, he's been with the LSU Department of Pathology for over fifty years—over forty of those as the head of the department.

Under Dr. Strong's leadership, the Department of Pathology became a renowned leader in clinical research. In this, Dr. Strong has led by example. His focus has been cardiovascular pathology, and his work has been legendary. In 1958 Dr. Strong and fellow faculty member Dr. Henry McGill journeyed to Africa to study atherosclerosis in non-human primates. Their studies showed that baboons could be used to study atherosclerosis. Along with Dr. Russell Holman, Chairman of Pathology at the time, they showed the profound effect that diet changes could have on the development of atherosclerosis.

In the 1960s, Dr. Strong taught baboons how to smoke cigarettes. This seemingly strange feat allowed him to test the effects that smoking had on the heart. In 1976, Dr. Strong was the first researcher to link smoking to heart disease. It was not the last time that Dr. Strong and the Pathology staff would play a vital role in enhancing the public's knowledge about one of our most dangerous scourges.

Later, Dr. Strong participated as a principal investigator in the Pathobiological Determinants of Atherosclerosis in Youth study. This groundbreaking twelve-year study proved that heart disease risk factors are important from an early age. Dr. Strong and colleagues showed that cholesterol levels, smoking, and the buildup of scar tissue and arterial blockages have to be controlled from an early age in order to cut down on heart disease cases.

Dr. Strong became Departmental Chair in 1966. His immediate predecessor was Dr. Henry C. McGill, who left to help organize the new University of Texas Medical School at San Antonio. Dr. McGill had been appointed in 1960 following the untimely death from lung cancer of Dr. Russell Holman, who had been Chairman since 1946.

Dr. Strong's love for LSU is boundless, and his work on behalf of his alma mater has been tireless and effective. He organized the first Alumni giving program "The Alumni Challenge Fund" in 1966 at the Class of '51's reunion. This was pivotal in the evolution of the modern Office of Alumni Affairs. He also functioned as Chairman of the School of Medicine's Long Range Planning Committee, which produced the plan to move much of the campus from its Tulane Avenue location to its current site on Bolivar and Gravier Street. He has been honored many times for his work. He was named the first Boyd Professor at the School of Medicine, the highest scholarly recognition that can be bestowed on a faculty member by the LSU System. The Boyd Professorships program was established by the LSU System in 1952. It is named for two brothers, David French Boyd and Thomas Duckett Boyd, who between them were President of the LSU System for 50 years. Dr. Strong has also been recognized internationally, receiving the Gold Medal Award from the International Academy of Pathology in 2002.

A Chair in Pathology was dedicated in Dr. Strong's name by the Committee of 100 – Champions of Excellence in 1992 in recognition of his service to the School and the profession.

Perhaps the most unusual honor awarded to Dr. Strong came in 2008 from the Emperor of Japan who chose him to receive "The Order of the Rising Sun, Gold Rays with Neck Ribbon." The award, established in 1875 and rarely presented to a non-Japanese citizen, honored Dr. Strong for his efforts to promote exchange between Japanese and American research scientists.

In 2009, Dr. Strong elected to step down as Chair after a 43-year run. A national search was conducted and Dr. Richard VanderHeide, Professor of Pathology at Wayne State University School of Medicine, a noted cardiovascular researcher, was named to succeed him.

෫০৪

Warren Summer, MD

He arrived at LSU in 1983 after serving for many years on the faculty of Johns Hopkins School of Medicine. He had graduated with honors from Georgetown University, trained in internal medicine in New York, in pulmonary disease at Georgetown, and had been in charge of Pulmonary Physiology at the National Naval Medical Center before moving to Hopkins.

He made an immediate impact at the School of Medicine both in the clinical and research arenas through the receipt of many major grants and participation in countless projects. Author or co-author of over 200 articles and 67 book chapters, he is internationally recognized for his body of research work.

Both in the public and the private sector, Warren became a sought-after consultant, and his diagnostic skill and meticulous follow-up earned high praise.

Over the years he has held many important positions in the American Thoracic Society and the American College of Chest Physicians, where he served as Governor of the Louisiana Chapter. He has been an invited lecturer at the University of Alabama, University of Wisconsin, and George Washington University, to name but three, and has received The Breath of Life Award from the American Thoracic Society.

At LSU he has served on numerous faculty committees, helped to educate countless students and residents, run major hospital departments at MCLANO and University Hospital, and been the mentor in chief for many pulmonary and critical care fellows.

His mentorship of younger faculty has been outstanding. Juzar Ali, **Ben DeBoisblanc ('81)** and **Peter DeBlieux ('88)** have been appointed to important positions at University Hospital and Steve Nelson has been named Dean of the School of Medicine.

A grateful School of Medicine named Warren as the first **Howard Buechner, MD, ('43M)** Professor of Medicine, when that professorship was created.

When he stepped down as Section Chief, Dr. Judd Shellito, another outstanding protégé was named to replace him. The Committee of 100 – Champions of Excellence of the Medical Alumni Association dedicated the Warren Summer, MD, Professorship of Medicine in 2010.

೮೦೦೪

Austin Sumner, MD

Following an eleven-year run as Department of Neurology Head by long-time faculty member Dr. Earl Hackett, the administration decided, on his retirement, for an external search to find his successor. The search committee soon zeroed in on Dr. Austin Sumner, who had been serving as Professor of Neurology at the University of Pennsylvania.

He had gone to Penn after a stint on the faculty of the University of California. A New Zealand native, he had graduated from the University of Otago and had then trained at the National Hospital for Neurology and Neurosurgery in London, England, before making his way to the U. S.

An expert in peripheral neuropathy he would serve on six occasions as a Visiting Professor at other universities and on the Editorial Board of eight journals.

He would be recognized for his leadership by being named the first Richard M. Paddison, MD, Professor of Neurology at the School of Medicine.

In acquiring the talents of Dr. Sumner for the School of Medicine, the Health Sciences Center has been equally lucky to have had Dr. Jane Sumner, an outstanding nursing educator, join the faculty of the School of Nursing.

In addition to building the Department of Neurology, Dr. Sumner would provide steady leadership to the LSU Healthcare Network and the Professional Practice Association. He would author over 60 scientific articles and numerous book chapters.

In his research work he would often collaborate with Dr. John England, whom he recruited to the Department. Dr. England served at LSU from 1992-2001. He then moved to Montana to serve as Chairman of Neurology at Deaconess Billings Clinic. Dr. England returned to LSU in 2007 to become Dr. Sumner's successor when Dr. Sumner retired as Chairman of the Department.

෨ଓ

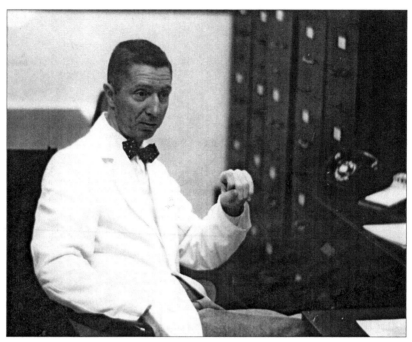

Dr. Swartzwelder

J. Clyde Swartzwelder, PhD

A native of Massachusetts who came south for a PhD in Parisitology from Tulane, Dr. Swartzwelder began a 38-year career on the faculty in 1937. It was interrupted by a four-year stint in the Army as a malaria control specialist in the South Pacific.

He retired in 1975 as Chairman of Tropical Medicine and Parisitology, a position that he had held from 1960, when Tropical Medicine morphed from a Division of Medicine to a full-fledged department. He was succeeded by Dr. David Clyde, a specialist in Tropical Medicine from Great Britain, but remained on the faculty for several more years.

During his years at LSU he worked closely with Dr. Frye and also with such distinguished scientists as Dr. Henry Meleney and Dr. Antonio Pena Chavarria and others in Panama and other Central American countries. His research interests included amebiasis, Chagas disease and the development of antihelminthics. He co-authored *Tropical Medicine* with Dr. Frye, authored 140 articles and was a contributor to the *Manual of Clinical Microbiology* and *Dorland's Medical Dictionary*.

Dr. Swartzwelder died in 2002 at the age of 91.

ಲೊ‌ಞ

Theodore Francis Thurmon III ('62)

On January 3, 2005, when **Theodore "Ted" Thurmon ('62)** suffered a heart attack that claimed his life, Louisiana lost a native son who pioneered the study of medical and clinical genetics in Louisiana.

A Baton Rouge native, Ted received his undergraduate degree from LSU in 1958, and his MD from LSUSM-NO four years later. After an internship in pediatrics at the US Navy Hospital in Pensacola and residency at the US Navy Hospital in Philadelphia, he trained under Dr. Hope Punnett in the emerging field of cytogenetics. After two years of training, Ted completed a one-year fellowship in medical genetics at Johns Hopkins under Dr. Victor A. McKusick, who had done groundbreaking genetic research among the Amish.

In 1969, Ted accepted the position of Director of the new Birth Defects Center in the Department of Pediatrics at LSUSM-NO and thus became the first true medical and clinical geneticist in New Orleans. His role was crucial in establishing genetic services by the State. He successfully recruited the noted geneticist Yves Lacassie to the department to aid him in his work.

Because most of his patients lived in rural areas of Louisiana, had limited resources and could not travel long distances to see a specialist, Ted drove up and down country roads to set up satellite clinics, mainly in Acadiana. Ultimately, he organized multiple clinics, which led to identification of many rare autosomal recessive disorders, including Tay-Sachs disease, in the Acadian population. He did an enormous amount of field work at courthouses and churches throughout Acadiana, patiently sifting through birth, marriage and baptismal certificates to prove consanguinity in families affected by rare disorders. In so doing, he also established the labyrinth of family connections that established the Acadians as a population for genetic study.

He taught medical and clinical genetics to several generations of medical students, residents and pediatricians at the LSUHSC-NO and Shreveport, where he moved in 1986, and authored two genetics books. An exceptionally well-rounded and knowledgeable geneticist, Ted's interests and publications covered a wide spectrum of issues in human, medical and clinical genetics, including new laboratory techniques, molecular biology and epidemiology.

೫ාඥ

Mervin Lee Trail, MD

When he served as Chairman of the Department of Otolaryngology at LSU, Merv Trail kept a simple sign in his office. It read "No Whining." Merv wasn't a whiner and he didn't like them. But he seemed to like just about everything else and everybody. If Merv had an enemy, no one ever knew it.

After graduating from the University of Maryland, serving in the Navy and training in Otolaryngology at Johns Hopkins, he journeyed south in 1968 at the urging of Dr. Charles Berlin and Dr. Irving Blatt, who was at that time Chairman of ENT at LSU. He joined the clinical faculty at the school and also threw himself into the civic life of his adopted city.

He would soon make profound marks on both the school and the city. At the school he would become a "geographic full time" faculty member and become Director of Residency Training. From there he would go on to become Professor in the Department.

Mervin Lee Trail, MD

In 1991 he become the founding director of the Stanley S. Scott Cancer Center at LSU and in 1993 would also become Departmental Chairman. In 1994 he was tapped to be Chancellor of the LSU Health Sciences Center succeeding Dr. Perry Rigby.

All the while he was making his mark on the civic and cultural life of the city. He served on the board of the New Orleans Tourist and Convention Commission, playing a leading role in luring Super Bowls, NCAA Final Fours, the Republican National Convention and the U.S. Olympic Trials to the City of New Orleans. He was a leader in the carnival organization Bacchus.

In 1997 he guided bills through the Louisiana Legislature that gave control of ten of the state's Charity Hospitals to LSU. They would prosper under his overall guidance.

In late December 2000 he suffered a severe stroke that proved fatal a few days later. LSU and the state lost a great and inspirational leader. The Medical Alumni Association, his "kids," the residents he trained and his many friends dedicated a Chair in Otolaryngology in his memory, and the LSU Board of Supervisors at the urging of the legislature named the Clinical Sciences Research Building the Merv Trail Building. It is the only time in the history of the school that an honor of such magnitude had ever been bestowed. No one deserved it more.

சு

Ronald Welsh, MD

Ron Welsh arrived at LSU in 1957 after a stint as Chief of Pathology at the U.S. Public Health Service Hospital in Galveston and a part-time teaching position at his University of Texas alma mater.

His training after graduation in 1951 had been through the Public Health Service in New Orleans and Baltimore. He was well familiar with the city and the School of Medicine, so it was easy for Russell Holman, the Chief of Pathology, to lure him to take a faculty position. The wide variety of clinical material at Charity and the presence of Jimmy Rives in Surgery and Edgar Hull in Medicine, two men he admired, helped the recruitment.

In only six years he rose to the rank of Professor of Pathology. This meteoric rise was fueled by his remarkable skill as a surgical pathologist, a skill noted both at Charity Hospital and in the private community where he was a sought after consultant, and by his work with the American Cancer Society. He was particularly cited for his work in the early diagnosis of cervical cancer.

He served for 17 years as Chair of Professional Education Committee of the Louisiana Division of the American Cancer Society and for four years on the Board of Directors of the American Cancer Society.

He served as Consultant to the AMA Council on Scientific Affairs for 20 years and to the Veterans Hospital in New Orleans for over 25 years.

The author of numerous articles in the scientific literature he has served on the editorial board of both the *American Journal of Clinical Pathology* and *Pathologist*. A grateful School of Medicine Alumni Association dedicated the Ronald A. Welsh, MD, Professorship of Pathology to him in June 1998.

80(3

Marilyn Zimny, PhD

Few educators in the School of Medicine commanded more respect and loyalty from faculty and students than Dr. Marilyn Zimny. Born in 1927 in Chicago, Dr. Zimny came to LSU in 1954 after receiving her PhD in anatomy from Loyola University in Chicago. Ten years later, she became a full professor.

Marilyn Zimny, PhD

Her academic prowess was evident from the beginning. She garnered large amounts of federal research funding for her projects and collaborated with faculty and students from around the School of Medicine. Her research spanned a gamut of topics which took her all over the world. She studied electron microscopy in Alaska and investigated mammalian hibernation at the Massachusetts Institute of Technology and in Helsinki, Finland. She maintained a long-term interest in the metabolism of hibernating animals. Students who helped with her research were affectionately known as her "ground squirrels." One of her most famous was **Larry Hollier, MD ('68)**, who would eventually become the Chancellor of the Health Sciences Center. Marilyn's specialized studies in degenerative arthritis, metabolism, and sports medicine made her a versatile asset in the research arsenal at the School of Medicine. She had 125 scientific publications, including 66 papers and 59 abstracts, making her not only a prolific writer but also an established authority in the Anatomy community nationally.

Nor were LSU students the only beneficiaries of her expertise. Dr. Zimny was also a member of the LSU team that helped the University of Costa Rica establish that country's first medical school in San Jose in the early 1960s. At the 25th anniversary of that school's first graduating class, Dr. Zimny was honored for her guidance and teaching excellence.

Dr. Zimny became the LSU School of Medicine's first female department head in 1975, when she was named head of the Department of Anatomy succeeding the late Dr. Melvin Hess. By this time, two decades' worth of students had learned at her feet, but her service to the Medical School and the entire Medical Center was far from over.

It was Dr. Zimny's personality as much as her teaching method that made her one of the most beloved figures in the history of the School of Medicine. With an imposing manner and a booming voice, Marilyn was a force to be reckoned with. She was a talented story teller, especially after she had imbibed a favorite libation "a Jack Daniel's Old Fashioned: very sweet, with extra Angostura bitters."

A close friend, Dr. Michael Levitsky of the Department of Physiology, once made the mistake of trying to match Marilyn drink for drink at a banquet. He failed.

Medical students named Zimny their favorite pre-clinical teacher three years in a row in the 1970s, while dental students named her their Most Popular Teacher in 1979. Dr. Zimny was also honored with the Distinguished Faculty Service Award as well as the 1987 Distinguished Faculty Fellowship and was inducted as an honorary member in the LSU chapter of Alpha Omega Alpha. In 1995, Dr. Zimny was recognized with a professorship of anatomy established in her name by the medical school's alumni; the following year, she was presented with the Women in Medicine Award.

National organizations also valued her leadership abilities. She served as president of both the Association of Anatomy Chairmen (AAC) and the Southern Society of Anatomists. She also served in several other leadership positions with the American Association of Anatomists throughout the 1980s. While with the AAC, Dr. Zimny was also Women Liaison Officer to the Association of American Medical Colleges continuing her work on behalf of women in medicine across the country.

In 1990, she was appointed Dean of the School of Graduate Studies and Vice-Chancellor for Academic Affairs, positions that she held until 1998, when she retired. Dr. Zimny was replaced as Anatomy Chairman by Dr. Sam McClugage who served as Interim Head for eighteen months until Dr. Ranney Mize assumed the Chair.

Two years after she retired, Dr. Zimny was called upon to serve as Interim Vice President for Academic Affairs with the LSU System and responded eagerly to the System's needs. She served in that position for nearly two years.

More than anything else in her career, Dr. Zimny treasured the rapport she cultivated with her students, and the success that these were able to achieve because of her tutelage. And she maintained contact with the School of Medicine until Katrina struck.

Severely affected by Hurricane Katrina, Dr. Zimny's health began to fail. Her physician diagnosed a recurrence of a malignant melanoma that had been treated years before. Chemotherapy was attempted initially but she then opted for comfort care only. Dr. Zimny died in January 2006 at the age of 79. In her will she provided funds to establish two professorships to support the Graduate School at the Health Sciences Center.

ഇൻ

ALUMNI HISTORY

and ACTIVITIES

*Left to right: Department of Pathology members in the 1950s: Drs. Henry McGill, **Jack Charles Geer** ('56), Russell Holman, and **Jack Strong** ('51). Drs. McGill, Strong, and Geer were known as "The Three Amigos." Dr. Geer became Chair of Pathology in Alabama, Dr. McGill in San Antonio, and Dr. Strong here. Dr. Holman served as head of the Department of Pathology from 1946 until his death in 1960.*

Alumni in Academics

Many alumni have distinguished themselves in academic careers. **William McCord ('39)** served for 11 years as President of the Medical University of South Carolina and was honored by the United Nations for his work in international healthcare. **Ralph Sanchez ('50)** became nationally known for his pioneering work in Continuing Medical Education, which efforts he started while at LSU when he was Professor of Family Medicine. He then moved to East Carolina School of Medicine where he continued his work until 1989. He was the first recipient of the Willard M. Duff Award from the Accreditation Council for Continuing Medical Education after the award's establishment in 1995.

Arthur Herold ('47) was honored many times for his research on diabetes by the American Diabetes Association, but in 1993 he was recognized for something quite unique. He was recognized as the second longest insulin user in the United States, having begun to receive insulin in 1923 at the age of two when his physician father diagnosed him with diabetes.

Ike Muslow ('48) went from being Professor of Medicine at the SOM in New Orleans to Professor of Medicine at Shreveport. He succeeded Dr. Edgar Hull as Dean there when Dr. Hull retired. When the Health Sciences Center in Shreveport was formed as a separate campus, he was named Vice Chancellor.

If **Jack C. Hughston ('43)** didn't invent the specialty of Orthopaedic Sports Medicine he was certainly one of its earliest and most successful pioneers. After a Charity internship and service in the army, he served a residency in Orthopaedics at Duke University, where he worked extensively with crippled children and developed an interest in athletic injuries. In 1952 he became team physician for the Auburn University football team.

He later opened a Sports Medicine Clinic in Columbus, GA, which ultimately grew to nine locations in two states; started the first Orthopaedic Sports Medicine Fellowship in the United States; opened the first-of-its-kind Sports Medicine Hospital; and served on the clinical faculty of several schools.

Able assistance was provided to him over time by **Champ Baker ('72),** who trained under Dr. Hughston and then succeed him as President of the Hughston Clinic. Dr. Hughston passed away in 2004.

Another outstanding sports medicine specialist is **James R. Andrews ('67)**. A champion at LSU (B.R.) in pole-vaulting and a world-class sailor, he serves as Clinical Professor of Orthopaedics at the University of Alabama, Birmingham, is founder of the Andrews Sports Medicine and Orthopaedic Center in Birmingham, and is Chairman of the American Sports Medicine Institute.

He serves as Orthopaedic consultant or Medical Director for six area colleges and has performed over 40,000 operations, many on professional athletes including Peyton Manning, Eli Manning, Michael Jordan, Shaquille O'Neal and Drew Brees.

Joseph Rozas ('57) was not only instrumental in the creation of the University of Nevada School of Medicine but served as its first Chairman of Ob/Gyn. A Chair was dedicated in his honor at the School. **Bettina Hillman ('55)** not only served as Professor of Pediatrics for many years at the SOM in Shreveport but received the Jerome Glaser Distinguished Service Award from the American Academy of Pediatrics in 1999.

Randall Marcus ('75) not only served as Professor of Orthopaedics at Case Western Reserve School of Medicine but also served as a Director of the American Board of Orthopaedics Surgery. **Barrett G. Haik ('76)** serves as the Hamilton Professor and Chairman of the Department of Ophthalmology at the University of Tennessee Memphis School of Medicine and a Regent of the American College of Surgeons. Before his appointment in Memphis he was Professor of Ophthalmology at Tulane.

Luis Balart, Jr. ('73) served as Professor of Medicine at LSU, following in the footsteps of his father, Luis Balart, Sr., MD, and then moved to Tulane. He was elected President of the American College of Gastroenterology, following there in the footsteps of a revered former LSU faculty member, the late G. Gordon McHardy.

A number of the original faculty of the School of Medicine came from Tulane to head departments at LSU. Over time we have often returned the favor. Both **Ed De Mouy ('57)** and **Hal Neitzschman ('65)** have served as Professor and Chair of Radiology there. Additionally, Hal served as President of the Medical Alumni Association. **Rich Strieffer ('77)** served as Professor and Chair of Family Medicine at Tulane and has been a national leader in his specialty, and **Ron Amadee ('81)** has served as Professor and Chair of Otolaryngology at Tulane Medical Center.

Terence Flotte ('86), a world-class geneticist, served as Professor and Chairman of Pediatrics at the University of Florida before moving on to become Dean at the University of Massachusetts School of Medicine. Another luminary in Massachusetts from LSU is **Arthur Day ('72)**, Professor of Neurosurgery at Harvard and Chair of Neurosurgery at Brigham and Woman's Hospital in Boston. Dr. Day took part of his training at Carraway Methodist Hospital in Birmingham, Alabama, which was founded by the father of LSU grad, **Benjamin Monroe Carraway ('35)** and grandfather of **Robert Carraway ('72).**

Female graduates have also distinguished themselves. **Pattie Van Hook ('52)** not only served as Assistant Dean at the School of Medicine in Shreveport but was also first woman to serve as President of the Louisiana State Medical Society.

Susan Day ('75) currently serves as program director for the Department of Ophthalmology at California Pacific Medical Center. She was President of the American Academy of Ophthalmology, served on the American Board of Ophthalmology, and is a sought-after pediatric ophthalmologist.

Mary Lipscomb ('67) serves as Professor and Chairman of Pathology at the University of New Mexico School of Medicine.

Mary Ella Sanders ('75) was not only an outstanding radiation oncologist but managed to serve at various times as Vice Chancellor at the Health Sciences Center in New Orleans, and later on the faculty of the School of Medicine in Shreveport. She also distinguished herself at different times as Chairman of the Board of Regents for Higher Education, President of the Medical Alumni Association, and Chairman of the Board of the LSU Health Sciences Foundation.

James Evans ('67) amassed an outstanding career as an administrator, surgeon, surgical oncologist and military physician. After serving his residency at LSU he took a fellowship at Roswell Park Memorial Institute in surgical oncology. Rising through the ranks he became Chair of Surgery at Mercer Medical College, Professor of Surgery at Shreveport, and finished his career at the State University of New York at Buffalo. He also found time to rise to the rank of Colonel in the U.S. Army Medical Corps, act as Advisor to the Veterans Administration, and be Chief Surgeon for the NATO Winter War Games staged by the U.S. Army. In between he found time to author 78 medical articles, 77 abstracts and 14 book chapters and monographs.

When **Stephen Mathes ('68)** died from amyotrophic lateral sclerosis in late 2007 the world lost one of its most innovative and productive plastic surgeons. His interest in the specialty began when, as an Army surgeon during Vietnam, he was called on to treat many wounded GIs. He joined the staff at the University of California, San Francisco, where he remained for 26 years, rising to Professor of Surgery and Chief of the Division. He authored six books, 223 articles and book chapters, was a visiting professor in 25 countries, and trained 62 plastic surgeons.

Described as a physician, technologist, researcher, and educator, **Brian Bergeron ('84)** has made his mark as the guru of the intersection of business and technology, concentrating on bioterrorism threat assessment. He serves as President of Archetype Technologies, is on the faculty of Harvard School of Medicine, editor of *Servo Magazine*, and is the author of 21 books and 50 technical articles.

He began his technology career at age nine when he began studying electronics, and by age 11 he was a licensed radio operator. He went on to build satellite communication systems, study at both LSU and Tulane as an undergraduate, and, while in medical school, open his first technology company. He has provided scientific support for computer-based testing done by both the National Board of Medical Examiners and the American Board of Family Practice.

Warren Jones, ('78), after retiring as a Captain in the U.S. Navy Medical Corps, became Associate Vice Chancellor at the University of Mississippi Medical Center, Professor of Family Medicine and Director of the Mississippi Area Health Education Centers. Another notable Mississippian is **William Rock ('69),** Professor of Pathology, who had previously served on the LSU faculty.

John Milam, ('60), Professor of Pathology at U.T. Houston; **Gordon Bernard, ('76)** Chief of Pulmonary/Critical Care at Vanderbilt; **Oscar Cruz ('87),** Chairman of Ophthalmology at St. Louis University; **Kevin Hardy ('80),** Professor of Medicine and Chief of Rheumatology at the University of Mississippi; and **Robert Bourge ('79),** Professor of Medicine, Radiology and Surgery at the University of Alabama, Birmingham, have all had outstanding careers.

O'Neill Barrett ('53) served for many years as Professor and Chairman of Medicine at the University of South Carolina School of Medicine. **Henry M. Selby ('43)** rose to prominence in New York as Chief of Radiology at the Sloan-Kettering Cancer Institute. He maintained a devotion to his alma mater, establishing a major student scholarship program, and in collaboration with his classmate and close friend, **D. Eldredge Bourgeois ('43),** established the Selby-Bourgeois Award. This award, the first of its kind at the School, recognized a faculty member for excellence in undergraduate teaching.

Other notable academics included **Roy Sessions ('62),** who served as Chairman of Otolaryngology first at Cornell Medical Center and then at Georgetown University. **Lawrence Kahn ('45)** served as Professor of Pediatrics at Washington University in St. Louis. **Harold Katner ('80),** an expert in Pediatric AIDS research, served as Professor at Mercer University. **Robert Dawson ('74)** served as Chief of Neuroradiology at Emory and **Jessie Hano ('61),** an outstanding nephrologist, was Professor of Medicine at Loyola of Chicago.

In 2009 **Charles Perniciaro ('83),** one of the nation's foremost experts in dermatopathology, was named "Practitioner of the Year" by the Florida Society of Dermatology and Dermatologic Surgeons. He had previously served on the LSU faculty and the faculty of Mayo Medical School and the University of Florida. Since 2001 he had been Chief of Dermatopathology for Bernhardt Laboratories.

೮౮೧ಌ

Alumni in Art and Literature

Said by one authority to have had more on-air television time than any other physician in history, **Walt Larimore ('77)** has parleyed his experience as a family physician, his writing and broadcasting talent and his strong Christian faith into a most unique career. Host for five years of "Ask the Family Doctor," a popular cable television show on the Fox Health Network, he has been seen by millions of Americans. As an author or co-author of eighteen books and 600 articles, he has received a number of literary awards. Much of his work has involved providing the lay public with medical information. In recognition of his work the American Academy of Family Physicians named him "America's Outstanding Physician Educator" in 1999. He currently serves as Vice President of Focus on the Family.

Other outstanding authors include **Bill Booth ('66),** who wrote the well-received *Blood of a Stranger,* a medical mystery.

Jean Persons ('50) wrote *From Dog Sleds to Float Planes: Alaskan Adventures in Medicine*, which told of her medical practice in one of the most remote and dangerous areas of that vast state.

Johnson Adeyanju ('89) authored a well-received medical mystery *Deadly Revenge*.

David Krueger ('73), after graduating from LSU in 1973 and training in psychiatry in Denver and psychoanalysis in Houston, practiced and taught for 26 years before founding Mentor Path, an executive coaching, publishing, and wellness firm. He has authored 15 books, including *Success and the Fear of Success in Women*, which was named to the Master List of the 100 Most Influential Professional Books of the 20th Century.

It isn't often that a medical student can claim authorship of a successful first book, but **Marc Matrana ('06)** did just that in 2005 when *Lost Plantation: The Rise and Fall of Seven Oaks* when published when he was a junior at LSUSOM. The book recounted the history of Louisiana's Seven Oaks Plantation, a plantation once owned during pre-Civil War times by the family of his late great-grandmother. This led him to an even more ambitious project: the history of 60 plantations (featuring plantations from every Southern state) all now destroyed. This book, *Lost Plantations of the South*, was published in 2008.

U. H. "Hank" Stoer (D'43) had a lifetime interest and hobby in drawing, painting, and photography that became a second career in 1985. In that year he retired as Chief of Pathology and Director of Laboratories at Schumpert Hospital in Shreveport, a position he had held for 30 years. His works have been avidly collected, he has served as president of several art societies in the Shreveport area and he has had a one-man show at the Karpeles Museum in Shreveport.

Thomas Guidry ('44) always prided himself on being a history buff and enthusiastic photographer. When he retired from medical practice in his adopted hometown of Natchez, Mississippi, he began a new career, collecting and restoring ancient deteriorating photographic negatives of people and places, many long gone, in and around Natchez. In all he collected and restored 75,000 negatives, preserving priceless history.

Sam Scurria ('62) began his art career in grammar school but put it and his interest in music on hold for 38 years. Both careers have since flourished, his art career as a noted watercolorist and his musical career as a saxophonist with two different orchestras, a 17-piece jazz band and a 30-piece classical orchestra. In addition, he has given generously of his time, providing music education to disadvantaged children, and as a hobby has collected and restored antique cars. His son Phil followed in his footsteps as a physician, graduating from LSU in 1986.

A. J. Friedman ('76) had a long-time interest in painting but it took the intervention of Hurricane Katrina and a temporary exile to Waycross, Georgia, to kick his artistic career into high gear. In Georgia and subsequently after returning to Louisiana, he has become not only a prolific but popular painter, with several shows and numerous collectors vying for his work.

Milburn Calhoun ('55) has for forty years been the owner of Pelican Publishing Company, which has published many best sellers.

෨ඁ

Alumni in Community Service

Being a great doctor made **Jack A. Andonie** ('62) an icon in the New Orleans area medical community, and that did lead to some of his fame. But what really propelled him toward renown, especially in the LSU community, was his innate decency.

It all began with a chance encounter with the then LSU football coach, Charlie McClendon. He was having a bad year and people were calling for his head. Jack wrote to and called Coach McClendon to offer words of encouragement. A friendship developed, they had dinner together, and Andonie, a Loyola University graduate, became an LSU booster – a big-time LSU booster –, and a collector of LSU sports memorabilia.

In time Andonie's house became overrun with memorabilia. By 1996 he would have amassed 13,000 separate items.

Back in the early 1980s, having at that time been the obstetrician for the wife of Governor Edwin Edwards' campaign manager, Jack invited the campaign manager to his home to show him his collection of LSU artifacts. The manager asked for permission to bring the Governor by. Jack agreed; the Governor came and was so impressed that he appointed Jack to the LSU Board of Supervisors. Jack served from 1984 to 1990 and then was reappointed in 1994 with terms that will not end until 2012.

Jack A. Andonie ('62)

So many people were impressed with Jack's memorabilia that the LSU System proposed the creation of the Jack and Priscilla Andonie Museum to house the 13,000 items on the Baton Rouge campus. With the full approval of his children, Jackie, Jon and Patrick, he donated the collection and the museum was built.

Jack's devotion to LSU has extended magnificently to his alma mater, the School of Medicine. He has served on the Alumni Board, ultimately as President, been named

Alumnus of the Year, and has had a Professorship in Ob/Gyn created in his name by friends and admirers.

He and his wife Priscilla live in New Orleans and although he has retired from his Ob/Gyn practice, he remains active in the work of the Hospice of New Orleans Program and in the work of the Catholic Archdiocese. He is on the Board of Holy Cross College and is an avid collector, now of religious art and saintly relics.

As a woman and as a physician, **Mary Lou Applewhite ('55)** was a trailblazer and she blazed those trails in many arenas. She was active on campus in Baton Rouge as an undergraduate and her devotion to its College of Basic Science led her to serve on the Alumni Board of Baton Rouge campus for many years, and as its President in 1991.

In 1999, she was named Alumnus of the Year in Baton Rouge, and when the College of Basic Science inaugurated a Hall of Distinction in 2007, she was the first inductee. A campus dormitory will also be named for her.

She has been active in the Department of Dermatology at the School of Medicine and an outstanding supporter of the Medical Alumni Association. She served for many years on the Council on Aging and as its President in 1978. She was President of the Louisiana Dermatological Association in 1980.

But perhaps her biggest groundbreaking occurred in 1992 when she became the first woman ever appointed to the Louisiana State Board of Medical Examiners. She retired from the Board in 1999, having served that year as its first female President. Now retired, she lives in New Orleans and continues to support the Medical Alumni Association.

After graduating from LSU (B.R.) in 1950 and being named "Air Force ROTC Distinguished Military Graduate," **Milton Charles Chapman ('59)** served five years in the Air Force. He graduated from the SOM in 1959, was named to Alpha Omega Alpha National Honor Medical Society, trained in Pediatrics, and then embarked on a 35-year career as a practicing physician.

Most people would count that a successful career. Not Milton. He served 12 years as a delegate to the AMA, gave advice on medical issues to three different Louisiana governors, served as President of Shreveport Medical Society and the Louisiana State Medical Society, and was named Chairman of the LSU Board of Supervisors. He helped found and served for 11 years on the Board of Directors of the Louisiana Medical Mutual Insurance Company, was recognized by President Ronald Reagan for founding "Operation Care," a program to provide healthcare to unemployed workers in Shreveport, was named to the LSMS Hall of Fame, and was named Alumnus of the Year by the School of Medicine in 1993.

Few alumni of the School of Medicine have had more distinguished careers than **Purnell Choppin ('53)**. A 1953 graduate, honored by the alumni for having the highest average in the graduating class and with two other prestigious awards in hand, he journeyed up river to St. Louis and did an internship and residency in Medicine at Barnes Hospital in St. Louis, Missouri.

After service in the Air Force, he became an investigator at the Rockefeller Institute, concentrating on virology research. In this career choice he was strongly influenced by his association as a student with Dr. Harry Dascomb, Chief of Infectious Disease and Professor of Medicine at LSUSOM.

Dr. Choppin rose steadily through the ranks, ultimately becoming the Leon Hess Professor, Vice President for Academic Programs, and Dean of Graduate School at Rockefeller University. In 1985, he left to become the Chief Scientific Officer and Vice President of the Howard Hughes Medical Institute. In 1987, he became President of the Institute, one of the

Purnell Choppin ('53)

world's largest philanthropic organizations. He held that post for 12 years.

In 2000, he became a Principal in the Washington Advisory Group, which provides consulting to universities, governments and non-profit groups.

Because of his outstanding academic performance he has received 14 honorary degrees, delivered 25 named lectures, and has been recognized by the National Academy of Science and numerous other scientific organizations for his work in virology.

He has acted as a consultant to the National Institute of Allergy and Infectious Disease, the American Cancer Society, and the AIDS Advisory Committee of the National Institute of Health. He has served as the President of the American Society of Virology and Chairman of the Class for Medical Sciences for the National Academy of Science, among many other achievements. In 1987, the LSU Medical Alumni Association named him Alumnus of the Year.

In 1986 then newly elected Governor Buddy Roemer split the massive state bureaucracy known as the Department of Health and Human Resources into two smaller fiefdoms; The Department of Social Services and the Department of Health and Hospitals which was then given responsibility for all of the State Charity Hospitals.

In 1987, he also created the Louisiana Healthcare Authority (LHCA) as an advisory body to suggest ways to revitalize the Charity Hospital System, which was deteriorating because of inadequate funding, a shrinking bed census, outdated equipment, and a lack of community support.

The LHCA suggested that the hospital management be turned over to it and that nine advisory boards be created that would allow local citizens to plan for the future of each facility. This was accomplished in principle but it made little practical difference as conditions in Charity continued to deteriorate.

Staff left in droves and by 1990 the hospital closed beds, reducing the number to 430 the lowest bed count in its history. Bed closure caused slowdowns in the ER with long waits for all care, save for the most seriously ill patients. Disaccreditation loomed.

Roemer, unpopular for many reasons and up for reelection, found himself pitted against two serious opponents, Edwin Edwards, whom he had defeated four years earlier, and David Duke, an arch segregationist and anti-Jewish bigot who was a state senator from Jefferson Parish.

Money poured into Duke's campaign war chest from far right-wing groups and Neo-Nazis across the country. Roemer dropped to a weak third in the polls and Edwards looked vulnerable and hard-pressed to keep up with Duke's fundraising.

Into this arena stepped **Arnold Lupin ('59)**, a well known local internist and philanthropist, a former LSU Medical Chief Resident at Charity, who became a one-man fundraising organization for Edwards. This was not so much a tribute to Edwards' sterling character, an attribute many thought was in short supply, as it was a desire to see Duke lose. Eventually both Edwards, who ran under the banner, "Vote for the crook, it's important," and Duke would wind up in federal prison, but not before Edwards served an unprecedented fourth term as Governor, soundly trouncing Duke in a runoff.

Dr. Lupin, whom Edwards called his "secret weapon," was rewarded, if you can call it that, by being named Chairman of the LHCA with a mandate to "fix" Charity Hospital. He brought a no-nonsense approach to the task. His immediate proposal to solve the overcrowding problem in the ER was to improve triage of patients immediately on arrival and create a "fast-track clinic" to see minor and/or chronic problems immediately. This unclogged the ER, and the approach proved so successful that it was copied by several private hospitals.

At this time the state helped pull Charity back from the brink of disaster by buying Hotel Dieu Hospital, a 20-year-old medium-sized private hospital located a few blocks from Big Charity. It was renamed University Hospital. The $161,000,000 purchase from the Daughters of Charity provided mostly med/surgery beds but did give the LHCA a bit of breathing room for the moment.

Dr. Lupin's proposal to solve Charity's many lingering problems and to help LSU included a 200-bed addition to University Hospital, an office tower for LSU physicians and for Charity Hospital Clinics, the addition of a separate pediatric emergency room, upgrade of impatient pediatric and neonatology, and new labor and delivery suites. These latter proposals would help lure Medicaid patients to the facility, a needed source of revenue, and he also proposed that LSU private-pay patients be admitted to University Hospital.

The upgrades in Peds and OB and the Pediatric ER were soon accomplished. The other proposals never got far. Financial issues prevented some from going forward, and political infighting blocked others. Many things did improve under Lupin's guidance but with Edwards' term coming to an end, he stepped down.

Edwards' successor, Governor Mike Foster, opted for a different approach and turned operation of the Charity Hospital System (except Shreveport, which would have a separate governance system) to LSU Health Sciences Center in New Orleans and its Chancellor Dr. Merv Trail.

By the time he was 33 years old, **Charles C. Mary, Jr. ('61),** was the Director of Charity Hospital. It was a meteoric rise to the top. While still a resident in internal medicine on the LSU Service, he accomplished the until-then unheard of feat of being named an Assistant Clinical Director at the hospital.

Until Charlie asked to be named, these positions always went to senior surgery residents. On a rotational basis they slept in the hospital and made administrative decisions. Their major jobs were to do such things as referee intra-service fights over who would admit a highly desirable patient or who would admit a less-than-desirable one. They also approved the need for routine blood transfusions, blood often being in short supply after major trauma events.

Charlie reasoned that these things required routine medical knowledge and common sense, not technical surgical skill. He got the job and brought to it a deft touch when he had to say "no" and a strength of character when pushed to say "yes." His abilities did not go unnoticed; he was named an Assistant Director when his LSU training finished in 1965.

He became Medical Director when two things occurred in succession. The then Director, **Louis Burroughs ('53**), resigned after irregularities were discovered in the hospital purchasing department, and Dr. John Adriani, the Associate Director and Chief of Anesthesia, developed a bleeding ulcer. Offered an "acting" position by the Board, Mary pointed out that if he didn't have the skill to be Director, he hadn't the skill to be "Acting Director." Without an alternative, he was made Director, a beneficial choice for the hospital.

Many good things occurred under his watch, first as Assistant Director and then as Director. He was instrumental in establishing the Office of Hospital Infection Control, a very innovative concept at that time, with the help of Drs. John Seabury and Harry Dascomb of the LSU faculty. A burn unit and a leukemia unit were established and the admit room and emergency room were upgraded. He developed neighborhood clinics, averted a nurse's strike, guided the hospital through the desegregation of the inpatient and outpatient services, deftly handled a flood in the basement due to a broken water main, and corrected financial irregularities involving the radiology department.

When budget cuts threatened the hospital, he closed 454 beds and had them hauled to a parking lot and piled one on top of another and invited the media. The cuts were rescinded. He was named "New Orleanian of the Year."

In 1973 he was named Secretary of the newly created Department of Health and Human Resources. The Department, full of promise to reform healthcare in the public sector, quickly became mired in Louisiana politics. Charles Roemer, the Commissioner of the Administration, wanted DHHR to become a haven for political patronage. Mary did not. Additionally, he had been the one to blow the whistle on the Beasley Affair, which did not endear him to the Governor. His plans to accomplish great things in healthcare were routinely blocked by Roemer. Dr. Mary resigned in 1974 and opened a highly successful practice of gastroenterology and internal medicine. He was succeeded as DHHR Secretary by **William Stewart ('45),** the then LSU Medical School Chancellor, who had previously served as United States Surgeon General under President Lyndon B. Johnson.

Dr. Mary rounded out his career as a civic leader, philanthropist, and radio talk show personality. Two of his children, **Mignon ('98)** and **Charles III ('96),** followed in his footsteps.

At Charity, Dr. Mary was succeeded by Associate Director, **Isidore D. Brickman ('62).** Dr. Brickman lasted only briefly, refusing to sign a formal affiliation agreement with Tulane and LSU, believing it not in Charity's best interest.

Dr. Stewart replaced Brickman with Lee J. Frazier, a 28-year-old Assistant Director who had a Masters in Hospital Administration but little practical experience. His tenure as director was brief.

It isn't often that a single physician has the opportunity to help transform the health of an entire country but that was the opportunity presented quite by accident to **I. Ricardo Martinez ('65),** PhD, Clinical Professor of Dermatology at LSU.

In 1991, ninety percent of the populace having voted for independence, 5,000,000 former Russian citizens formed the Republic of Georgia. The new country, bordering Turkey and about the size of West Virginia, immediately sought advice from American business people. One who responded was businesswoman Dolly-Dean Martinez.

While she found no investment opportunities in Georgia she noted a lack of trained healthcare professionals. She prevailed upon her husband to become involved in reforming healthcare and medical education in Georgia. Dr. Martinez immediately got involved and soon led a group of 11 physicians to the capital, Tbilisi, meeting there with members of its Medical Academy and the Dean and faculty of the Georgia State Medical School.

Lectures and technical demonstrations took place and this lead to the formation of the American-Georgian Academy of Medicine and Surgery, with Dr. Martinez as its first President. Many visits to Georgia by American physicians and many visits to America by Georgian physicians followed. Several of the Georgian physicians came to LSU for training in ophthalmology, surgery, obstetrics and otolaryngology as well as dermatology. Dr. Martinez oversaw the translation of American medical texts into Georgian and the delivery of medical supplies and large pieces of equipment to Georgia, greatly improving healthcare and medical education in that country.

He was lionized for his work not only by physicians from the Tbilisi Medical Academy but by the country's Parliament and also its President, Eduard Shevardnadze.

You have got to work really hard to acquire the title "Dr. Duck" but that is the title proudly borne by **L. J. Mayeux ('77).** He's been an excellent Marksville, Louisiana, physician and long-time Avoyelles Parish Coroner, but his passion for wildlife preservation, specifically ducks, a 30-year-long avocation, is what has brought him to international prominence. Because of his dedication, he not only was named National President of this million member organization but had a wildlife habitat in Canada named in his honor.

૮૭૦૪

Alumni in Military Service

Most alumni are aware that **William Stewart ('43)** served as Surgeon General of the United States. America's "Chief Medical Officer," he was Surgeon General by being commander of the U.S. Public Health Service.

What fewer alumni may realize is that the United States has more than one Surgeon General. It has one for the Army, one for the Navy, and one for the Air Force. More interestingly, an LSU School of Medicine alumnus has at one time or another occupied each of these positions.

Quinn H. Becker ('56) served as Surgeon General of the Army from 1985 to 1988. An orthopedist by training, he began his career in 1962 after completing an Army-sponsored residency in Shreveport. He served in Germany and Vietnam, and in various capacities in the U.S., and received numerous badges of honor, including the Bronze Star, Combat Medic Badge, and the Distinguished Service Medal. He was named Alumnus of the Year in 1991.

Rear Admiral **Daniel B Lestage, MD**, a 1963 graduate of the School of Medicine, amassed 32 years of active duty before his retirement in 1992. A specialist in Public Health and Preventive Medicine, he served in many capacities both in the United States and in Europe. He additionally held important positions as the first Chief Executive of the Champus/Tri Care Program, Associate Dean of the

Dr. Quinn Becker

Eastern Virginia School of Medicine, Vice-President of Blue Cross Blue Shield of Florida, and Chair of the Aerospace Medical Association. He lives in Florida in retirement.

A 1964 graduate of the SOM, Lt. General **Edgar R "Andy" Anderson, MD**, spent over 30 years in the U.S. Air Force, where he attained "Top Gun" status in gunnery and bombing. A specialist in both dermatology and public health, he was also a medical test pilot and parachutist. He served in many locations and in many capacities, including Surgeon General 1994-1996. On his retirement in 1997, he became Executive Vice President of the American Medical Association, serving in that capacity for a number of years. He also served as CEO of the Harry S. Truman Medical Center in Kansas City.

Lt. General Edgar R. Anderson, Jr.

He continues to be active in medical affairs, and has been designated a "Louisiana Legend" by National Public Broadcast.

Many other alumni have had outstanding military careers. Hundreds served during World War II, eight making the ultimate sacrifice. From Korea to Vietnam to Desert Storm (where 26 alumni and four faculty served) through Iraq and Afghanistan, many have answered when duty called.

It is impossible to highlight the careers of more than a few of them. One graduate who would almost certainly have attained Surgeon General Rank had he not died at the age of 43 was **Robert Leonce Hullinghorst ('39)**. He had been a career officer, having served in many capacities during WWII, and serving in high administrative capacities at the Army Medical Field Service School and Walter Reed Army Medical Center. At the time of his death, he was deputy commander of the Surgeon General's Research and Development Organization.

No account of the military exploits of LSU graduates would be complete without discussing the career of **E. Ralph Lupin ('55)**. During his Ob/Gyn residency he volunteered for active duty and was posted to England for 2 ½ years under an excellent commanding officer who was also an obstetrician/gynecologist. Within 10 months Dr. Lupin succeeded him as Chief, a testament to both his medical skill and command abilities.

On his return to New Orleans he remained in the Air Force Reserve, set up a private practice, and became immersed in community activities such the Vieux Carre Commission, which devotes itself to the preservation of the historic French Quarter.

He eventually switched from the Air Force to the Louisiana National Guard, where he rose to the rank of Brigadier General and was put in command of all military medical assets in the state. He also distinguished himself in philanthropy through the Lupin Family Foundation.

Although he was by then retired, when Katrina struck he volunteered to return to active duty. Assigned to the Superdome, he was placed in command of all medical assets and stayed at his post until the Superdome evacuation was complete.

Colonel **Paul J. Azar, Jr.** ('70) distinguished himself in a variety of ways. He had a 30-year career in active military and reserve duty, graduated from the Army War College, served during Operation Desert Storm, and still managed to become one of Louisiana's most outstanding ophthalmologists.

After training in ophthalmology on the LSU Service, he did fellowship study under the auspices of the NIH in strabismus surgery and corneal pathology, and did a stint at the Armed Forces Institute of Pathology in Corneal Pathology. He founded the Azar Eye Clinic in Lafayette in 1975.

He has been active in the Medical Alumni Association for decades, having served as President in 2007, is Clinical Professor of Ophthalmology directing the residency program at University Hospital in Lafayette, and has been active in organizing Continuing Medical Education programs locally and nationally.

Perhaps his most important contributions came in the immediate aftermath of Hurricane Katrina. A long-time member of the Lafayette Cajundome Commission, he immediately volunteered as a staff physician when hundreds of disaster victims, many in need of emergency care, were evacuated there. He found a scene described by others as utter chaos.

Calling on his army training and experience, he began to issue orders

*Colonel **Paul J. Azar, Jr.***

to military and civilians alike, was promptly named "Medical Director" of the Cajundome, and brought order and calm to the scene. He then arranged to take ophthalmology residents displaced from New Orleans into his private practice so that they could continue their training under the supervision of him and his partners, helping to save the entire department training program from disaccreditation.

In his Cajundome experience, which would provide 750,000 meals and triage 25,000 people over 60 days, Dr. Azar was assisted by local nephrologist and Alumni Board member, **Andy Blalock ('98),** who had previously served as Chair of the Resident Section of the American Medical Association.

Dr. Blalock noted the slow response of both the Red Cross and the National Guard to both Katrina and Hurricane Rita, which came ashore a few weeks later. He was convinced that things could be improved and became the driving force behind the formation of the Louisiana Emergency Medical Unit (LEMU). This was designed to enhance emergency care and provide quick response to major disasters in a nine-parish area across the southern part of the state.

The unit was formed in early 2006 when a fundraiser was held in Washington, DC, in conjunction with Louisiana's Annual Washington Mardi Gras. In 2008 it was called upon twice, responding to both Hurricane Gustav and Hurricane Ike. In both instances it was a resounding success, providing immediate deployment and free care to the ill or injured. In both instances it beat the Red Cross and National Guard to the scene.

In addition, LEMU has caused the Louisiana legislature to consider providing civil liability relief to responders during a declared emergency.

Another notable alumnus is **Robert Morrow, Jr. ('69),** who ended a 33-year military career in 2002 but continues to be a force in the Lafayette Louisiana Orthopedics community.

After an internship in Texas he did a four-year orthopaedics residency in the Air Force and a hand-surgery fellowship in New Mexico. When his commitment to the Air Force ended, he switched services to the Army, commanding the 420th Medical Detachment at Fort Sam Houston Texas from 1987-1993. In that capacity he served in Operation Desert Storm, the successful liberation of Kuwait from Iraq. In the process, he earned five commendations, including one each from the Government of Kuwait and the Kingdom of Saudi Arabia.

He closed out an illustrious medical career as Deputy Commander of the 807th Medical Brigade based in Seagoville, Texas.

Nick Broussard ('81) ended a 20-year career in the U.S. Navy as Chief of Staff at the National Naval Medical Center in Bethesda Maryland.

After graduating from the School of Medicine in 1961, **Charles Raborn ('61)** trained as a pediatrician in Army hospitals. He remained either on active duty or in the reserves for

40 years and also practiced his chosen specialty for 30 years. Called back to active duty, he served in Desert Storm.

That all might have been enough for most people but not Dr. Raborn. He helped set up several Kid Med Clinics, working closely with the Department of Health and Hospitals. Then, under the auspices of the Medical Mission Board of the Southern Baptist Convention, he has made many mission trips to Venezuela, Cuba, Mexico and Antigua caring for the poor of those countries.

Finally he has been, for over 35 years, an outstanding woodcarver, with photographs of his works adorning magazine covers, and the woodcarvings themselves being displayed in libraries and museums throughout the state.

Patriotism and a love of country motivated **Charles Chappuis** (`79) to join the Louisiana Air National Guard in 1998. A gifted surgeon, he first trained at LSU under Dr. Isidore Cohn, Jr., and then did a fellowship in transplant surgery at the Lahey clinic in Boston. Dr. Chappuis currently serves as Chief of Surgery at University Medical Center in Lafayette, La.

Since joining the Guard he has risen to become "State Surgeon" with the rank of Colonel and has served three tours of duty in Iraq as Commander of a Military Battalion providing care to U.S. military, Iraqi soldiers and civilians, and even prisoners of war.

Between tours of duty he continues to serve as Clinical Professor of Surgery at the School of Medicine.

Few people decide on their life's work as a nine-year-old but that is what **Alvin Cotlar** ('57) did when, in 1942, he decided on a career in the military. His first efforts, the planting of a "victory garden" at his elementary school, were modest, but his interest continued in high school as a member of the Junior ROTC program, and then at Tulane as ROTC Battalion Commander.

Four years of medical school and four years of surgery residency later, he was off to several army duty stations, including airborne training and a parachutist badge at Fort Benning, Georgia. Service in Germany and Fort Bragg, North Carolina, followed but ultimately he joined the faculty of the school, then later opted for a stint in private practice.

In 1981, at nearly 50 years of age, he decided to finish his surgical career, this time in the Air Force as a Lieutenant Colonel and as a flight surgeon in F105 fighter planes. Service in the U.S. and Germany followed, along with a promotion to Colonel and then deployment to Saudi Arabia for Desert Storm, which earned him a Bronze Star and numerous other awards.

Stationed ultimately at Keesler Medical Center in Biloxi, Mississippi, he retired in 1998 at age 66, the eldest then serving Colonel in the entire Air Force. On retirement he was awarded the Air Force Legion of Merit, his proudest decoration. He stayed at Keesler on contract as a civilian for several years and is finishing out a notable career on the staff of the Biloxi VA Medical Center.

Lest readers think that LSUSOM has contributed only male graduates as military trail blazers, please consider the career of **Jacqueline Morgan ('65)**, who after years in private practice entered the U.S. Air Force as a Major in 1980. Assignments at Barksdale Air Force, Sembach and Ramstein Air Bases in Germany were a prelude to her being the first woman medical officer to serve as a Department of Defense medical facility commander when she headed the hospital at Incirlik Air Force Base in Turkey.

From there she became Commander of the 92nd Strategic Hospital in Fairchild, Washington. Other assignments included the Office of the Surgeon General and the Uniformed Services University of the Health Sciences, where she obtained a Master of Public Health degree.

When she retired in 2000, she was not only a Senior Flight Surgeon but the first woman to serve as Command Surgeon. After retirement she served three years on the Department of Veterans Advisory Committee on Women Veterans and now lives in retirement in Seattle, Washington.

William "Brent" Klein ('86) (no relation to the senior author) has compiled an outstanding record in the USAF, and along the way has added both a Master of Public Health and Master of Business Administration to his credentials, which also include certification in Occupational Medicine and Aerospace Medicine. He has logged over 1,700 flying hours in 38 different types of air craft that included flying F16 combat missions over Kosovo.

During the Iraq War, he served as commander of the 332 Expidiatory Medical Group, the largest Air Force Hospital in the region. He is currently Chief of Aerospace Medicine at Moody Air Force Base in Georgia. He has received the Legion of Merit, Bronze Star and Air Force Commendation Medal, among many decorations.

It is said that because of service during the Vietnam War, the School of Medicine class of 1979 boasted more military veterans than any class since the years immediately following the Second World War or the Korean conflict. Few could boast a more varied or distinguished career than **Steve Oreck ('79)**, who spent 37 years in the Navy, first as an officer in Naval Intelligence and then as a physician serving principally in field hospitals supporting Marine Corps Unit as an orthopaedic surgeon. He served in Saudi Arabia and Kuwait during Operation Desert Storm, was called to Washington to be Senior Medical Watch Officer for the Marine Corps Combat Operations Center, and retired with the rare designation of Fleet Marine Force Medical Officer. He lives in retirement in Madison, Wisconsin.

Fred Kelly ('51) became interested in flying as a child and by age 17, in 1943, he was in a Naval Aviation Cadet Program. As the war wound down he elected college and then medical school. But the lure of flying drew him back to the Navy after a year of internship, and he became a Naval Flight Surgeon. In time he became both a naval aviator and a flight surgeon.

Assigned to the Navy Missile Center, Point Mugu, California, he began to do research in bioinstrumentation, developing an electrode to gather electrocardiographic data on pilots in flight.

He worked closely with the NASA space program and was called on to head the medical team that investigated the death of the astronauts killed when NASA attempted to launch the Apollo I space flight in January 1967, an attempt that ended in a fatal fire in the cockpit of the space craft. He continued to work with NASA and ultimately retired from the Navy in 1975. He then worked on the space program as a civilian until 1983, when he became an advisor to the Saudi Arabian Air Force. In addition, he has written several books, a nonfiction account of the space program and two fictional works dealing with space exploration. He lives in retirement in Florida.

The Air Force bug bit **Dwight Smith ('64)** in medical school and led him to do an Air Force Internship, a residency in dermatology, a training program in aviation medicine and then study National Security Management, where he was designated "outstanding graduate." He ultimately served two tours of duty in Vietnam, earning among other awards the Bronze Star, Legion of Merit, Air Medal and Vietnam Service Medal with five battle stars. On retirement from the Air Force, he served as Chairman of the Department of Dermatology at Wright State University School of Medicine and Chief of Dermatology at the VA Hospital in Dayton, Ohio. He retired in 1994.

With the "Doctor Draft" in effect, **Larry Fontenelle ('62)** opted for the Air Force, where he trained in general and cardiothoracic surgery before being assigned to Keesler AFB Hospital. He rose rapidly in the ranks, becoming a full Colonel by age 36.

At Keesler he became Chairman of the Surgery Department, developing an outstanding educational program and developing a surgery residency program at the Biloxi VA Hospital. On retiring from the Air Force after a 20-year career, he became Chief of Surgery at the Biloxi VA, supervising residency programs in surgery, ENT, GU, eye anesthesia and neurosurgery, and serving in that capacity for 20 more years. He was the first retired Air Force Officer to receive the "Excalibur Award" from the Society of Air Force Clinical Surgeons.

Garland McCarty's 27-year military career began on graduation in 1967, and included training in neurology that allowed him ultimately to become Chief of Neurology at Brooke Army Medical Center. He also graduated from both the U.S. Army War College and the U.S. Army Command and General Staff College. He commanded research centers in the United States, Thailand, Brazil, Africa and Germany, and became Deputy Assistant Surgeon General for Medical Research and Development. He then became Commander of Army

Medical Research during Operation Desert Storm. Ultimately he acted as Command Liaison to the Academy of Health Sciences at San Antonio, Texas, and retired as Colonel in 1994.

Before **Richard A. Keller ('86)** went with diploma and AOA membership in hand for internship and dermatology residency at Brooke Army Medical Center, he had already had a significant military career. While at Marion Military Institute in Alabama, where he completed both high school and junior college, he was named cadet captain and commissioned through the ROTC program. First as a member of the Army Medical Service Corps and then as a member of the Army Medical Corps, he served in many ways in many locations before he retired as a full colonel in 2003.

During his service he graduated from the Command and General Staff College, became Chief of Dermatological Surgery at Water Reed Army Medical Center, became Senior Army Medical Officer for the 43rd Presidential Inaugural Parade, and received a host of medals and acted as consultant to the Surgeon General.

Perhaps his finest hour came during the Cuban Refugee Crisis when he and his unit stationed in Guantanamo Bay became responsible for six refugee camps that provided 53,000 sick call visits for 14,000 Cubans in a three-month period and dealt successfully with a mass infestation of lice and scabies. At that time he was also responsible for the medical care for a Haitian repatriation project.

On his retirement Dr. Keller began a career in the VA System in Texas, where he lives with his wife Judith.

Colonel **James Gregory (Greg) Jolissaint ('86)** began his army career in 1977 when, after receiving his undergraduate degree from LSU (B.R.), he joined the army, became an Army Ranger, earned an Expert Infantry Badge, and became a parachutist.

After graduation from LSUSOM, he trained in family practice in Georgia and then embarked on a remarkable career in military medicine that would see him serve during the fighting in Kosovo and Kuwait and see him receive the Legion of Merit, the Army Commendation Medal, the Kosovo and Kuwait Campaign Medals, and receive a special award, the Samil Medal from the President of South Korea for his service to that country.

When the decision was made to close the aged and inadequate Walter Reed Army Medical Center and move its functions and personnel to the National Naval Medical Center in Bethesda, Maryland, Dr. Greg Jolissaint was placed in charge of the operation to merge the clinical support and administrative functions of those institutions and the Army Hospital at Fort Belvoir, Virginia.

ℰ⃝ℛ

Alumni in Politics and Government Service

Any recounting of the involvement of alumni at the federal level of government must begin with the story of **John Cooksey ('66),** who served in the U. S. Congress for three terms (1997 – 2003).

Before and after his election and occasionally during his terms, he was a highly regarded practicing ophthalmologist in Monroe, Louisiana. He pledged on election that he would serve only three terms and he remained true to his word.

Even before he was elected to Congress he distinguished himself and endeared himself to Louisiana physicians by spearheading the comprehensive reform of medical malpractice in the state with the passage of Act 817 in 1975. He has also served on the clinical faculty of the School of Medicine in Shreveport and has been active in church work and given generously of his time to provide care to those who could not afford it, including leading five medical mission trips to

John Cooksey ('66)

Africa. In 1999 LSU School of Medicine named him Alumnus of the Year.

The second alumnus to make it to the U. S. Congress is **Dr. Charles Boustany ('82).** A noted Lafayette, Louisiana, cardiovascular surgeon, now retired after 20 years of practice, Dr. Boustany was first elected in 2004 and has been reelected since then. He has been a champion both for healthcare issues and for issues related to energy and agriculture.

The two newest additions to the Halls of Congress from the alumni are **R. Parker Griffith ('70)** and **William Cassidy ('83).** Both were state senators at the time of their election, Griffith from Alabama and Cassidy from Baton Rouge.

Griffith, a retired radiation oncologist, has been a champion of early childhood education and small businesses in Huntsville.

Dr. Cassidy was cofounder of the Baton Community Clinic, which provides dental and healthcare to the working uninsured. He is on the faculty of the School of Medicine and a strong supporter of the Pennington Biomedical Research Center.

Although they did not hold elected federal offices, other alumni have served in important positions. In 1999, **Ricardo Martinez ('80)** was named National Highway Safety Administrator. He was honored by the AMA and received the Nathan Davis Award, an award given to a government official who has "promoted betterment of public heath." He worked to prevent accidental injury or death in children by use of child safety seats.

In 2000, **Fred Rodriguez ('75)** was named Chief of Pathology Services for the entire Veterans Administration System. He served in that capacity for seven years.

In 1988, **Jerry Thomas ('79)** was elected to the Louisiana State House of Representatives. He had previously served as coroner of Washington Parish and was on the faculty of the Department of Family Medicine, directing the program in Bogalusa. He was eventually elected to the Louisiana State Senate in 1999.

Pat Sullivan ('61) served three terms in the Colorado State Legislature.

The Louisiana Legislature has also been graced over time with the presence of other alumni of the School of Medicine. Among them are: **Michael Robichaux ('71), Don Hines ('59)** and **William Cassidy ('83). Mike Robichaux ('71)** not only served in the State Senate but had previously distinguished himself both as an outstanding ENT surgeon and as an LSU Football All-American.

But for sheer variety of service in government at the state and local level no one can top **Don Hines ('59)**. After graduation and internship he was a medical officer in the U.S. Navy, receiving the Naval Commendation Medal for his part in the rescue of three downed navel airmen.

A family physician, he served on the Avoyelles Parish School Board from 1972-1993 and served as President on two occasions for a total of five years. In 1993 he was elected to the Louisiana State Senate, serving as President from 2004-2008. Required to step down from the Senate because of term limits, he serves as Executive Director of the Louisiana Rural Health Information Exchange, which provides electronic links to the LSUSOM Shreveport for rural healthcare providers who need consultation services.

In 1994, **Elmore Rigamer ('66)** was named Deputy Assistant Secretary of State for Medical Affairs. He was particularly noted for his interest in mental health and oversaw programs to serve the needs of diplomats and their families on Foreign Service.

In 2003, the School was notified that **Charles "Jiggs" Weldon ('51)** had died and was buried in Thailand. He was the author of *Tragedy in Paradise: A Country Doctor at War in Laos*. He achieved legendary status as the Chief Medical Officer for the U.S. Agency for International Development. He helped fight the takeover of Laos by Communist rebels and their North Vietnamese allies. In this he was assisted by his wife Pat and classmate **Walt**

Majewski ('51). Jiggs was a World War II vet who was one of the first to go ashore during the liberation of Guam from the Japanese. A classmate once said that Jiggs never got over being a Marine.

For length of service in government few alumni of the school will outdo Orleans Parish Coroner **Frank Minyard ('55),** who has served in that capacity since April 1, 1974. An Ob/Gyn by training he was drawn to run for the office by a desire to bring better civil and criminal justice to the citizens of Orleans Parish.

He was prompted to run for office because he saw a real need to improve conditions in the city. He established the first prison drug treatment program in the U.S. at Orleans Parish Prison in 1974, worked to establish mandatory seat belts laws and safety regulations for children in motor vehicles, and established a nationally recognized forensic toxicology laboratory among many other accomplishments.

In addition to an active private practice, Dr. Minyard also managed to serve in the U.S. Navy Reserve, rising to the rank of Captain before his retirement, and as drug consultant to the then Chief of Naval Operations, Admiral Elmo Zumwalt, for four years.

In his spare time, Dr. Minyard has authored 27 medical articles and three books. He is also both an accomplished musician and President of JAZZ ROOTS Foundation, which has raised thousands of dollars for hundreds of local charities.

In his work as coroner he was aided greatly by the late **Monroe Samuels ('50),** who served the coroner's office as chief pathologist for an incredible 50 years.

For nearly 30 years Dr. Minyard has served on the LSU clinical faculty in both Emergency Medicine and Clinical Pathology, and is regarded as an expert witness in forensic medicine both in state and federal court.

A pediatrician and pediatric cardiologist by training, **Larry Hebert ('59)** currently serves as Executive Medical Director of Unisys Corporation in Baton Rouge. Prior to that, he served for many years as Medical Director of the Department of Health and Hospitals overseeing four DHH Sections: Public Health, Mental Health, Substance Abuse and Developmental Disabilities.

Before that, he served as State Health Officer and Director of the Office of Public Health, supervising 2,500 employees. Preparation for that position included serving as Medical Director of Earl K. Long Hospital.

Other services included a six-year stint as President of the 450 member Louisiana Pediatric Society. But perhaps his finest achievement was drafting the Louisiana Child Protection Statute, which was passed by the legislature and has been used as a model for other states to formulate their child protection statutes. It has been used throughout the state to protect children from being neglected or physically or sexually abused. He has also produced "Health Call," a television show on Baton Rouge station WBRZ for which he received an Excellence in Medical Journalism Award.

Many years ago the noted American humorist James Thurber wrote a short story, "The Secret Life of Walter Mitty," which told the amazing adventures of its hero. The adventures occurred only in Mitty's mind. It's too bad that Thurber didn't write about the adventures of **Hypolite Landry ('58)**. They might not have been as funny, but they were all real.

Dr. Landry matriculated at the School of Medicine after World War II Army service in the Field Artillery, and he eventually became a family physician in Baton Rouge. He practiced until 1978, when he closed his practice to devote himself full time to another job he had assumed in 1972, coroner of East Baton Rouge Parish.

Dissatisfied with the way that office was being run, he offered himself to the people and won election. He held the job for 27 years. It expanded considerably under his administration. Initially he discovered that the coroner was often called on to deal with people suffering from drug addiction or alcoholism. He also discovered that there were no facilities in Baton Rouge to do this, so in typical fashion, he cajoled $100,000 and the use of two buildings from the state and set up a 21-bed treatment center, the first ever in Baton Rouge. To combat other public health problems, he set up a rape crisis center and a child abuse center.

Most people would consider that enough but not Dr. Landry. In 1964, a pilot, a son of a patient, interested him in flying. Soon thereafter, he bought a small plane, was appointed to the Airport Commission that oversaw Baton Rouge's Ryan Airport, and then the flying bug really bit. In 1969, he decided to fly a single-engine Beechcraft Bonanza around the world solo. And that is exactly what he did, setting 14 records in 23 days. Not many people have done that.

He retired in 1998, but continues to fly at the age of 82 and also amuses himself collecting antique cars and musical instruments and riding his *ten* motorcycles.

The political bug bit **Reggie Goldsby ('69)**, a family physician in Amite, Louisiana, in 1975 when he ran for and was elected Mayor of Amite and served for four years. Running again in 1985, he was again elected. When his term is up he will have served as mayor for an astounding total of 32 years.

Certified on six separate occasions by the American Board of Family Practice, he serves on the faculty of the School of Medicine as a full professor at Earl K. Long Hospital.

Another alumnus with a long and distinguished record is **A. John Tassin ('69)**. A four-year term in the State Senate from District 28 was only the start of his career in public service. His long-time interest in raising, training, and racing quarter horses led later to his appointment by then Governor Dave Treen to the State Racing Commission, a then newly formed blue ribbon group. He served with distinction for three years.

Later, under the administration of Governor Buddy Roemer, he was appointed to the State Ethics Commission where he ably served for a total of six years.

George B. Mowad ('55)

It was a tragic end to a remarkable career of public service when **George B. Mowad ('55)** was killed in an auto crash in 2000. A family physician serving on the board of Huey P. Long Hospital in Pineville, he was on his way from a meeting at the hospital to his office in Oakdale, Louisiana, when he died in a head-on collision. He had practiced there for 40 years, a remarkable run, but he had managed to sandwich in a 20-year stint as Oakdale's mayor. During his tenure he was instrumental in convincing the Department of Justice to build its largest detention center in the U.S. in Oakdale. It was completed in 1985. Shopping centers, new home subdivisions, and a new hospital were built because of his efforts. He then convinced the government to construct a Federal Deportation Center at Oakdale and through successful lobbying at the state and federal levels, funds for a new city hall, library, and police station were obtained.

In addition to all this, he found time to act as a mentor to medical school students from both LSU and Tulane interested in family medicine and was on the faculty of both schools.

After serving as Director of the Lafayette Parish Department of Health for many years, **Brian Amy ('80)** was named Executive Director of the Mississippi State Department of Health. He also served for many years on the Medical Alumni Board of Directors.

The late **Sarah Braud ('51)** was a practicing pediatrician in Houma, Louisiana, until she became Lafourche Parish Health Officer. Eventually, she served until retirement as State Health Officer.

Mark Dawson ('77) not only served as Acadia Parish Coroner by also was on the Louisiana State Board of Medical Examiners.

෨෬

Alumni Missionaries

Many LSU graduates have provided distinguished humanitarian service through participation in medical missionary work. In the case of **Edward Sauter ('86)**, his work took place during two senior class rotations when he, as a Brother of the Sacred Heart as well as a medical student, served in the order's medical missions in Meru, Kenya and Gulu, Uganda. Parasitic diseases and burn injuries were common in his experience, and anesthetic agents were in short supply. Perhaps his most challenging and satisfying case involved a man with a huge jaw tumor that he diagnosed (clinically) as Burkitt's lymphoma. He located a single dose of cyclophosphamide long past its expiration date. Having nothing else to offer, he administered the drug. The tumor disappeared. After graduation, Dr. Sauter trained in surgery and oncology and is presently serving as Professor of Surgery and Associate Dean at the University of North Dakota School of Medicine.

His strong Baptist faith motivated **G. Dewey Dunn ('60)** to help the less fortunate in other countries, and his fluency in Spanish propelled him to make many trips to Central America. Indeed, his 30 trips to Venezuela earned him the nickname "Dr. Venezuela" and the respect of many LSU Alumni, including **Leland Albright ('69), Charles Norwood ('63)** and **Charles Raborn ('61)**, who all participated with him on mission trips. Other destinations included Ghana, West Africa, Haiti, the Philippines, Paraguay and Hong Kong, where he was able to work with **Don Langford ('57)**, a missionary surgeon working there.

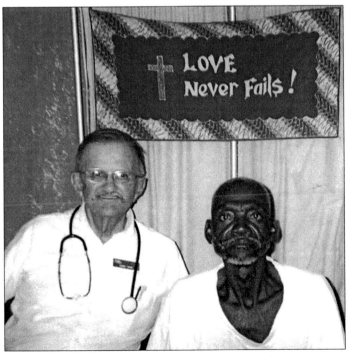

Dewey Dunn with a patient in clinic in Ghana, spring 2009

Dr. Dunn, who has worked in the VA Hospital System and

currently lives in Nashville, Tennessee, and teaches at Vanderbilt University School of Medicine, credits the pioneering efforts in missionary work of **Charles Black ('38)**, a Shreveport ophthalmologist, for inspiring his own efforts. Dr. Black has made over 50 mission trips to such diverse places as Mexico, India, Indonesia, Brazil, Yemen, Ghana, Kenya and Nigeria, often spending one or two months at a time.

Other graduates who have served notably include: **Oliver Gililand ('56)**, a medical missionary for 22 years in India and Indonesia; **Bert Oubre ('68)**, who, as International Medical Director of Voices of the Martyrs, built medical centers across Asia and Africa; **Charles Rogers ('86)** in Mongolia; **Van Joffrion ('64)** in Madagascar; **Sidney Tate ('69)** in Zambia; **David McGehee ('81)** in Russia; and **Burton Lindau (`50)** in Africa.

ৰো৪ব

The Formation of
the Modern Medical Alumni Association

The 75th Anniversary of the School of Medicine in 2006 coincided with the 23rd Anniversary of the Committee of 100 – Champions of Excellence, the most generous support organization for the School of Medicine and the catalyst for the formation of the modern medical alumni association.

Attempts to form an Association had been made earlier, once before World War II and later in the 1940s under **Chester Fresh ('35),** and in the 1970s, under **Frank Rieger ('50).** No attempt lasted more than a few years because the organizational structure was weak and depended solely on volunteers. This approach proved unsustainable over time. Only when the School appointed a full-time faculty member to the job of managing Alumni Affairs did things begin to take on a permanent shape.

The dream of developing endowed professorships, commonplace at most private medical schools was one that Dr. Richard Paddison, the appointed Coordinator of Alumni Affairs, had had for some time, but it took the leadership of two close friends, **Bernard Samuels ('57),** a well known local ob/gyn; and **Cy Vaughn ('57),** a famous (he invented an artificial heart) Phoenix, Arizona, heart surgeon, to get it off the ground. The idea was simple: find 100 alumni who would pledge $1,000 a year for 10 years, amass $1,000,000 over time, and dedicate four professorships, one each in medicine, surgery, ob/gyn, and pediatrics, and name each one for a famous faculty member. One would be dedicated every year for four years. What would happen in year five never came up for discussion.

The funds would be invested, someone on the faculty would be named to the professorship and income from the professorship would pay for research, travel, or other support. Aside from the problem of what would happen in year five, the funds would have to be deposited in the LSU Foundation in Baton Rouge, the only 501(c)3 then existing in the LSU System, an arrangement that did not sit well with some potential donors.

Cy and Bernard, who would be named Alumni of the Year in 1986, went looking for the first 25 donors and were having some success when Dr. Paddison had a serendipitous lunch meeting with the man who would become, quite by accident, his successor. The conversation in early 1984 with **Russell Klein ('59)** turned to the reunions in June. Klein's class was scheduled for its 25th anniversary reunion and he offered to help. Paddison asked him to put together the Scientific Session and raise money from his class to help make the first Committee of 100 banquet a success.

Since the Committee had decided to honor Dr. Edgar Hull, a revered figure, Klein agreed and soon raised $20,000 by getting people, including himself, to join the Committee. The banquet was a success, the Scientific Session was well received, the reunions went off without a hitch, and Klein left on a two-week vacation.

When he walked into his office on the first day back, he found Paul Larson, the Dean, waiting for him. Paul without preamble said that immediately after the reunions Dr. Paddison became ill and planned to retire in December; Paul wanted Klein to take his place. Larson explained that no one in the school knew more about the Office of Alumni Affairs or the Committee of 100 than Klein. Actually no one else on the faculty knew anything about the office so there wasn't a lot of competition for the job.

Klein agreed to consider it. This was a career change, but the need for a vibrant Alumni Association was obvious to him. With the blessing of his wife to consider the job, he went to Paddison's office to chat with the real power, Paddison's long-time assistant, Ms. JoAnn Roloff, who had proved invaluable in setting up the reunions, the Scientific Session, and the Committee of 100 Banquet.

Clearly she had talked with both Paddison and Larson.

"Are you taking the job?" she asked.

"If I do will you stay on?"

"I will, if you take the job," she answered.

That settled that. Klein took the job on January 1, 1985.

The existence if the Committee of 100 – Champions of Excellence of the LSU Medical Alumni Association, as it was ponderously known, presupposed that there was an Alumni Association. There was not. But this time two people stepped forward immediately to help, **Julius Mullins Sr. ('36),** a retired but well known Baton Rouge physician, the founding father of Women's Hospital in Baton Rouge and the unofficial School of Medicine historian, and **Henry Jolly ('40),** the Chairman of Dermatology, a man who commanded everyone's respect.

Together, they speedily helped organize a volunteer board that, in addition to Drs. Mullins and Jolly, consisted of **Claude Craighead ('39), Ewing Cook ('69), Robert Batson ('71), Charles Eckert ('64), Frank Incaprera ('50), E. Ralph Lupin ('56), Barbara Morgan ('73),** and **Mary Ella Sanders ('75).** In June 1985, Julius was formally recognized as the first modern Alumni President. Jolly would succeed him in June 1986. The organization continued as a volunteer group until 2004, when it was formally incorporated and recognized both by the LSU System and the Internal Revenue Service.

Over time, the Committee of 100 continued to add hundreds of members, and continued to dedicate professorships. A second giving group, the 500 Club, was formed later, to concentrate on fundraising for basic science departments.

Two things also happened that greatly changed the face of fundraising at the School of Medicine. The Louisiana Board of Regents for Higher Education developed a matching grant program that would provide a dollar for every two dollars raised for Professorships and they went a step further by authorizing the creation of million dollar and ultimately two million dollar chairs. The Alumni Association has been able to access this fund many times, adding millions to the School's endowment.

A second opportunity presented itself when the University of New Orleans decided, with the perhaps grudging approval of the LSU Board of Supervisors, to form a foundation separate from the Baton Rouge campus. The Alumni Association, urged by then Dean Robert Daniels, seized the opportunity to create a Medical Center Foundation to provide an alternative to depositing money in Baton Rouge. This was accomplished in 1988 and a group of community leaders and medical professionals have served on the Foundation Board since then. Its first President was Dr. Jolly.

Since its formation the Alumni Association has not only created numerous Chairs and Professorships it has inspired others to do so, has created numerous scholarships and awards for students and faculty, and has provided numerous other services to the school, including creation of the Isidore Cohn, Jr., MD, Student Learning Center, the **Russell C. Klein, MD ('59)**, Center for Advanced Practice, and the Institute of Professional Education (IPE). The Institute is designed to facilitate the development and presentation of continuing education programs. Surpluses generated in this way by the IPE are made available to departments and other school units to improve their operation.

The Institute was originally formed under the guidance of Mr. Joseph D'Angelo, who came over from Tulane, and Mr. Louis Castaing, who had worked at LSU in Learning Resources for many years.

The Institute operated as a subsidiary of the LSU Health Sciences Center Foundation for many years. When the Alumni Association formally incorporated, ownership shifted to it from the Foundation.

Mr. D'Angelo retired in the aftermath of Katrina, was succeeded briefly by his longtime associate, Barbara Hollingsworth, and permanently by Rebecca Norwood, a New Orleanian who had worked in New York in CME for many years.

In the aftermath of Hurricane Katrina, the Alumni Association was also responsible for much fundraising, which helped the School in its darkest hour, and it made possible the celebrations that marked the School's Diamond Jubilee in January 2006, a remarkable feat given that Katrina had occurred just four months earlier.

The Alumni Association has been blessed with uniformly strong leadership since its modern inception. Presidents and their terms include **Julius Mullins ('36)**, 1986-1987; **Henry Jolly ('41)**, 1987-1988; **Claude Craighead ('39)**, 1988-1989 (who had also been a President in the 1940s and 1970s); **Frank Incaprera ('50)**, 1989-1990; **Barbara Morgan ('73)**, 1990-1991; **Bernard Samuels ('57)**, 1991-1992; **Mary Ella Sanders ('75)**, 1992-1993; **Jack Perry Strong ('51)**, 1993-1994; **Earl Rozas ('64)**, 1994-1995; **Kenneth Adatto ('68)**, 1995-1996; **Harold Neitzschman ('65)**, 1996-1997; **Mack Thomas ('62)**, 1997-1998; **John McLachlan ('62)**, 1998-1999; **Mario Calonje ('59)**, 1999-2000; **Bennie Nobles ('71)**, 2000-2001; **Ewing Cook ('69)**, 2001-2002; **Cathi Fontenot ('84)**, 2002-2003; **Mark Juneau ('73)**, 2003-2004; **Jack Andonie ('62)**, 2004-2005; **Cherie Niles ('87)**, 2005-2006; **Paul Azar ('70)**, 2006-2007; **Lee J. Monlezun ('69)**, 2007-2008; **Jim Leonard ('63)**, 2008-2009; and **Gerard Peña ('82)**, 2009-2010.

Over time, Professorships honoring Drs. Mullins, Jolly, Craighead, Strong and Andonie were created by the Alumni Association. Dr. Rozas created one honoring his father, Kai Rozas, and Dr. Adatto create one honoring his father, Dr. Carl Adatto, a long-time and nationally known faculty member in the Department of Psychiatry.

ഇ‍ൻ

Source Material

Books

Fred Allison: *My Medical Autobiography* [privately printed and distributed, 2005]

Douglas Brinkley: *The Great Deluge: Hurricane Katrina, New Orleans, and the Mississippi Gulf Coast*. Harper Perennial, 2007.

Albert Cowdry: *Fighting for Life: American Military Medicine in World War II*. Free Press, 1994

Harnett Thomas Kane: *Huey Long's Louisiana Hayride: The American Rehearsal for Dictatorship 1928-1940*. Pelican Publishing Company, 1971.

Rudolph Matas History of the Louisiana State Medical Society, Vol. I, by Mary Louise Marshall; Vol. II by Hathaway Gibbons Aleman. Hope Haven Press, 1957.

John Salvaggio: *New Orleans' Charity Hospital: A Story of Physicians, Politics, and Poverty*. LSU Press,1992.

This I Remember: Reminiscences of the 50th Anniversary Conclave, LSU School of Medicine, 1981.

John Wilds: *Crises, Clashes and Cures: A Century of Medicine in New Orleans*. Orleans Parish Medical Society, 1978.

T. Harry Williams: *Huey Long*. Vintage, 1981.

Charles Wiltse: *The Medical Department: Medical Service in the Mediterranean and Minor Theaters*. United States Army in World War II. The Technical Services. U. S. Government Printing Office, 1965.

Records

Archival Records: Charity Hospital of Louisiana

Archival Records: LSU Health Sciences Center

Archival Records: State of Louisiana

Archival Records: U. S. Army

Archival Records: U. S. Government

Publications

Academic Medicine

Catalogs and Bulletins: LSU School of Medicine 1931-present

James Duffy: *Huey Long and the Spite School Controversy* (Master Thesis)

Journal of the Louisiana State Medical Society (various issues)

Journal of the American Medical Association (various issues)

LSU Baton Rouge Alumni News (various issues)

LSU Medicinews and other alumni publications 1974-present

New England Journal of Medicine

Newsweek magazine

The New York Times Magazine

The Pharos of Alpha Omega Alpha

The Tiger: Student Newspaper 1931-1941

The Tiger Rag: Student Newspaper 1950-1967

U.S. Government Guide to Subversive Organizations (1951)

Yearbooks: LSUBR and/or LSUHSC 1931-present

Reports

From Dean Beryl Burns to Major General Campbell Hodges, President of LSU
From Dean Rigney D'Aunoy to James Monroe Smith, President of LSU
From the American Medical Association to the LSU School of Medicine and System
From the American Association of Medical Colleges to the LSU School of Medicine and System
To the American Medical Association from the LSU School of Medicine and System
To the American Association of Medical Colleges from the LSU School of Medicine and System
From the American Association of Medical Colleges to its members (1944): "Effects of the Accelerated Program of Medical Schools on Curriculum, Faculty and Students"

Center and Department Historical Records

Eye Center
Neuroscience Center
Department of Dermatology
Department of Medicine
Department of Neurosurgery
Department of Ob/Gyn
Department of Otolaryngology
Department of Pathology
Department of Pediatrics
Department of Physiology
Department of Surgery

Collected Papers Of

G. John Buddingh, MD
Howard Buechner, MD ('43)
Alice Baker Holubek, MD ('36)
Joe E. Holubek, MD
Edgar Hull, MD
Robert Marier, MD
I. Ricardo Martinez, MD ('65), PhD
Charles C. Mary, Jr., MD ('61)
Julius Mullins, Sr., MD ('36)
William Dosite Postell (School Librarian)
Jerold Schenken, Sr., MD

Newspaper Articles

Baton Rouge Advocate
Houston Chronicle
New Orleans City Business
New Orleans Times Picayune
New Orleans States
New Orleans Item
New Orleans States Item
New York Times

Oral and/or Written History

Karl Adatto, MD; Edgar Anderson, MD ('64); Jack Andonie, MD ('62);, Mary Lou Applewhite, MD ('55); Vikki Ashley, PhD; T. Benton Ayo, MD; **Paul Azar, MD ('70)**; Charles Berlin, PhD; Haydee Bazan, PhD; Nicolas Bazan, MD, PhD; **Quinn H. Becker, MD ('56)**; Thompson DeWitt Boaz, MD ('39); John Bobear, MD; Fred Brazda, PhD; Michael Carey, MD; **Bill Cassidy, MD ('83)**; Louis Castaing; **Fred Cerise, MD ('88)**; Milton Chapman, MD ('59); Charles Chappuis, MD ('79); **Purnell Choppin, MD ('53)**;, Isidore Cohn, Jr., MD; Allen Copping, DDS; Roland Coulson, PhD; Alvin Cotlar, MD ('57); Claude Craighead, MD ('39); Van Culotta, Jr., MD ('74); Joseph D. Angelo, MHA; Robert Daniels, MD; **Walter Daniels, MD ('59)**; Harry Dascomb, MD; George Davis, PhD; **Ben deBoisblanc, MD ('81)**; Herbert Derman, MD ('43); Robert DiBenedetto, MD ('52); Richard DiCarlo, MD ('87); Wilfred Dolan, MD ('49); G. Dewey Dunn, MD ('60); Homer Dupuy, MD ('38); Fred Eigenbrod, MD ('38); Cathi Fontenot, MD ('84); Reggie Goldsby, MD ('69); Helen Hartman; **Samuel Hartman, MD ('41)**; **Larry Hebert, MD ('59)**; Thomas Hernandez, PhD, MD ('47); Charles Hilton, MD ('76); Don Hines, MD ('59); **Larry Hollier, MD ('68)**; Ernestine Bass Hopkins, MD; **Frank Incaprera, MD ('50)**; J. Gregory Jolissaint, MD ('86); Fred Kasten, PhD; Herbert Kaufmann, MD; **Richard Keller, MD ('86)**; Fred Kelly, MD ('51); David G. Kline, MD; **David Krueger, MD ('73)**; **Hypolite Landry, MD ('58)**; Walt Larimore, MD ('78); Paul Larson, MD; **Daniel B. Lestage, MD ('63)**; **Fred Lopez, MD ('90)**; Ron Luftig, PhD; **Arnold Lupin, MD ('59)**; **Ralph Lupin, MD ('56)**; **George Lyons, MD ('54)**; Patricia Magee; **Alice Hull Maier, MD ('62)**; Robert Marier, MD; Jorge I. Martinez-Lopez, MD ('50); Marc Matrana, MD ('06); Garland McCarthy, MD ('67); Sam McClugage, PhD; **Abe Mickal, MD ('40)**; Bobbie Millet; Lindy Mills; **Frank Minyard, MD ('55)**; Emel Songu Mize, PhD; Ranney Mize, PhD; Joseph Moerschbaecher, PhD; **Jackie Morgan, MD ('65)**; **Robert Morrow, MD ('69)**; Norman Nelson, MD; Steve Nelson, MD; Thomas Nolan, MD; **Daniel Nuss, MD ('81)**; **Heck Olinde, MD ('54)**; **Steven Oreck, MD ('79)**; Richard Paddison, MD; Donald Palmisano, MD; **Joseph K. Perloff, MD ('51)**; Robert Plaisance, MBA; **Warren Plauché, MD ('57)**; James D. Rives, MD; **Fred Rodriguez, MD ('75)**; JoAnn Roloff; Robert Roskowski, PhD; John Ruby, PhD; **C. V. Sanders, MD ('64)**; Edward Sauter, MD ('86); Lou Peveto Scott, RN; John Seabury, MD; **Dwight Smith, MD ('64)**; Ronnie Smith, MBA; **William Stewart, MD ('45)**; Jack Perry Strong, MD ('51); Warren Summer, MD; David Tarver; **A. John Tassin, MD ('69)**; Claude Tellis, MD ('70); Dwayne Thomas, MD ('84); Mack Thomas, MD ('62); Marilyn Zimny, PhD.

Other Source Material

Annotated photo collection of **Robert Simmons, MD ('36)**
Minutes of Faculty Council, LSU School of Medicine
Letter of Resignation Emmitt Lee Irwin MD to Arthur Vidrine MD
Official Diary – 64th General Hospital
Special Collections, Hill Memorial Library, Louisiana State University, Baton Rouge
The admittedly fallible memory of the lead author

Photographs

Photographs from The Historic New Orleans Collection (used by permission), pp. 1 and 13.
Photographs appearing on the following pages courtesy of LSUHSC New Orleans Libraries Photographic Archives (LSUHSC-NO © 2009): 2, 4, 5, 7, 24, 27, 30, 33, 38, 40, 88, 97, 104, 112, 116, 126, 135, 146, 150, 163, and 170

The future is now...

Scenes from the Isidore Cohn, Jr., MD, Student Learning Center and the **Russell C. Klein, MD ('59)**, Center for Advanced Practice

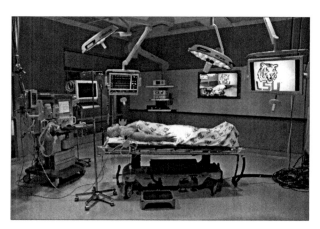

ABOVE: Simulated operating room in the Student Learning Center

Lions-LSU Clinics building, home of the two centers

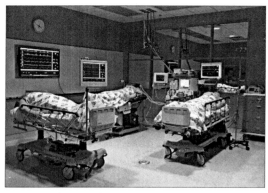

LEFT: Simulated emergency room in the Student Learning Center

LEFT: Center for Advance Practice

RIGHT: Simulation Room, Center for Advanced Practice

About the Authors

RUSSELL C. KLEIN, MD, was born in New Orleans in 1935 and attended Loyola University and Louisiana State University School of Medicine graduating with a MD degree in 1959.

He served an internship and a year of medicine residency at Charity Hospital before being called to active duty in the United States Army.

Upon discharge he returned to New Orleans, completed his medicine residency and a stint as Research Associate to the late John Salvaggio, MD. He then served a year of pulmonary fellowship at LSU under Dr. John Seabury. Subsequently, he moved to Boston for further training at Harvard Medical School and the Pulmonary Unit at Massachusetts General Hospital.

In 1967, at the urging of the late Dr. Edgar Hull, he returned to New Orleans and joined the faculty of the Department of Medicine at LSU in the Pulmonary Section working under Dr. Seabury and Dr. John Barry Bobear, achieving the rank of Professor in 1982.

In addition to teaching, patient care and research at LSU, Dr. Klein was asked to be in charge of the design and construction of the first modern medical intensive care unit at Charity Hospital and served as its Medical Director from 1977-1982, was also Director of Respiratory Care at Hotel Dieu Hospital for eleven years and Director of the School of Respiratory Therapy at Delgado College for six years. He is a Fellow of the American College of Physicians, a Laureate Award winner of the Louisiana Chapter and a Fellow of the College of Chest Physicians.

Active in organized medicine since 1967 he served as President of Orleans Parish Medical Society in 1991 and as a member of the board of La State Medical Society since 1993. In 1996 he was elected Vice Speaker of the LSMS House of Delegates and was elected Speaker in 2000. He served as President Elect in 2007 and President in 2008.

From 1985 until 2009 he was responsible for all Continuing Medical Education at LSU School of Medicine.

Dr. Klein is married to the former Donna Guinn, an RN and attorney specializing in health care law. They have two children.

ഇരുവ

VICTORIA BARRETO HARKIN, MA, was a student worker at the LSU School of Medicine for almost five years, leaving only to pursue a Master's Degree in History from the University of New Orleans. But the pull of the school was too strong, and Victoria returned to help the Office of Alumni Affairs research, write and assemble the School's 75-year history.

When Hurricane Katrina struck the city of New Orleans, Victoria joined the Alumni Office staff in Baton Rouge and continued work on this history, which would now also document the resurrection of the school from the floodwaters of the storm. Thankfully, her office in the 1542 Tulane Avenue building back in New Orleans safely held some of the school's oldest records, dating back to 1939. These records safe, Victoria helped Dr. Russell Klein reconstruct some of the most important events in the school's history.

She is a graduate of Loyola University New Orleans, where she graduated Summa Cum Laude with a Bachelor of Arts in History. Victoria published two papers while still in college; she specializes in the study of the U.S.'s Cold War history and Northern South America. She also earned a Masters of Arts in History from the University of New Orleans, graduating with a perfect grade average.

Victoria now lives and teaches in central Iowa. She is married to Kelly Harkin, and they are the proud parents of Aleutia (a pretty cute beagle).

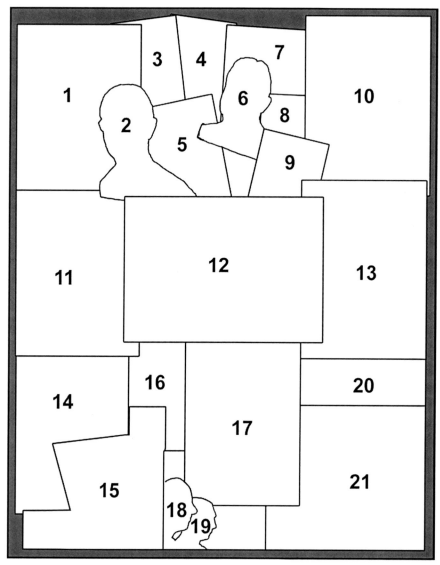

Identities in back cover montage

1. Percy Rosenbaum, MD
2. Harry Dascomb, MD
3. Urban Maes, MD
4. Abe Mikal, MD
5. James D. Rives, MD
6. Arthur Vidrine, MD
7. Fred Brazda, PhD
8. J. Sherburn Anderson, MD (first physician ever to graduate from the School of Medicine)
9. Bill Frye, MD, PhD
10. Edgar Hull, MD
11. John Salvaggio, MD
12. Seal on the original Medical School building
13. Robert Simmons, MD, Associate Dean and Professor of Public Health
14. Students in the Charity Hospital amphitheater
15. Julius Mullins, MD, taking a history at Charity Hospital in 1936
16. Charles Mayo Goss, MD
17. Urban Maes lecturing in the "pit"
18. Jack Strong, MD
19. J. Clyde Schwartzwelder, PhD
20. Students in the Charity Hospital amphitheater
21. *left to right:* Thomas Hernandez, PhD, MD, and Ronald Coulson, PhD

LaVergne, TN USA
31 August 2010
195309LV00001B/2/P